S0-ARC-847

Universal Human Rights

Philosophy and the Global Context

Series Editor: Michael Krausz, Bryn Mawr College

This series addresses a range of emerging global concerns. It situates philosophical efforts in their global and cultural contexts, and it offers works from thinkers whose cultures are challenged by globalizing movements. Comparative and intercultural studies address such social and political issues as the environment, poverty, consumerism, civil society, tolerance, colonialism, global ethics, and community in cyberspace. They also address related methodological issues of translation and cross-cultural understanding.

Intellectual Property: Moral, Legal, and International Dilemmas (1997) by Adam D. Moore
Ethics of Consumption: The Good Life, Justice, and Global Stewardship (1998) edited by David A. Crocker and Toby Linden
Alternative Visions: Paths in the Global Village (1998) by Fred Dallmayr
Philosophical Reflections on the Changes in Eastern Europe (1998) by William L. McBride
Intercultural Philosophy (2000) by Ram Adhar Mall
Philosophical Questions: East and West (2000) edited by Bina Gupta and J.N. Mohanty
Formal Transgression: John Stuart Mill's Philosophy of International Affairs (2000) by Eddy M. Souffrant
Limits of Rightness (2000) by Michael Krausz
The Empirical and the Transcendental: A Fusion of Horizons (2000) by Bina Gupta
The Human World in the Physical Universe: Consciousness, Free Will, and Evolution (2001) by Nicholas Maxwell
Tolerance: Between Forbearance and Acceptance (2001) by Hans Oberdiek
Persons and Valuable Worlds: A Global Philosophy (2002) by Eliot Deutsch
Yesterday's Self: Nostalgia and the Immigrant Identity (2002) by Andreea Deciu Ritivoi
Ethical Questions: East and West (2002) edited by Bina Gupta
Universal Human Rights: Moral Order in a Divided World (2005) edited by David A. Reidy and Mortimer N.S. Sellers

Universal Human Rights

Moral Order in a Divided World

Edited by
David A. Reidy and Mortimer N. S. Sellers

ROWMAN & LITTLEFIELD PUBLISHERS, INC.
Lanham • Boulder • New York • Toronto • Oxford

ROWMAN & LITTLEFIELD PUBLISHERS, INC.

Published in the United States of America
by Rowman & Littlefield Publishers, Inc.
A wholly owned subsidiary of The Rowman & Littlefield Publishing Group, Inc.
4501 Forbes Boulevard, Suite 200, Lanham, Maryland 20706
www.rowmanlittlefield.com

P.O. Box 317, Oxford OX2 9RU, UK

British Library Cataloguing in Publication Information Available

Library of Congress Cataloging-in-Publication Data

Universal human rights : moral order in a divided world / edited by David A. Reidy and Mortimer N.S. Sellers.
p. cm. — (Philosophy and the global context)
Includes bibliographical references and index.
ISBN 0-7425-4860-0 (hardcover : alk. paper) — ISBN 0-7425-4861-9 (pbk. : alk. paper)
1. Human rights. 2. International relations. I. Reidy, David A., 1962– II. Sellers, M. N. S. (Mortimer N. S.) III. Series.
JC571.U638 2005
323—dc22

2005002652

Printed in the United States of America

∞™ The paper used in this publication meets the minimum requirements of American National Standard for Information Sciences—Permanence of Paper for Printed Library Materials, ANSI/NISO Z39.48-1992.

For our wives, Frances and Kathy,
with love and gratitude.

Contents

1

Introduction

David A. Reidy and Mortimer N. S. Sellers

Human rights talk is now ubiquitous. Human rights claims permeate political, legal, and even commercial practices. And human rights stand at the center of philosophical inquiry into global or international justice, one of the most active and productive areas of philosophical inquiry in recent decades.[1] Yet it is often not very clear what human rights talk is about or is intended to accomplish or could accomplish in a world as divided as our own. The aim of this book is to bring some clarity to this important and contested new discourse of universal human rights.

Nearly all governments of the world have now expressed their commitment to "fundamental human rights, . . . the dignity and worth of the human person, [and] . . . the equal rights of men and women" everywhere.[2] Through the Charter of the United Nations, nearly all states have formally committed themselves to promote,[3] realize,[4] and "take action"[5] to achieve human rights and fundamental freedoms for all "without distinction as to race, sex, language, or religion."[6] The General Assembly of the United Nations proclaimed "the equal and inalienable rights of all members of the human family" in a "Universal Declaration" of the particular human rights[7] to which "everyone is entitled"[8] from birth.[9] Most states have given binding legal effect to most, in some cases all, of these listed rights through multilateral treaties,[10] in their own constitutions,[11] or both.

The nearly universal recognition by governments of a nearly identical list of "universal" and "inalienable" rights neither confirms that such rights exist nor guarantees their effectiveness. Many governments do little to secure the rights of their subjects. Many violate the very rights they have solemnly promised to uphold and would fall from power if they were to respect even a minimal list of universal human rights. Many governments still maintain control through illegitimate and unjust force. In this regard, it is even more remarkable that so many governments pay lip service to or ratify treaties endorsing human rights, for these are often the very rights that may ultimately undermine their hold on power.

This formal recognition by governments of "universal" and "fundamental" human rights no doubt reflects the general appeal of "human dignity" as an ideal to people everywhere and a general convergence in understanding what this ideal requires. This apparent consensus falls apart, however, as soon as the task becomes explaining the nature of universal human rights, reconciling human rights into a coherent system or systems of norms that may be fairly invoked to adjudicate diverse conflicts in diverse circumstances, enforcing judgments regarding human rights violations, or marking the limits, if any, of universal human rights. It is these tasks to which this volume is dedicated and around which it is organized.

The first and most fundamental of these tasks is to explain the moral nature or structure of human rights and the consequent basis of their universal validity. While the vast majority of governments, collective peoples, and individual persons recognize and affirm more or less the same universal human rights, they frequently differ as to the nature, structure, justification, and origins of these rights. These disagreements often have important implications. Whether and how human rights may be internationally enforced or whether and how they might trump national civil or constitutional rights will often depend on how one settles these disagreements.

The three chapters in part I consider the nature, structure, justification, and origin of human rights, with an eye to the sorts of issues regarding the priority and enforcement of human rights that turn on how one settles such matters. Some scholars have tried to avoid these philosophical inquiries into the nature and justification of human rights by building the superstructure of human rights practice on a narrow "overlapping consensus" between states over a particular list of human rights. Notwithstanding the obvious appeal of this approach, the fact remains that in the absence of a fuller account of their nature and justification even recognized human rights are likely to wither on the vine or fall prey to competing concerns in moral and political life. Human rights claim a priority and a universality that are unlikely to sustain themselves in the absence of good reasons, publicly expressed and affirmed.

The priority and universality of human rights, even if well-grounded, do not entail that human rights will never come into conflict with one another or require different institutional arrangements or practices in different contexts. Ultimately, universal human rights must be vindicated as particular rights for particular individuals in particular societies. Human rights reflect universal values in vastly different circumstances. They will often require or permit different interpretations, systematizations, and applications in diverse particular contexts.

The three chapters in part II consider the tensions that inevitably arise in securing universal human rights as particular rights for particular persons in particular contexts. While some human rights may be universal in the strong sense that they apply in more or less the same way to all people everywhere, many are universal in only the weaker sense of setting out core normative considerations and fundamental normative limits applicable to all people everywhere, considerations and limits that permit a substantial degree of discretionary judgment and thus reasonable disagreement. And, of course, even human rights that are universal in the strong sense will often require context-dependent interpretation. This will happen, for example, when an atypical context either generates a conflict between two rights or makes inadequate standard institutional efforts at securing some particular right. The fact is that the practice of universal human rights introduces into the theory of human rights many contextual variables. The challenge for philosophers and other theorists of human rights is to deal effectively and coherently with these variables without compromising the universality of human rights in theory or practice.

As the object and artifact of an emergent global and legal practice, human rights have followed a natural progression. They first receive articulation through various declarations, treaties, and legislative enactments. This first step invites philosophical and theoretical reflection on the nature, structure, justification, and origin of human rights. Human rights are then put into practice: violations and violators are identified, and conflicts are adjudicated. This is the second step in the natural progression of human rights practice. It invites philosophical and theoretical reflection on the application of universal human rights as particular rights for particular persons living under particular institutions in particular societies. Identifying human rights violations and adjudicating human rights claims, however, are incomplete unless and until human rights are in fact enforced. Violators must be punished; victims must have their rights restored. This is the third stage in the development of the global and legal practice of human rights: the enforcement stage.

The three chapters in part III deal with issues arising out of the enforcement of universal human rights. Among these issues are those associated with responsibility for war crimes, the permissibility of coercive intervention by one state into the domestic affairs of another state to secure human rights, and the relationship between independent states and new international bodies such as the International Criminal Court. These are matters traditionally discussed under the somewhat misleading heading of "just war theory," misleading since what is referred to is not so much a theory as a tradition of normative discourse.

Just war theory has received a great deal of new attention in recent years. This is in part the result of the very important work done by Michael Walzer, Oliver O'Donovan, David Luban, and other theorists concerned with the norms, including human rights norms, that govern just warfare, work often responsive to particular wars (such as the Vietnam War or the first Gulf War).[12] But it is also in part the result of the end of the Cold War. The Cold War effectively blocked genuinely humanitarian interventions in the name of human rights as well as the sort of ad hoc tribunals created by the United Nations for adjudicating international crimes committed in the former Yugoslavia and Rwanda. But with the end of the Cold War, the political context for thinking about just war has changed at a fundamental level, and the path has been cleared for new and bolder thinking about the enforcement of human rights, whether through military or nonmilitary but nevertheless coercive interventions, using economic, diplomatic, or other pressures to influence the behavior of states. Within this new and bolder thinking, the key tasks include (1) setting out the conditions under which domestic human rights violations may justify or even require coercive intervention by one or more members of the international community and (2) identifying the constraints that human rights impose on any exercise of coercive force by a state, including the force exercised in a just war of self-defense.

The central challenge in dealing effectively with the enforcement issues raised by the global and legal practice of human rights is that of avoiding a cure worse than the disease itself. Military intervention is always a costly undertaking, as are almost all coercive exercises of economic and diplomatic power. At both the theoretical and institutional levels, then, there is a real danger in authorizing enforcement norms and practices that create as great or more dangerous a threat to international peace and security than the rights violations they seek to correct.

Some human rights theorists—for example, Michael Walzer and Michael Ignatieff—have suggested that under certain extreme conditions, universal human rights must or may yield to other moral considerations, such as collective self-defense.[13] The two chapters in part IV address the challenge to universal human rights posed by the most extreme circumstances, as when a people or state faces its potential destruction by an unjust aggressor or finds itself confronted with apparently nihilistic and undeterrable terrorists bent on and capable of killing mass numbers of "enemy" civilians to vindicate some theological vision or indulge some irrational hatred. Even seemingly absolute prohibitions against the intentional killing of civilians or the use of torture may weaken when a people faces its own potential destruction through warfare or mass terrorism.

While it is not unnatural to think that more extreme circumstances or threats justify more extreme responses and thus potential departures from core human rights norms, there may still be certain standards from which no derogation should ever be permitted. The status and role of human rights in warfare generally and in the "war on terror" more specifically form a controversial matter. While taking different positions on this matter, the authors of the two chapters in part IV agree that human rights deserve moral consideration, even when they are justifiably or excusably overridden in the face of extreme circumstances.

The role that human rights play in bringing moral order to a divided world determines the progression of the discussion in this volume, from the general and theoretical concerns with which the volume begins to the specific and practical concerns with which it ends.

In chapter 2, Alistair Macleod argues that questions about the nature of human rights are intimately bound up with questions about their rationale. Arguments offered to support the existence of human rights also determine their content and scope. Thus, there is little reason to suppose that human rights might be grounded in a shallow "overlapping consensus" between different cultural attitudes and practices, unless cultural differences themselves turn out to be superficial and moral consensus runs deep. Of course, if this is the case, then it should be possible to articulate the deeper moral consensus. Articulating this deeper consensus is, or should be, a basic aim of philosophical discussions about human rights.

Macleod recognizes human rights as those moral rights that are ascribable to all human beings. They derive from the respects in which all human beings are alike. Rights normally promote some basic interest of the right holder by burdening another person or persons in a way that is distributively just. Thus, any theory of human rights entails a theory of distributive justice. And a theory of distributive justice in turn requires a theory of basic human interests or well-being, drawing on such universal needs as health, food, housing, physical security, education, and the like. These needs are best met through social institutions, and indeed it is in society that humans typically thrive best. Thus, human rights derive from the social rules necessary to ensure that the basic interests of all individuals are met. Human rights therefore set a basic standard of justice applicable to all societies.

In chapter 3, Rex Martin adds that human rights are, or ought to be regarded as, civil rights in the sense that they can only be enjoyed in the context of some specific society. Basic civil rights are those rights that have been enacted as legislation, confirmed by judicial review (or some similar checking device), and institutionally and politically vindicated regularly over time within a particular political and legal system. They generally trump rights that are not universal or not locally well established in the foregoing sense. Human rights can be said to meaningfully exist, then, only as socially recognized practices, ideally manifest as basic civil rights. But this means that well-entrenched local norms may function as a sort of constraint on human rights, blocking their recognition or real existence in some cases. Martin defends this "social recognition thesis" against the alternative view that human rights exist as valid moral claims regardless of their social recognition. While it is not nonsense to speak of human rights (in the manner of Alistair Macleod) as valid moral claims, it is wrongheaded on Martin's view to speak of human rights as normatively binding "rights" where the other basic commitments and beliefs central to the relevant social, political, and legal context block recognition of the right as a right. Just as a justified legal claim counts as a legal "right" only if it is legally recognized and affirmed in some meaningful sense within the relevant institutional context, so too a justified moral claim counts as a human "right" only if it is socially recognized and affirmed, ideally as a basic civil right, in the relevant social/political/legal context.

Martin suggests, then, that rights that cannot be acknowledged, because they are blocked in a given society by a competing and superior normative claim (and not mere self-interest or lack of understanding) should not be regarded as normatively binding there. Human rights—not only their enforcement but also their very existence as rights—depend, then, on being socially recognized and maintained as basic norms (ideally, as basic civil rights) governing social relations. Through international human rights declarations and covenants, states undertake to recognize and maintain specified rights. These declarations and covenants do not typically grant human rights to individual persons directly. Rather, they contribute to the constitution of regional and international patterns of conduct between states grounded in the recognition and maintenance of human rights, ideally as basic civil rights within the legal systems of all state parties.

Martin concludes that rights do not properly exist and could not in any case be identified or protected outside the social practices established to recognize and maintain them. These practices are national and, increasingly, international. Accordingly, human rights exist, with determinate content and scope, as basic civil rights in particular societies, in particular political-legal systems. There they are justified as mutually beneficial to all citizens and are recognized and maintained by determinate social practices. Human rights are merely nominal outside the institutional arrangements that support them, and for the time being, these are nation-states joined for shared purposes in regional and international associations or federations.

In chapter 4, David Duquette faces directly the tension between universal human rights and the cultural circumstances of different societies, a tension mediated by Rex Martin through his social recognition thesis. While recognizing universal human rights as valid moral claims rooted in particularly important aspects of individual human dignity (and therefore not dependent for their existence on legal formalities), Duquette recognizes the role of social recognition in grounding the social significance or force of universal rights. Socially unrecognized abstract moral claims, even if valid, cannot function as rights. Because of the great diversity in human communities, universal human rights are likely to be recognized socially in various ways. This does not undermine the moral objectivism of universal human rights; rather, it merely confirms the contextually bounded nature, the relativism, of giving social recognition to such rights. This relativism, however, is not an invitation to reduce moral argument to little more than simple assertions of cultural prejudice or frank ethnocentricity. Instead, moral arguments regarding human rights must appeal to human dignity and universal human nature. But humility and caution must attend the move from this universal appeal to particular claims about human rights in specific historical contexts. Human rights represent particular collective responses to historically contingent threats to basic human values and interests as these threats have arisen in specific political and economic circumstances. They are at once universal and relative. They share in a basic relation to universal human dignity, grounded in human nature. But they vary in light of the social circumstances calling for and framing their social recognition, circumstances within which what is vindicated in one society as a human right might conceivably be trumped in another society by other weighty normative considerations. All the important work to be done regarding human rights, then, is a posteriori, pragmatic, and historically informed. Human rights are particular expressions of human dignity achieved by diverse societies confronting diverse challenges in their own particular ways.

One of the great affronts to human dignity around the world is the oppression, domination, and maltreatment of women, or patriarchy. Human rights are often presented in international law and political theory as, among other things, a remedy to this moral deficiency. Women's rights are understood to be human rights. More recently, however, worries have arisen over whether human rights as they have developed over the last fifty years are themselves expressions of a distinctively male moral point of view or are otherwise problematic as a core tool to be put to use in the dismantling of patriarchal oppression, domination, and maltreatment of women. Some theorists have complained that the "human" in human rights is typically a male with male interests. Others have complained that the priority assigned to "rights" by the human rights movement is bound up with a distinctively universalist, essentialist, and morally unattractive male point of view.

In chapter 5, Lucinda Peach sets out these two general orientations toward women's rights as human rights: the liberal universalist and the feminist contextualist, identifying the merits and demerits of each and the ways in which each presents itself as a corrective to the other. She pays special attention to the ways in which any acceptable deployment of human rights in the struggle to end patriarchy must take seriously the socially constructed and variable nature of gendered identity, and thus patriarchy, in different social contexts. Peach argues for a pragmatic feminist approach to human rights, one that transcends the differences between a liberal, universalistic, legal, and rights-based approach to ending patriarchy and the sort of multifaceted, pluralistic, contextually specific approach suggested by those who insist that gender, both male and female, is always socially and locally constructed. Peach's pragmatic feminist stance suggests that in the struggle to end patriarchy women and their allies ought to act from within their own particular local contexts and self-understandings—specifically, to view human rights as no more than potentially valuable tools, tools to be used when they work and to be set aside when other, more productive tools for dismantling patriarchy and improving women's lives lie ready to hand.

It is not enough, of course, for human rights to be identified, articulated, and justified. They must be given real effect. Giving human rights real effect often requires the adjudication of conflicting claims, as for example when parties disagree over whether a particular right is a human right, whether a particular right is outweighed by a competing human right or some other claim, or whether some particular pattern constitutes a human rights violation. In chapter 6, Helen Stacy undertakes to develop a distinctive approach to the adjudication of human rights claims by taking seriously the particularity of any adjudicative judgment. She proposes a judicial "ethic of listening," the aim of which is to ensure that in rendering judgments regarding human rights, and thus the moral requirements of respect for universal humanity, judges remain attentive to the fact that it is always a particular conflict between particular persons with their own particular individual and social self-understandings that they are called upon to resolve. Responsible judging requires listening to and often taking positive account of the diverse self-understandings of human rights claimants. This is an important corrective, Stacy argues, to the dominant view of adjudication as a sort of scientific inquiry into the legal truth.

Western and international courts frequently face human rights claims that come from utterly different intellectual or cultural traditions. Claims of minority cultural identity often seem to shield abuses of power, yet they can also represent sincere expressions of individual (or collective) self-understanding, even self-determination. When asserted in the context of a human rights conflict, such claims often present judges with no common or shared collective self-understanding in terms of which the conflict might be resolved. Stacy maintains that judges should resist the temptation to treat human rights as a universally shared self-understanding of what it is to be human. Rather, judges should adjudicate such conflicts by deploying human rights so as to realize a unique and intersubjective justice between the parties. Judges will be able to do so only if they truly listen to the parties, trying sympathetically to understand the divergent points of view. In this way, judges in the act of adjudicating bring together in human rights practice both the shared universality and the diverse particularities of all concerned.

In chapter 7, William Nelson considers the challenges not so much of adjudicating universal human rights claims in particular contexts, as of institutionally realizing human rights in a world as diverse and complex as our own. He focuses broadly on the universal human rights to political participation or democracy, on the one hand, and to a certain level of economic well-being, on the other. Governments and other institutional actors have positive duties to realize human rights as well as negative duties not to violate them. But these duties must be reasonable and fairly distributed. Otherwise, the rights in question will be mere "manifesto rights," aspirational goals that underwrite no enforceable duties. But, as Nelson points out, it is not possible to specify a reasonable and fair distribution of the duties imposed by any particular human right without taking account of the great differences—economic, social, cultural, and otherwise—between nations or states. Taking account of these differences need not drive us to say that human rights impose no duties. Rather, they require us to recognize that what universal human rights demand of any particular agent, particular government, or other institutional actor will depend on a host of contextual facts.

Turning to the political right to democracy and the economic right to a certain level of material well-being, Nelson argues that any judgment regarding the content of the right in question, or whether existing institutional arrangements secure it, must pay close attention to the context not only of the alleged right holders but also of those said to be duty bound to act in this or that way by the right in question. Nelson suggests that it is likely that the human right to democracy in practice will prove to be conditional, imposing different duties in different cases, as will the human right to a certain level of material well-being. What rights require will turn on what a reasonable or fair distribution of burdens or duties would look like. And given the diversity of institutional actors, this will likely result in different duties for different actors in different cases. Still, Nelson insists, there are many duties we can justifiably attribute, as fair and reasonable, to various institutional actors, even after taking account of the great diversity of their contexts. For example, wealthy states and international organizations such as the World Trade Organization and the International Monetary Fund are, Nelson maintains, by virtue of the human right to basic material well-being, duty bound to reform their current practices in concrete ways. Rich states should stop supporting dictators through trade and arms sales. The First World should open its markets to Third World agricultural products. All governments and institutions should put the basic interests of the international community before the wealth of their own elites.

In chapter 8, Steven Lee turns from the difficulties of implementation to the vagaries of enforcement. Many human rights are now well known, both in the abstract and as applied to particular cases, but are still violated with impunity under the cover of local state sovereignty. For example, the genocide against the Tutsi minority in Rwanda took place in the full view of the international community, which nevertheless did nothing to stop or even mitigate the disaster. Lee inquires whether human rights violations of this magnitude can ever justify enforcement or preventive measures ("humanitarian intervention") by foreign governments or institutions. He concludes that respect for national sovereignty should be no more than a rule of thumb, which can be overruled when serious human rights violations warrant outside intervention. This humanitarian intervention exception to national sovereignty depends on questions of proportionality and (1) epistemological considerations concerning the severity of the human rights violations; (2) the expectation of resistance, which raises the cost of intervention; (3) the risks of self-interested intervention; and (4) the danger of creating precedents for intervention, which might encourage the use of force against states for nonhumanitarian reasons. When the disease of human rights violations "shocks the moral conscience of mankind," then the rule of thumb against intervention may be superseded by the humanitarian intervention exception to national sovereignty, provided the other conditions are satisfied. But it is one thing to say that humanitarian intervention is morally permissible in some cases, another to say that it is wise, all things considered, and yet another to say that it is morally obligatory. Lee concludes by recognizing that the growing consensus that humanitarian intervention may sometimes be morally permissible invites further research and thought on when a permissible moral intervention would be wise, all things considered, or perhaps even obligatory.

In chapter 9, Larry May considers the possibility of international judicial prosecutions for mass human rights abuses, such as genocide. Criminal trials usually seek to hold individuals accountable. Genocide, however, is perpetuated by organized groups and institutions. Nevertheless, May argues that prosecutions of individuals for genocide are conceptually and normatively justified. Individuals can be responsible for collective crimes when they share in the criminal plan. What distinguishes genocide from ordinary crimes is the individual's underlying aim of destroying a group. The criminal acts themselves may be fairly inconsequential, provided the requisite intent remains. May suggests that guilt for crimes committed collectively, such as genocide, may be widely shared by members of the collective, such as a state. Shared responsibility involves the responsibility not merely of those who directly cause harm but also of those who cause harm indirectly and are in other ways complicit in a crime. Holding individuals responsible makes it clear that individuals are in fact the perpetrators of these collective crimes. This does not mean that all individuals are equally responsible. May concludes that punishment should be distributed in proportion to the degree of complicity or contribution to the criminal enterprise.

May informs his analysis with details drawn from recent war crimes trials arising out of the genocides in the former Yugoslavia and in Rwanda. These trials were conducted by ad hoc tribunals. In recent years attention has focused on the need for a permanent tribunal to prosecute international criminals, including those guilty of war crimes. In chapter 10, Kenneth Henley discusses the legitimacy of trying international criminals in an international criminal court. The Rome Statute of the International Criminal Court establishes a tribunal of last resort to enforce the most serious international crimes. This challenges some conceptions of state sovereignty that would place all the activities of a state within its own borders beyond the reach of international law. Henley argues that if human rights exist and can be clearly identified, they ought to be impartially enforced. An international criminal court would offer the rule-of-law virtue of objectivity, when justice is not available in a state's own national courts. Henley suggests that the danger of politically motivated prosecutions in international courts can be diminished by retaining complementary local jurisdiction over international crimes and by requiring judicial acquiescence in all international investigations. The concept of human rights posits enforceable individual claims that belong to all human beings, simply in virtue of their humanity. Henley echoes Rex Martin in asserting that a human right is defective if it remains unrecognized, unmaintained, and unenforced. An international criminal court promises to strengthen the status of human rights as civil rights, putting pressure on all states to recognize and enforce human rights within their own domestic institutions. The existence of an international tribunal within which rights might be vindicated need not diminish the sovereignty of states or threaten the status of human rights as basic civil rights within all nations. The international tribunal offers just another complementary enforcement mechanism and thus contributes to an international human rights regime centered on sovereign national jurisdictions.

In chapter 11, Stephen Nathanson begins this volume's final section, on human rights in extremis. He raises the question whether terrorism can ever be morally justified. The standard answer to this question, which Nathanson affirms, is that terrorism can never be morally justified because it involves the killing of innocent persons. But this immediately invites the question of whether war can ever be morally justified, since it too involves, or often involves, the killing of innocent persons, as for example when innocent civilians are killed as a result of a military bombing operation. What makes war different from terrorism? Isn't one man's just war another man's terrorism?

Nathanson argues that what makes terrorist killing different is that it involves the intentional targeting of innocent civilians as a direct means to a political end. The unintentional killing of innocent civilians in a just war is different; it is an accidental consequence of an otherwise justifiable activity (as when fighting a just war of self-defense). But the killing of innocent civilians in an otherwise just war is not made morally acceptable simply by being unintended, Nathanson maintains. If it were, then the September 11 terrorists might excuse their killing of innocent civilians by claiming that they meant only to destroy the World Trade Center towers and the Pentagon as buildings (which happened to have civilians inside). But what then makes the killing of innocent civilians, "collateral damage," sometimes morally permissible in a just war? It cannot be the consequences of such killings, nor can it be the magnitude of the threat faced, for then in either case terrorist killings might turn out to be morally permissible, too.

Nathanson concludes that the unintentional killing of innocent civilians in an otherwise just war is morally permissible only if it is both unintended and arises after all feasible steps have been taken to eliminate all civilian casualties. It is not enough simply not to intend to kill innocent civilians. One must intend, and take all feasible steps, to protect them, even if that means increasing one's potential military losses or reducing one's prospects for military success. It is this norm that terrorists violate but that good soldiers and armies honor. And it is for this reason that terrorism is never morally permissible but that warfare sometimes can be.

In chapter 12, Jonathan Schonsheck takes up another issue raised by terrorist killings. That is whether certain antiterrorist countermeasures (including torture) otherwise forbidden by universal human rights might be morally permissible given the unique threat posed by terrorist killings. Schonsheck argues that suicide terror attacks are sui generis and dissimilar from ordinary acts of war or terrorism as well as ordinary crimes. They are harder to deter, because the perpetrators are eager to die, and harder to prevent, because terrorists have no single sponsor to conquer or imprison. Terrorism, or more specifically suicide terrorism, requires instead that fundamental legal and moral categories, including universal human rights, be developed to accommodate a new reality.

Schonsheck argues that to possess human rights, one must belong to the human moral community and that this belonging is not given by one's merely being biologically human. Suicide terrorists, at least those of the sort encountered in the September 11 attacks, are not, Schonsheck maintains, members of the human moral community. They have placed themselves outside of that community. Whatever normative constraints restrict the response to such terrorists are not human rights constraints, at least as regards the terrorists. Nevertheless, some moral constraints remain. These constraints arise not from the human rights of the terrorists but rather from our own concern to preserve our own moral integrity as members of a moral community committed to human rights. We (prima facie) ought not torture suicide terrorists, not because of what it would do to them but rather because of what it would do to us.

To enjoy human rights, one must respect, or evidence a capacity and disposition to respect, human rights. By systematically rejecting the human rights of others, suicide terrorists of the now familiar sort should be understood as having repudiated their own reciprocal human rights. In this sense, human rights, for Schonsheck, are not universal. They belong only to those who declare themselves members of the human moral community by demonstrating a reciprocal respect for the human rights of others.

While the authors in this volume address a range of issues and advance a range of positions, they nevertheless achieve a substantial consensus on the nature, application, enforcement, and limits of universal human rights. This consensus, often latent and unarticulated in international political practice, plays a large part in the recent movement in international relations toward a more coherent and robust human rights practice. But as evidenced by the chapters in this volume, disagreements remain in theory and in practice. It is one of the pressing tasks of this generation to continue working to find a just and principled resolution of these disagreements so as to promote and more fully realize human rights as the universal rights of all particular persons within the human moral community.

NOTES

1. See, for example, Allen Buchanan, *Justice, Legitimacy, and Self-Determination: The Moral Foundations of International Law*, Oxford University Press, 2004; Darrell Moellendorf, *Cosmopolitan Justice*, Westview Press, 2002; Charles Jones, *Global Justice*, Oxford University Press, 1999; Jack Donnelly, *Universal Human Rights: In Theory and Practice*, 2nd ed., Cornell University Press, 2003.
2. *Charter of the United Nations* (June 26, 1945), *Preamble*.

3. *Ibid.*, Article 1(3).
4. *Ibid.*, Article 13(1)(b).
5. *Ibid.*, Article 56.
6. This language is repeated in Article 55(c) and Article 76(c). Cf. Article 62(2).
7. *Universal Declaration of Human Rights*, General Assembly Resolution 217 (December 10, 1948).
8. *Ibid.*, Article 2.
9. *Ibid.*, Article 1.
10. E.g., the *International Covenant on Civil and Political Rights* (1966), entered into force March 23, 1976; and the *International Covenant on Civil and Political Rights* (1966) and the *International Covenant on Economic, Social, and Cultural Rights* (1966), entered into force January 3, 1976.
11. E.g., *Constitution of the United States*, Amendments I–X (ratified December 15, 1791).
12. See Michael Walzer, *Just and Unjust Wars*, 3rd ed., Basic Books, 2000; Oliver O'Donovan, *The Just War Revisited*, Cambridge University Press, 2003; David Luban, "A Theory of Crimes Against Humanity," 29 *Yale Law Journal* 85 (2004), and "The War on Terrorism and the End of Human Rights," 22 *Philosophy & Public Policy Quarterly* 9 (Summer 2002).
13. See Michael Walzer's *Just and Unjust Wars*, *supra*, as well as his more recent *Arguing about War*, Yale University Press, 2004. See also Michael Ignatieff's *The Lesser Evil: Political Ethics in an Age of Terror*, Princeton University Press, 2004.

I

THE NATURE OF HUMAN RIGHTS

2

The Structure of Arguments for Human Rights

Alistair M. Macleod

There are a number of fundamental questions about human rights that cannot be addressed by careful scrutiny of such international documents as the Universal Declaration of Human Rights or the Covenant on Civil and Political Rights or the Covenant on Social, Economic, and Cultural Rights.[1] These include not only questions about the rationale for human rights (which might be readily conceded, in view of the paucity of argumentative material to be found in such documents) but also, somewhat more controversially, questions about the content—and even about the very existence—of human rights. For example, what the Universal Declaration of Human Rights says about the human rights to which recognition was given by the international community in 1948 does not settle questions either about their content or about their existence. The reason is that human rights—if they exist at all and regardless of what their content might be—are not rights that owe their existence or their content to the recognition accorded them in internationally endorsed documents or to institutional arrangements for their interpretation and implementation. Human rights are a species of moral rights—and moral rights are institution-determining rather than institution-determined rights. They are rights that we invoke in making judgments that purport to evaluate institutional arrangements. They are thus among the supra-institutional standards to which we appeal when we are endeavoring to determine the adequacy or defensibility of existing or contemplated laws, policies, and institutions.[2]

It is possible, of course, for talk about human rights to be shorthand for talk about the rights to which formal recognition has in fact been accorded in such human rights documents as the Universal Declaration of Human Rights or the international Covenants on human rights. But this will be the case only because, in the context at hand, reference is being made to the rights itemized in these documents. In a precisely analogous way, talk about the right to freedom of the press may, in certain contexts, be properly construable as talk about the right to freedom of the press embedded in the law or constitution of some particular country, even though, in other contexts, it is taken to be an important moral right that may or may not be adequately recognized in the law or the constitution. The question whether or not there is a legally (or constitutionally, or internationally) recognized right to X is definitively answerable, at least in principle, by pursuing the appropriate set of questions about the provisions of the law or the constitution in some specific jurisdiction or hitting upon the correct interpretation of the relevant clauses in such international human rights documents as the Universal Declaration of Human Rights or the human rights Covenants. And the same is true of questions about the content and scope of the rights to which express recognition is accorded in these ways. Nevertheless, there are questions about the existence, content, and scope of human rights that cannot be answered at all—let alone definitively—by interpretive exercises of any of these kinds. The reason is that they are questions about rights that are not constituted, even in part, by the recognition (if any) that is accorded them. It is consequently possible to be a skeptic about human rights—to deny that there is any such thing as a human right—without betraying any ignorance of the express provisions of the well-known international documents to which the nations of the world are signatories. And it is possible to be a critic of the content of the human rights doctrines embedded in these documents well after all the necessary homework has been done on what these documents actually say or on how they ought to be interpreted.

THE RATIONALE FOR HUMAN RIGHTS

Questions about the existence and about the content and scope of human rights are intimately bound up with questions about their rationale—that is, with questions about the structure of the arguments proffered in their support. Once we become puzzled about which rights deserve to be characterized as human rights, or once we begin to wonder whether there is any such thing as a human right, the only way forward is to try to determine the shape of the argument or arguments on the basis of which this or that determinate human right ought (allegedly) to be given recognition.[3]

There is a venerable tradition—the natural rights tradition—which, in one of its strands, might be invoked in criticism of this thesis. Human rights, it might be claimed, need only to be formulated in a perspicuous way for questions about their existence or content to be taken care of. Appropriately articulated statements about the existence of human rights are self-evident (it might be held), and there is no need, accordingly, for any inquiry to be conducted into the rationale for such rights.

This familiar traditional view certainly contrasts sharply with the view put forward here. If it proved to be possible to sponsor statements about the existence of human rights (to X or to Y or to Z) that had the status of self-evident truths, it would indeed be otiose to embark on an inquiry into the shape of the argument(s) needed for the establishment of the existence of human rights. It would be unnecessary to do so, since we would already be in a position to affirm the truth of determinately specified human rights statements. It would also be impossible, since it makes no sense to try to set out the reasons for supposing self-evidently true statements to be true. There is obviously no overlap between the class of self-evidently true statements—whatever one's view about its membership—and the class of statements that can be shown to be true because they follow in some logically approved manner from (or because they can be supported in some logically defensible way by reference to) other statements whose truth can be assumed or ascertained.

However, there are at least two reasons for rejecting the self-evidence account of statements about human rights. The first is that doctrines of self-evidence are epistemologically suspect if the statements said to be self-evident are not "analytic" statements,[4] and—Locke's notorious view to the contrary notwithstanding—moral statements, including statements about the existence of human rights, cannot be classified as "analytic" in any plausible sense of the term. The second is that the giving of reasons for thinking this or that claim about the existence of a determinate human right to be true seems to be both possible and necessary. People who claim that the right to freedom of expression is a fundamental human right, for example, do not typically advance the claim without having any reasons in support of the claim. On the contrary, they typically have such reasons, difficult though it no doubt is to articulate them in a comprehensive and fully accurate way. Moreover, such reasons must be supplied, sooner or later. That this is the case is particularly clear when questions have to be faced about the precise content (or scope) of the putative right. Why, for example, does the right to freedom of expression not include the right to make false slanderous statements about other people? It is a revealing fact about the reaction this question elicits that it is only the least articulate (and perceptive) defenders of the right to freedom of expression who will be tempted to say that it is "intuition" that enables us to draw a line between the situations in which the right can be properly invoked and the situations in which it is inappropriate to try to appeal to it. In this sort of context, the issue (it should be clear) is one about the proper content and scope of the right to freedom of expression. It is not about how a putative right to freedom of expression of *virtually unlimited scope* is to be curtailed in particular situations—either situations in which this putative right happens to come into conflict with some other putative right or situations in which some weighty "rights-independent" moral principle happens to have an application.[5]

More serious challenges to the view that claims about the existence and content of human rights are inextricably bound up with questions about their (supposed) rationale are implicit in the approaches to human rights issues recently recommended by Michael Ignatieff and Amy Gutmann. In his recent Tanner Lectures at Princeton,[6] Michael Ignatieff advocated a "minimalist" approach to human rights, one that not only forgoes divisive "foundational arguments" about human rights but also classifies as human rights only those rights that "protect human agency"—where by "agency" he means "more or less what Isaiah Berlin meant by 'negative liberty.'"[7] In her editorial introduction, Amy Gutmann denies that a minimalist approach to human rights in the international domain can have the sort of "negative liberty" rationale that Ignatieff suggests might suffice, pointing out that "protecting human agency" is not possible unless certain rights that are not "negative" rights—such as the right to subsistence—are also given recognition as human rights. At the same time, she agrees with Ignatieff that advocacy of a "maximalist" agenda on the international human rights front—one that seeks to represent human rights either as "guarantors of social justice" or as instruments for the realization of "comprehensive conceptions of the good life"—"may make it far more difficult to achieve the broad intercultural assent to rights that an international human rights regime requires to be effective."[8]

Despite her agreement with Ignatieff about the indefensibility of a "maximalist" position, Gutmann goes on to argue against too "minimalist" an account. She points out that a human rights regime "needs to avoid a minimalism so sparing that its enforcement would leave the most vulnerable people without what is (minimally) necessary to protect their ability to live a minimally decent life by any reasonable standard."[9] She also thinks that it may be "easier to enlist agreement on a set of human rights that combine protections of negative freedoms with subsistence and maybe even other welfare rights."[10]

Gutmann also adopts an interestingly different approach from that of Ignatieff to the question whether it is important to the correct identification of human rights for questions to be taken up about the "foundations" of human rights—questions about "why we have rights."[11] She disagrees with Ignatieff about the desirability (and indeed the feasibility) of avoiding "foundational" questions altogether, holding—surely rightly—that

Ignatieff's "protection of human agency" argument is itself a foundation-providing argument. However, she thinks it would be a mistake to rely on it as the sole foundation for human rights, partly because—contrary to what Ignatieff seems to take for granted—it is not in fact sufficiently uncontroversial (transculturally) to provide an adequate basis for international human rights but also because there is a better way to handle potentially divisive "foundational" arguments. In her view, the preferred alternative to avoidance of foundational arguments is to give recognition to a multiplicity of such arguments. Indeed, this is the way in which she thinks a human rights regime in the international domain can be squared with the fact of "moral pluralism."

Invoking the Rawlsian notion of an *overlapping consensus*,[12] Gutmann claims that human rights can be a matter of international agreement, even though the arguments for them are multifarious. Indeed, there can be agreement about human rights even if the arguments for them are mutually inconsistent and not merely diverse. Provided that they "converge" on a (more or less) agreed set of the rights to be given recognition as "human rights," the diversity of the supporting arguments—and the fact that there neither is, nor can be, a consensus about their cogency—should be accepted with equanimity. Gutmann's defense of this general strategy is similar to that described by Charles Taylor in a recent paper.[13] In this paper, Taylor "begins with the basic notion that an unforced world consensus on human rights would be something like a Rawlsian 'overlapping consensus,' in which convergent norms would be justified in very different underlying spiritual and philosophical outlooks."[14]

While Gutmann's critique of Ignatieff's attitude toward "foundational" arguments for human rights is persuasive, the alternative approach that she herself favors—along broadly Rawlsian lines—is not without its difficulties. A lot depends, of course, on the kind of consensus that is needed about the existence, or about the content, of proposed "human rights." For example, if the aim in some context is simply to get international agreement for the recognition of certain named and delineated rights—a daunting enough task in itself—it may not matter whether the reasons particular countries have for being parties to the agreement are sharply divergent. What matters is only that there be a consensus about the desirability of giving recognition to the named rights. But if the aim is to secure agreement about which the rights are that deserve to be recognized as "human rights"—and if there is to be some basis for the hope that an international consensus will prove to be stable and enduring—it may not be possible to distinguish so sharply between the question whether given rights are to be given recognition as "human rights" and the question why they ought to be accorded this sort of recognition. The reason is that in the case of moral rights generally—and thus also in the case of "human rights"—their content is determined by the arguments that can be mounted in their support. Indeed, so close is the connection between questions about the existence and content of human rights on the one side and questions on the other about the reason there are for supposing them to exist and to have the content they do, that it would be natural to anticipate that whenever there are deep differences about the (supposed) foundation-providing arguments for human rights, there will tend to be disagreement also about the rights to which recognition is to be accorded under this head. Thus when theological foundations are posited by religious sponsors of human rights—foundations, for example, in the form of "the will of God" as revealed in the pages of some sacred text or as disclosed in some religious tradition—it is unlikely that there will be broad (interfaith) agreement about which these rights are.[15]

If attention is restricted to those rights about which there is a (potential) consensus, it will be found that the arguments that underpin their existence do not have the specifically theological (or religious) character they are often represented as having, both by those who operate within the religious traditions in question and by such outsiders as Gutmann. For example, if a crucial part of the proffered rationale for certain human rights turns out to be the securing for all of some of the fundamental conditions of individual well-being—and if the elimination of deep injustices in the distribution of the conditions for the living of a decent life turns out to be central to the perceived rationale for human rights of certain sorts—stripping away the religious language in which ostensibly theological foundation-providing arguments are sometimes couched will serve to show that, at bottom, these arguments are little more than theologically embellished versions of "core" moral arguments that are (or could well be) a matter of international (intercultural, interreligious) agreement. The moral kernel of these arguments is often obscured by the theological husk in which they are encased. It seems to be a mistake, for example, to suppose that there are as many different foundation-providing arguments for human rights—the right not to be tortured, say, or the right to an equal opportunity to live a decent life—as there are different religions or cultures. It clearly does not follow from the fact that Christians, Muslims, Jews, and secular humanists all consider torture and (say) racial discrimination to be violations of fundamental human rights that they do so for fundamentally different reasons, reasons that reflect the beliefs they hold that are distinctively Christian, or Islamic, or Jewish, or humanist. Again, if the members of a culturally plural society—Canada, for example—all agree that such institutions as slavery and apartheid involve gross breaches of human rights, why should we expect the reasons for which they have these shared convictions to be as diverse as their most fundamental beliefs as Christians, Muslims, Jews, or humanists? An alternative hypothesis, surely, is that while their shared belief in the wrongness (indeed, the injustice) of these institutions is nested within a system of beliefs they have as Christians, Muslims, Jews, or humanists, this particular belief cannot be regarded as deriving from the parts of these belief systems that are distinctively Christian, Islamic, Jewish, or humanist. That is, it is not obvious that it is by reference, ultimately, to distinctively Christian, Muslim, Jewish, or humanist beliefs that beliefs about the injustice of slavery (or of apartheid) would be thought to be justified—even by those who are committed to these systems of belief. It is not because God forbids slavery (or apartheid) that slavery (or apartheid) must be seen to be an unjust institution. On the contrary, within religious traditions (such as the Christian, the Islamic, and the Jewish) that conceive of God as (among other things) a just God, it is because slavery and apartheid are unjust institutions that they are (deemed to be) contrary to the will of (the Christian, the Islamic, and the Jewish) God.[16] Similar arguments can be run to show that when, within a particular culture, there is condemnation of slavery or apartheid, the reason for the condemnation need not be (at the most basic level)—and indeed typically is not—some idiosyncratic, culture-specific reason. To suppose that it must be would be to saddle cultural theorists with a daunting task—the task of identifying, for any given cultural tradition, the culture-specific reason that the members of that tradition happen to have for thinking that slavery and apartheid are unjust institutions.

Doubts about the defensibility of Gutmann's ostensibly Rawlsian ("overlapping consensus") approach to the establishment of an international consensus about human rights are wholly consistent with agreement about the great importance that attaches to efforts to secure such an international consensus. The aim, however, should be to establish a consensus that extends to (at least the most basic of) the reasons for thinking that recognition should be accorded to certain named and delineated human rights.

THE STRUCTURE OF ARGUMENTS FOR HUMAN RIGHTS

Human rights are an important subclass of moral rights. They comprise the rights that are ascribable to people simply as human beings. They must, accordingly, be seen as rights possessed by all human beings. And when it comes to the question of the rationale for the supposition that there are such rights—that all human beings actually do have such rights—it is natural to assume that the answer will have to draw attention either to respects in which all human beings are alike or to respects in which the circumstances of their lives are alike (or both).

But in what respects must human beings be alike—and in what respects must the circumstances of their lives be alike—for the ascription to them of moral rights to be defensible or warranted?

Three facts about human beings and the circumstances of their lives form an important part of the backdrop to claims about the existence (and content) of such rights. It is at least partly in virtue of these facts that the ascription of such rights to human beings, simply as human beings, is justified. Not, of course, that the facts can be represented as entailing that human beings have rights. The relationship is much weaker and much more indirect. Nevertheless, each of these facts can be described in a way that connects it with an important ingredient in the arguments on which we tacitly rely when we affirm the existence of human rights.

Before attempting to identify some of these familiar facts about the human condition, let me briefly describe the three principal ingredients in arguments for human rights to which, perhaps somewhat obliquely, they might be held to point. When arguments for human rights are set out in a reasonably full and explicit way—and it goes without saying that this is often unnecessary, given the comparative obviousness of some of these rights and the comparative obviousness, too, of the considerations that might be cited in their support—it will be found that they incorporate, in some form, subclaims of at least three different kinds.

First, there is the claim that protection of the putative right in question can be expected, in normal circumstances, to promote some vital interest of the right holder—that is, to contribute in some way, direct or indirect, to the right holder's well-being or welfare. It is not insignificant that in the editorial introduction to their recent book on the East Asian challenge to doctrines of human rights,[17] Joanne Bauer and Daniel Bell believe that they can take for granted—as uncontroversial—that the "essential purpose" of an international human rights regime is "to promote and protect vital human interests." It is a view of the fundamental purpose served by human rights that is challenged by none of the contributors to their collection, very diverse though the cultural traditions to which they belong in fact are. Nowhere do they suggest that the consensus about this fundamental purpose can be called into question by the issuing of reminders about the differences of view there are between (some) Westerners and (some) East Asians about (certain) questions of "value." Rather, the question that they all take up is whether the existing international human rights regime is "flexible enough to accommodate fully the needs of the non-Western, in this case East Asian, peoples."[18]

The second claim that is built into arguments for human rights is that the burden of promoting the right holder's interest falls upon persons other than the right holder and *not* upon the right holder. Thus if A is said to have a right to X, it is assumed that responsibility for the securing of the benefit to A that respect for the right is thought to procure does *not* fall upon A.

The third principal ingredient in arguments for human rights is the claim that the imposition on persons other than the right holder of the burden of promoting the right holder's interest (through the doing of whatever has to be done if the right is to be respected) must be consonant with principles of distributive justice. That is, if A has a right to X—and if this means, in part, that persons other than A are duty bound in normal circumstances to do whatever may be needed to ensure that A is secured in the possession of the right—then it must be possible to show that it is not unfair to ascribe such duties to all those against whom A holds the right.

Any reasonably full version of an argument defending the existence of a human right to X thus embodies a claim to the effect that all of three conditions are satisfied.

1. The interest (or welfare or well-being) condition requires that the X to which there is a right be something that, in normal circumstances, will serve the interest of the right holder.
2. According to the nonresponsibility condition, it must be reasonable to suppose that the right holder ought not to be regarded as personally responsible for the securing of X (responsible, in effect, for the securing of the benefit ostensibly securable by X).
3. According to the justice (or fairness) condition, the imposition of duties on persons other than the right holder—the duties that must be discharged if the right to X is to be protected—does not place unfairly heavy burdens upon them.

An argument purporting to show that A has a human right to X can consequently fail if one or more of these conditions is not satisfied. Thus, if the X to which A allegedly has a right is something that, in normal circumstances, cannot reasonably be expected to contribute to A's well-being or welfare or interest, it will be false that A has a right to X. Again, if it can be shown that it is up to A—one of A's responsibilities (and a fortiori something well within his or her power)—to do whatever may be necessary to procure the benefit X can be expected to yield for A, then again, it will be false that A has a right to X. Finally, if it can be shown that—even though the securing of X for A would confer a palpable benefit upon A, and even though it cannot plausibly be maintained that responsibility for securing X ought to fall upon A—ascribing to persons other than A responsibility for securing X for A would saddle them with duties that are unfairly burdensome, then, once again, A cannot be said, defensibly, to have a right to X.

Let me now rehearse briefly the three (familiar) facts about the human condition that can be linked to the principal ingredients in arguments for human rights.

The first of these facts is that all human beings seek to live lives over time that will enable them—among other things, no doubt—to achieve their own well-being on some reasonably determinate, even if in content somewhat variable, conception of what their well-being consists in. A good deal of the detail of these conceptions of well-being will of course be heavily indebted to the cultural traditions within their community or the society with which they identify. But alongside the differences there are in the tradition-influenced aspirations that help to give shape to their lives, the conceptions of the good by which they are guided can be expected to have some important common features. For example, if a satisfactory life is assumed to be a life in which at least some measure of personal well-being is secured over time, there will be found to be agreement across societies and cultures about such components of a satisfactory life as (1) maintenance of health and avoidance of disease, (2) satisfaction of basic economic needs (for food, clothing, shelter, etc.), and (3) the development, through education of the appropriate sorts, of a wide range of natural capacities. Ill health and debilitating disease, grinding poverty, and stunted development of latent capacities are everywhere recognized to be evils. They are among the things that all human beings have an important stake in eliminating from their lives.

A second fact about human beings and the circumstances of their lives is that they are unable to live satisfactory lives on their own. That is, they are unable to live lives in which at least some measure of well-being is achieved simply by doing the things it is wholly within their power, as individuals, to do. Despite the variation there is in the capacities that individuals have, and despite the variation there is in their personal qualities (of temperament, personality, and character), human beings are alike in that it is true of all of them that the living of a satisfactory life would be out of the question for them if, *per impossibile*, they were left, throughout their lives, to fend for themselves and to rely exclusively on their own resources.

A third fact about human beings and the circumstances of their lives is that at least some of the most important things needed for the living of a satisfactory life are securable through cooperation with other people. Collective strategies consequently have an indispensable role to play, not only in the pursuit by the members of a community or society of certain collective goals, but also in the efforts that individuals make over time to achieve their own personal well-being.

These familiar facts about human beings and the circumstances of their lives can be brought to bear on the articulation of the structure of arguments for human rights, in that, when viewed in a certain way, they can be used to highlight the principal ingredients in such arguments.

The first fact—about the stake that all human beings have in securing their own well-being—provides part of the backdrop to the central thesis of the so-called interest (or welfare) conception of rights. According to this account, a right has to be seen (at least in part) as a device for securing the interest (or welfare or well-being) of the right holder. While it is a deficiency of this view that it is sometimes represented as embodying the whole story about the rationale for rights, it does highlight one of the crucial conditions that must be fulfilled if a well-founded claim about the existence of a human right to X is to be advanced. In particular, it throws light on one of the most striking features of rights, which is that those to whom they are ascribed have a personal stake in their recognition.

One way of underscoring this sort of point about the connection between rights and interests—or the connection, indeed, between the recognition of someone's right to something and the securing of that person's interest—is to draw attention to the distinction we ordinarily draw between moral duties and moral rights. The distinction is quite a sharp one. One striking difference between moral duties and moral rights can be brought out by contrasting the relations in which duties and rights stand, respectively, to protection of the agent's interest. On the one hand, the ground of moral duties cannot plausibly be thought to be the protection of the interest of the duty bearer, as is clear, for example, from the contrast moralists have almost always drawn between duty and interest and from the distinction that is standardly drawn between what people are morally required to do and what it would be (merely) prudent for them to do. On the other hand, when it comes to an agent's rights, at least an important part of what we take for granted when we try to make sense of the strong personal stake a putative right holder has in demanding recognition of his or her (moral) rights is that there is an important link in practice between respecting people's rights and protecting their vital interests. Recognition of this link is reflected in the fact that when someone's right is not respected, compensation of the right holder (compensation of some sort or in some form) is normally thought to be called for. Compensation is due precisely because of the injury to the right holder's interest occasioned by the breach.

The second of the three "facts" about human beings and the circumstances of their lives is connected in a rather less direct way with another important part of what we suppose the rationale for human rights to be. If it is simply not possible for individual human beings, by the doing of things wholly within their power as individuals, to live a tolerably satisfactory life over time—that is, to achieve at least some measure of well-being over a lifetime—then, because *ought* implies *can*, it makes no sense to suppose that individuals, as individuals, ought to be held personally responsible for how well their lives go overall. It is tolerably obvious, in light of this feature of the human condition, that any extreme version of an "ethic of self-reliance" must be summarily rejected—any version, for example, according to which it is simply up to individuals, as individuals, to do whatever may be needed to make a success of their lives, with any shortfall in their achievement of this general goal being properly attributable to them as something for which they, as individuals, must take the blame. But sponsors of less extreme versions of the self-reliance ideal may also need to be reminded of the many respects in which even exemplars of the ideal are in practice indebted to others for the achievement of some of their most important personal goals.[19]

What light does this general point throw, even if only indirectly, on the structure of arguments for human rights? To see what the connection is, recall a second standard feature of talk about rights, which is that when someone has a right, the duties that can be "correlated" with the right are duties dischargeable by persons other than the right holder. Even though it is the right holder who is the beneficiary of effective protection of his or her right—and this is a function of the fact that part of the rationale for a right is the role it plays in the promotion of the right holder's interest or well-being—it is no part of the right holder's responsibility to do what may have to be done to secure that benefit.

It is true (but it is also of course irrelevant) that the possessor of a right to X may have to take personal responsibility for *exercising* the right (where X is an activity of some sort, for example) or for *claiming* the X to which there is a right (where X is something other than an activity). The only question in the present context, however, is whether *having* a right to X presupposes that whatever has to be done to ensure that the right holder has the right is one of the responsibilities of the right holder—which it is not.

It is indeed taken for granted, when A is identified as the possessor of a right to X, that it is not A who is to be called upon to do what needs to be done for the protection of the right; this is clear from the fact that one of the standard ways in which opposition to the claim that A has a right to X can be expressed is by saying that "on the contrary, it is A's responsibility to do whatever may need to be done for the securing of the benefit the putative right would confer if it were accorded recognition as a bona fide right." It is precisely because would-be defenders of the right to X may have to contend with this sort of assault on the claim that the right so much as exists that importance must be held to attach to the "nonresponsibility" condition for the ascription of a right. To counter this particular kind of opposition to the recognition of rights, one has to show that it is not reasonable to assign to the putative right holder the responsibility for securing the benefit associated with the putative right.

For example, if the X in "right to X" is privacy and if the sort of privacy to which a putative right holder, A, is laying claim could be secured for A either by the taking of elaborate steps by A or by the adoption of a number of (let us say) somewhat costly measures by persons other than A, one straightforward way in which a critic of the view that A has a right to privacy of the sort at issue might argue is to claim that it is A and not persons other than A who ought to shoulder the burden of ensuring that A enjoys this sort of privacy. A successful argument of this sort would of course undercut the claim that A has a right to X, simply because it is understood that whenever A does have a well-grounded right to X, part of what this implies is that the burden of securing X for A[20] must fall on persons other than A: it will never be the case that the burden falls on the right holder.

The potential importance to disputes about the existence of rights of the nonresponsibility condition can be confirmed by recalling that critics sometimes express their objection to what they think are extravagant claims[21] by complaining that there is, on the part of defenders of rights, much too much interest in people's rights and not enough in their responsibilities. Since the doctrine of the "correlativity" of rights and duties commits any defender of the claim that A has a right to X to ascribing a plethora of duties to persons other than A—all those duties that they must discharge if A's right to X is to be effectively safeguarded or respected—it is clear that the complaint must be taken to be that, in such situations, it is the failure to ascribe these responsibilities to the putative right-holder—namely, A—that is being objected to. The nub of the complaint is that persons other than A are being saddled with responsibilities that ought instead to be shouldered by A. Since it is common ground—as between critics and defenders of A's putative right to X—that ascription of the right relieves A of responsibility for the securing of a benefit that other people have a duty to provide, the dispute has to be seen as revolving around the question of whether, in the case at hand, the nonresponsibility condition of possession of a right ought to be deemed to be satisfied.

The third fact—about the degree to which individuals are dependent on the assistance as well as the forbearance of other people when they endeavor to achieve at least some measure of well-being in the course of living their lives—is related to the connection we normally assume exists between rights and justice. There is assumed to be a connection of this sort because, whenever people are said to have rights, questions must in principle be faced about whether it is fair for the correlative duties they entail to be imposed on all those against whom the rights are held. These are questions about whether it is fair—consonant with principles of distributive justice—for the putative right holders to expect others (other individuals, other groups, other agencies, etc.) to stand ready to perform, perhaps at considerable cost to themselves, the acts of forbearance or assistance that the rights in question may require.

Care must be taken, however, in specifying the nature of the connection between rights and justice. It should not be supposed, for example, that the notion of justice enters the picture rather naturally when there is talk about (moral) rights because justice simply consists in "respect for people's rights." Consider, for example, the view that justice is a matter of "giving everyone their due," when this is glossed (as it plausibly might be) as "arranging for everyone's rights to be respected." This view of the relation between rights and justice will not do because it assumes, falsely, that people's rights can be identified (for the purpose of spelling out what justice in fact consists in) independently of appeal to considerations of justice. The assumption is false because people cannot be said, defensibly, to have moral rights of this or that determinate kind unless it can be taken for granted that calling upon others to stand ready to carry out the correlative duties does not impose an unfairly heavy burden on them. Justifiable ascription of the rights in question presupposes that this justice issue has been dealt with. The relevant judgments of distributive justice are thus more fundamental than—and consequently cannot be explicated by reference to—judgments about the (moral) rights people have.[22]

What I have referred to as the "third" fact about human beings and the circumstances of their lives helps point the way to a better account of the connection between rights and justice. If the achievement by individuals of their own well-being depends in part on the contributions other people make to facilitating the achievement of their goals in life (sometimes only by refraining from interfering with their pursuit of these goals, sometimes by providing active assistance in various forms), questions are bound to arise about how far it is fair to require people to carry out all those duties (whether of forbearance or of active assistance) that are (necessarily) correlated with the rights of putative right holders. While A's having a right to X (against B, C, D, and so on) entails that B, C, D, and the rest must shoulder whatever responsibilities they may have to stand ready to discharge to ensure that A's right to X is protected, the question whether A has any such right is, in part, the question whether B, C, D, and the rest have any such responsibilities. In its most important form, this latter question can be glossed as the question whether it is fair—that is, in accordance with principles of distributive justice—for these burdens to be made to fall on B, C, D, and the rest.

That the fundamental issue here is one of fairness—an issue of distributive justice—can be brought out by noting both of the points already made about the rationale for rights. When A is said to have a right to X and the right is one that A holds against B, C, D, and the rest, A must be seen as enjoying a benefit (the benefit possession of the right confers on A, a benefit, moreover, for the securing of which A has no responsibility whatsoever[23]). B, C, D, and the rest, on the other hand, must be seen as bearing certain burdens (the burdens they must bear if they are to discharge the various duties entailed by A's right). The justice condition for possession of a right is only satisfied when conferment of this benefit on the right holder at the cost of imposition of various burdens on persons other than the right holder can be represented as consistent with principles of distributive justice. It is precisely because such "aggregative" principles as the social benefit maximization principle[24] to which mainstream utilitarians are committed do not require special attention to be given to questions about what would constitute a fair or just distribution of the conditions of a decent life among the members of a society that they are so widely regarded as having no interesting role to play in arguments about the (moral) rights of individuals.

SOME IMPLICATIONS

The account I have given of the structure of arguments for human rights has implications for several important issues that have arisen in recent philosophical debates about rights.

The first concerns the possible conflict there is sometimes thought to be between the "universality" that is generally regarded as a defining feature of human rights and the rights people might be taken to have to participate fully in the (very different) religious and cultural traditions that help to give shape and content to their distinctive ways of life. It is important to notice that on the view defended in this chapter, the notion of individual well-being (or welfare or interest) that plays so central a role in arguments for human rights can be applied simultaneously in ways that reflect both universal features of the human condition and the diverse cultures and ways of life that provide the context for the pursuit of their life goals by the members of a society. This means that there is no barrier to the accommodation both of such relatively "fixed-content" human rights as the right not to be tortured and of rights that get much of their content from distinctive features of the ways of life of diverse groups and societies. Provided a society's cultural (and political and economic) arrangements are consonant with protection and promotion of the well-being of all its members, and provided the conditions for the living of a life that reflects these arrangements are securable for all on a fair basis, the right to participate fully in (diverse) local traditions can be accorded recognition as a human right, despite the fact that it is (in a sense) a right with "variable content."

A second implication of the proffered account is that care must be taken not to attach the wrong sort of significance, within doctrines of human rights, to the distinction between (on the one hand) "civil and political rights" and (on the other) "social and economic rights." It need not be disputed, of course, that the distinction is useful enough as a classificatory device if it serves to mark the difference between the institutional arrangements that give effect to human rights in (say) the political domain and the institutional arrangements needed for the protection of human rights in (say) the economic domain. However, no assumption should be made about the greater importance in principle of rights of any of these different kinds. It should not be thought, for example, that greater importance attaches to the securing of the civil and political rights of human beings than to the protection of their social and economic rights. And a fortiori, it should not be thought that rights of certain of these sorts have a stronger claim to recognition as human rights than rights of the other sorts. Civil and political rights, for example, cannot be viewed, defensibly, as having a better claim to the status of human rights than social and economic rights.

A third implication of the view I have presented has to do with the ongoing dispute between advocates of the interest (or welfare) conception of rights and advocates of the autonomy (or choice) conception.[25] While I regard it as a deficiency of the interest or welfare theory that it seems to give no express recognition to the role played by (say) justice considerations in arguments for (moral) rights, it offers in my view a better account of the personal stake people have in the ascription to them of (moral) rights than the account given by those who hold that the basic rationale for such rights is protection of the autonomy of right holders.

The interest (or welfare) view is superior to the autonomy (or choice) view for at least three reasons. The first is that to restrict human rights to rights that help secure the autonomy of right holders is to identify human rights with a mere subclass of human rights. Such important human rights as the right to life, the right not to be tortured, the right to health care, and the right to education are not properly describable as autonomy rights, even though, of course, securing their recognition may be an indispensable condition of the protection of autonomy rights.

Second, the interest theory gives a better account of what underpins our recognition of the importance of autonomy rights, in two ways. For one thing, what makes it important for the autonomy of individuals to be accorded special protection is the crucial role that the exercise of autonomy rights plays in the securing of personal well-being. Not only is it the case that human beings typically take a special satisfaction in making their own decisions about the shape and direction of their lives, but it is only when they are left free to do so that judicious choices can be made about which activities will actually contribute to the living of a fulfilling and satisfying life. The other reason for thinking that the interest theory offers a more satisfactory account of the importance of autonomy is that it is only when autonomy considerations are seen to be subordinate in some sense to considerations having to do with the well-being or welfare of individuals that sense can be made of the distinction between, on the one hand, situations in which affording individuals autonomy (i.e. giving them choices) is a (perhaps indispensable) good and, on the other, situations in which it may be highly undesirable as well as impracticable to allow (let alone encourage) individuals to make their own decisions. Young children, for example, are human beings, and as such they have rights, but they cannot plausibly be said to have a full complement of autonomy rights.[26] Again, full autonomy rights cannot be ascribed to adults whose capacity for the making of interest-safeguarding decisions on their own is severely compromised (temporarily or permanently) either because of some disability or because of the impairment of decision-making capacities brought about by disease, addiction, or extreme psychological stress. We can make sense of the attitudes we adopt in these cases only if we recognize that the argument for granting individuals autonomy rights is contingent on its being at least likely that their exercise of these rights will make a contribution, in typical decision-making situations, to their achievement of personal well-being. No such rights ought to be extended—we are likely to believe—in cases where the putative possessors of the rights clearly lack the ability to make decisions that will safeguard their vital interests.

DISAGREEMENT ABOUT HUMAN RIGHTS

The account of the structure of arguments for human rights offered here has at least two other important (and related) implications—implications that are plausible to view as providing further support for the account itself. Not only does the account leave open, to some considerable extent, what a comprehensive list of human rights under given social, economic, and cultural conditions would be like, but it also helps to identify some of the key areas in which there may be disagreement about whether this or that putative right deserves a place on the list. When there is dispute about the existence—or about the content or scope—of some putative human right, the dispute will be traceable (if the analysis offered in this chapter is on the right lines) to one or more of three sources.

First, there may be disagreement about whether there is a human right to X because of uncertainty or dispute about whether the measures aimed at securing X for all human beings can in fact be represented, defensibly, as an effective (or even plausible) means of contributing to their well-being over time. And uncertainty or dispute about these matters may have its origins, in turn, in the sheer diversity of the economic conditions that prevail in different parts of the world or in the diversity of the social and cultural traditions to which individuals in different societies are committed.

Second, there may be disagreement about whether there is a human right to X because of uncertainty or dispute about whether it is or is not within the power of individuals, if they display sufficient initiative and are sufficiently persistent and self-reliant, to secure X for themselves. It will often be a matter of considerable difficulty determining how to cope with such questions, and some of them, indeed, may prove to be intractable. There are some easy cases. It is clear, for example, that for many of the unemployed in industrial economies in which a high unemployment rate is considered "normal," being economically self-supporting is not a real option. Other cases will be more difficult and may raise questions about the preferred interpretation of the virtue of self-reliance. Should individuals be required to do whatever they can to be self-reliant in the living of their lives no matter how demanding the ideal of self-reliance in this form proves to be? Or should self-reliance be recognized to be a virtue—a quality to be developed and emulated—only when a more balanced approach is adopted to the choice between go-it-alone strategies for the achievement of personal goals and strategies that require a willingness to cooperate with (and thus also to depend upon) other people?

Finally, there may be disagreement about whether there is a human right to X because of differences of view about whether, if the right is posited, a fair balance is being struck between what individuals might be asked to contribute to the securing of X (by making various kinds of effort themselves or by exploiting resources to which they already have access) and imposing on others the obligation to help them to secure X. Among the trickier issues here are those that involve cases where the securing of X calls for dividing up the responsibility for securing X but where there is difference of view, initially, about what the split ought in fairness to be between what individuals should be asked to do for themselves and what "others" should be required to contribute. For example, in specifying what the human right to health care might amount to, one may have to determine how much of the cost of health care should be paid for by individuals (perhaps in the form of fees or premiums) and how much of the cost should be borne by the public purse. As this last example shows, the fairness issues are complicated. In part, the reason is that the members of a society may be unequally well off in economic terms—so that the payment of fees or premiums may be a greater burden for some than for others. It is also that their needs for health care are likely to be unequal—and unequal, too, for reasons over which individuals have little or no control.

Once it is accepted that human rights are a subclass of moral rights, it follows that questions about their existence or content cannot be answered by an appeal to documents, even widely accepted documents such as the Universal Declaration of Human Rights (1948) or the international human rights Covenants (1966). Instead, such questions must be answered by considering the role played by human rights in (1) promoting the interest (or well-being) of the right holder, (2) imposing duties on persons other than the right holder, and (3) doing so fairly. Claims about the existence of a human right fail when any of these conditions have not been satisfied.

NOTES

1. The Declaration was adopted by the international community in 1948, and the Covenants received international endorsement in 1966.

2. For the distinction between "institution-determining" and "institution-determined" rights, see Macleod, "Rights, Law, and Justice," pp. 7–38, in *Legal Theory Meets Legal Practice*, ed. Bayefsky (Academic Publishing, Edmonton, 1987). The distinction is elaborated in section 6 (Rights and Justice), pp. 31–38.)

3. While recognition—in law, in constitutional documents, in international conventions, and so forth—is not crucial to the existence of human rights in the sense at issue in this chapter, it is of course a matter of the first importance to determine whether arguments can be mounted showing that recognition ought to be accorded these rights. And importance clearly attaches to determining what the appropriate forms of recognition are. It may, for example, be desirable but insufficient for judiciously formulated versions of these rights to be embedded in international documents to which all countries are signatories. It may also be necessary for effective legal instruments—both in domestic and in international law—to be established for the protection and enforcement of the rights in question.

4. While no particular account of what, precisely, the marks of a so-called analytic statement are is either offered or presupposed here, I have in mind—roughly—the sort of statement the contradictory of which is self-contradictory.

5. The general point here is that if—as seems obvious—there is no such thing as a (moral) right to make, knowingly, statements about other people that are both reputation undermining and false, the idea that the (moral) right to freedom of expression is a right of unlimited scope must be abandoned. Once this is noted, the question of what the boundaries are within which people can be said to have this right becomes an important—and inescapable—question.

6. *Human Rights as Politics and Idolatry*, edited by Amy Gutmann (Princeton University Press, 2000).

7. *Op. cit.*, p. 57

8. *Op. cit.*, x

9. *Op. cit.*, xii

10. *Op. cit.*, xii

11. This is one of Ignatieff's clarifying articulations of the "foundations" issue. (*op. cit.*, p. 55).

12. John Rawls, "The Idea of an Overlapping Consensus," *Oxford Journal of Legal Studies*, 7 (1987), 1–25.

13. "Conditions of an Unforced Consensus on Human Rights." This was Charles Taylor's contribution to *The East Asian Challenge for Human Rights*, edited by Joanne Bauer and Daniel Bell (Cambridge University Press, 1999).

14. *Op. cit.*, p. 143.

15. The basic point here is that theological disagreements—disagreements about what the "will of God" is—are bound to generate lists that differ at least to some extent of the so-called human rights that are held to be justified, most fundamentally, by reference to the "will of God."

16. If the injustice of slavery were to be regarded as—quite strictly—grounded in (or derivable from) the "will of God" (as "revealed" in this or that sacred text, e.g.), the common religious belief that God is to be seen as a just God would be undermined.

17. Joanne Bauer and Daniel Bell (eds.), *The East Asian Challenge for Human Rights*, (Cambridge University Press, 1999)

18. *Op. cit.*, p. 3.

19. The point that needs emphasis here is the considerable degree to which individuals are interdependent in the pursuit of personal goals. (That they are interdependent when pursuing collective goals is of course too obvious to need underlining.)

20. That is, the burden of ensuring that A's right is safeguarded.

21. Things would be different, of course, if rights were self-evident or if (as so-called rights-based theories seem to promise) rights could be shown to be "foundational" to a system of political morality. However, the fact that considerations of distributive justice provide part of the rationale for the ascription of moral rights to people can be cited, tellingly, in the refutation of both these views.

22. Courtesy of the "nonresponsibility" condition for the ascription of rights, that is.

23. According to this principle, the distribution of benefit and burden—as between A (the beneficiary of ascription of a right) and B, C, D, and the rest (the bearers of the burden imposed by the duties entailed by the right)—is a satisfactory distribution for the purpose of endorsement of the ascription of the right to A, provided it can be represented as being, for society as a whole, a net-benefit-maximizing distribution. Whatever we may think at the end of the day about the applicability or about the defensibility of the net-benefit maximization principle, it is clear that it can throw no light at all on what might make some determinate distribution of benefit and burden across society as a whole a fair, just, or equitable distribution.

24. See, for example, Wayne Sumner's discussion in his *The Moral Foundation of Rights* (Oxford University Press, 1987).

25. The tussle between interest and autonomy theorists on the battlefield of children's rights is explored in several of the essays in *The Moral and Political Status of Children*, a collection that was edited for Oxford University Press (2002) by David Archard and Colin Macleod.

26. There should be no embarrassment about conceding—what is undeniable anyway—that there are differences of view about the rights that merit recognition in any reasonably comprehensive catalogue of human rights. Such differences are only to be expected, given the complexity and diversity of the social, cultural, and economic conditions under which human rights regimes have to be established and given the difficulty, consequently, of devising appropriate strategies for the effective implementation of the principles of justice (and the conceptions of well-being) that provide the normative underpinnings for human rights.

3

Human Rights: Constitutional and International

Rex Martin

Basic civil rights, sometimes called fundamental constitutional rights, are, paradigmatically, those civil rights such as freedom of political speech or liberty of conscience that have passed the double test of being enacted by legislative majorities and of being affirmed and then supported over the years by checking devices, such as judicial review. These rights have survived the scrutiny of time, experience, and public discussion. They have been focused, revised, winnowed, and affirmed by the self-correcting character of the democratic process and now continue to enjoy a high level of consensus and social support. Basic rights, as understood here, are not to be superseded or significantly impaired in the normal case by rights that are not universal; by universal rights that are not well established in the ways just described; or by other normative considerations, such as national security, gross domestic product, or mere aggregate net welfare.[1]

Not all constitutional rights (for example, uninhibited freedom of contract or the right of persons to own and carry guns) will meet the standard set by the notion of basic civil rights, and some rights not thought to be constitutional rights, such as the right to a primary and secondary education, will in fact meet it. The standard set by basic civil rights is a normative, not a descriptive, theory of constitutional rights in a democratic system.

The account that follows is not intended as a conceptual analysis, broad or otherwise. Rather, it is an attempt to use the notion of basic civil rights as a structuring device, to develop a constructive theory of the main constitutive elements of the contemporary conception of human rights. That conception draws on and is informed by a number of traditional strands in our thinking. The theory proposed here suggests connections between aspects of various ordinary ways of thinking about rights and human rights, connections that should be preserved.

CONCEPTIONS OF HUMAN RIGHTS: TWO MAIN CAMPS

The vocabulary of rights and, in particular, of human rights may actually be used at any of several steps: that of mere claim, that of entitlement (where only the claim-to element is really settled), that of fully validated claim (where we have the idea of both a justified claim *to* something and a justified claim *against* some specific person[s] for it), and, finally, that of satisfied or enforced claim (where the appropriate measures required to support or fulfill the claim have been given effective embodiment). The presence of these possible stages has introduced a degree of ambiguity into assertions that a right or, in particular, a human right exists.

Accordingly, contemporary opinion varies significantly as to the point at which such assertions can most plausibly be thought to take hold. While some (such as Bernard Mayo) have said simply that rights are claims, others say they are entitlements (for example, H. J. McCloskey), and yet others (most notably Joel Feinberg) say they are valid claims.[2] Ranged against them have been those (such as Wayne Sumner) who emphasize that rights, even human rights, are basically established ways of acting or being treated.[3] And, last of all, some (for example, John Rawls and A. I. Melden) have treated rights as legitimate expectations and, hence, have landed more or less in the middle.[4]

For simplicity, and leaving aside legitimate expectations, the remaining views can be divided into two camps: the view that rights are justified claims and the view that they are socially recognized practices. The main case for each of these contrasting views is laid out rather briefly. But ultimately the argument comes down on the side of social recognition.

The starting point for the view that rights are (valid) claims is the common opinion that to have a right is to have a justification for acting in a certain way or for being treated in a certain way. Now, suppose that a candidate for rights status had all the rights-making features but one. Though accredited (in the sense of being justified), it was not established; it lacked the social acceptance or the official recognition that it ought to have.

Why should the lack of such recognition deprive it of rights status? Clearly, a morally justified claim can be valid as a claim even though it has not been answered, so to speak, by governmental or individual action, for the validity of the claim is in no way infirmed by the fact that the called-for responses have not been forthcoming. A morally valid justified claim can be purely a claim, for it is possible to conceive any such claim as one that holds in the absence of practices of acknowledgment and promotion and yet is fully valid as a claim.

The thesis that human rights are universal morally justified claims is understood by its proponents to be a way of asserting that human rights (simply insofar as they are justified or valid claims to ways of acting or of being treated and are applicable to all people) are rights, whether responded to or not. The proposed thesis stands or falls on the point that morally justified claims, simply in virtue of being morally valid, are rights and that human rights owe their status as rights solely to the element of justified claim.

On this view, human rights can be conceived without loss as morally justified or valid claims and nothing more. Thus, when a claim to something can be morally justified as holding good for all or almost all people and when this justification can serve as the ground of duties (incumbent on at least some people) to see to it that this something is relevantly done or provided, then we have a human right. J. S. Mill put the heart of the matter here nicely when he said, "To have a right, then, is, I conceive, to have something which society ought to defend me in the possession of."[5]

Accordingly, if the rights-making features were modeled on what was justified (what was accredited in that sense), the thing was already a right even before it was recognized and even before it became a practice. And when it was recognized, it would be recognized as a right (as something that was fully justified) and would not simply become a right in being recognized.

Human rights, on this account, are moral rights that are "held to exist prior to, or independently of, any legal or institutional rules"; that is, they are rights that are "independent of *any* institutional rules, legal or nonlegal."[6] The word *moral* seems to be doing much of the same work in this context that the word *natural* used to do. Describing rights as natural implied that they were not conventional or artificial in the sense that legal rights are, and the same is implied here by describing human rights as morally valid claims. This way of looking at such rights is widely thought to be one of the great virtues of the idea that human rights are justified or valid moral claims.

The opposing view is that rights are socially recognized practices, and a number of important figures in the history of political thought (for example, Jeremy Bentham and T. H. Green) as well as political thinkers working today belong in this camp.[7] The social recognition view rests on three main contentions.

The first of these is the contention that the notions of authoritative recognition (if not explicit, then at least implicit, as evidenced by conduct) and of governmental promotion and maintenance (usually on a variety of occasions) are themselves part of the standard notion of a legal right—that is, when we are concerned with rights that are more than merely nominal ones.

Now, the view we examined earlier attempts to provide a generic characterization of rights. (This is certainly true not only of Mill but also of Mayo, McCloskey, Feinberg.) Thus, on the social recognition view, the fatal flaw in the theory of rights as simply justified or valid claims (in any of its formulations) is the suggestion that practices of governmental recognition and enforcement in law can be dispensed with in the case of legal rights. Indeed, this is the very point at which both Ronald Dworkin and Joseph Raz, who might otherwise be taken to be sympathetic to some form of the valid claims thesis, desert that thesis when they emphasize the necessity of institutionally establishing ways of acting or being treated, if these are to count as legal rights.[8]

The second point put forward by the social recognition view is that it is desirable to have, if possible, a single unequivocal sense of rights: one that is capable of capturing both basic civil rights (as a special case of legal rights), on the one hand, and human (and other moral) rights, on the other, under a single generic heading.

Why should one think this? Well, if a characterization of rights was equivocal as between legal rights on the one hand and moral rights on the other so that it seemed to cover radically disparate things in each case, then people might begin to suspect that something funny or even dodgy was going on with talk of human rights. And some, thinking this, might go so far as to deny that there were such things as human rights, to deny that valid claims in and of themselves were really rights at all. Thus, Bentham said that natural rights are nonsense, and others have said similar things about human rights.[9]

It would be difficult for the valid claims characterization of rights to break free of such skeptical doubts, for these doubts arise from the very point at which the valid claims view has attempted to distinguish itself from the social recognition view by saying that rights are essentially valid claims or that valid claims in and of themselves, with nothing else added, are rights. More important, where one alleged that moral rights or human rights are radically different from legal rights on the exact point at issue (that features of recognition and maintenance are seemingly expected of active legal rights but not of moral rights), then it would prove difficult for valid claims theorists to identify the existence conditions (as Sumner calls them) of rights that totally lacked social recognition of any sort.

That is, it would be difficult to state the existence conditions for rights that totally lacked such recognition while at the same time holding onto the ideal that rights to identifiable ways of acting or of being treated should (1) provide significant normative direction to the conduct of people and (2) provide some kind of guarantee to the benefits that can reasonably be expected to accrue to right holders from these very ways of acting or being treated. By the same token, it would prove difficult to ascertain to the satisfaction of fair-minded observers that, in the face of such total lack, these conditions had in fact been met.

Now, if the argument sketched so far is convincing, then the view of rights as justified or valid claims (understood as a generic account of rights) does not provide an adequate generalized notion of rights, one that can comfortably include both legal and human rights. Legal rights cannot satisfactorily be accounted for under the heading of mere justified or valid claims. And we have just seen that alleging a radical disparity, as between legal rights and moral rights on the point currently at issue, may prove unavailing. Thus, we must consider the contention that the notions of social recognition (of some appropriate sort) and promotion and maintenance (usually on a variety of occasions) are themselves internal to the notion of any active right.

This raises the third point urged by the social recognition view. Here the argument is that all moral rights, as accredited moral rights, can themselves be construed as involving established practices of recognition and maintenance. The question is, why *should* we so regard them?

To answer this question requires a certain amount of logical pressure on the notion of a justified or valid claim. Two sample cases illustrate the problem. In each case there is present something like a moral claim, either a claim against a duty or a claim to something but not one that has been recognized.

Consider first, for example, a confessional state with a dominant and exclusivist religion. Here the beliefs that most people have (including their moral beliefs) could effectively block acknowledgment of something as a duty they have (for example, the duty to allow all persons there the free exercise of religion).

In this case, there is a disconnect between an accredited or a possibly accredited critical moral standard that might justify freedom of religion on the one hand and the way these people think that they are supposed to act on the other. The normative directive to act in a certain way (for example, to allow even persons of a minority religion the free exercise of their religion) is exactly what would be missing in the case at hand. It would not take hold; it would not be effective.

It is not (let us hypothesize) that the people in the confessional state summarily deny this accredited critical moral standard or that they simply fail to comprehend how it could underwrite freedom of religion. Indeed, they could very well accord it a sort of initial justified status. And such justified status (were it to hold up) would provide some normative direction to their conduct; at a minimum, it would allow them to conclude that a substantial denial of freedom of religion was wrong, and this judgment might in turn lead them to take corrective measures. And anyone else so reasoning would reach these same conclusions.

The point is, though, that acceptance by the people of this standard, concretely conceived, would be outweighed or negated by another consideration, by another competing principle, which for them has normative precedence. This is at least the hypothesis of our example.

The duty enjoined by the accredited principle (if it had been given full acceptance) is thereby effectively blocked. Its acceptance is blocked here neither by simple self-interest nor by intellectual incomprehension (nor by the claim that the principle, insofar as entertained, is not a moral principle). Rather, it is blocked here by a competing and, in this case, prevailing normative consideration.

A duty that is not or cannot be acknowledged in a given society will not be regarded as a proper duty, as one that normatively binds conduct.

A second and parallel argument could be developed about certain so-called claims-to (for example, claims to a specific liberty of conduct or to a specific way of being treated). When we regard rights as morally justified (as ways of acting or being treated that are justified by some accredited critical moral standard), we expect this standard to provide a basis for someone to be able to claim or demand some specific liberty or some specific way of being treated as something one is fully entitled to, morally speaking. But if that standard is similarly blocked in a given society, it could give rise to no morally legitimate expectation. Or, at least, it could not give rise to the one we are contemplating.

For example, consider the future victims of the Aztec practice of human sacrifice. Let us suppose they were made captive by the Aztecs and that they had precisely the same belief system (cosmological, religious, moral) as their captors. Here the beliefs that most of the captives had (including their moral beliefs) would effectively block the idea (were they able to form it) that they have a claim to life (a claim not to be killed) to which the Aztec priests must, if they act properly, yield in the instance at hand.

In this case, there is a disconnect between an accredited critical moral standard that might justify a specific claim not to be killed on the one hand and the actual claims-to (the moral entitlements) that people properly think they have. Here the Aztec captive would not be in a normative position to enjoy the substance of the liberty or the way of being treated in question (say, a right to life) or to lay claim to it as a moral right they have.

Again, it is not (let us hypothesize) that the people in the Aztec way of life summarily deny this accredited critical moral standard or that they simply fail to comprehend how it could underwrite a claim (on the part of captives) not to be killed. Indeed, they could very well accord that claim a sort of initial justified status. And such justified status (were it to hold up) would provide some normative direction to their conduct; at a minimum, it would allow them to conclude that the slaughter of captives was wrong, and this judgment might in turn lead them to take corrective measures. And anyone else so reasoning would reach these same conclusions.

The point is, rather, that acceptance by the people of this standard, concretely conceived, would be blocked for them (even if they could entertain it) by a competing consideration, by a cosmological principle, which for them has normative precedence. The entitlement enjoined by the accredited principle (if that principle could have been given full acceptance) is thereby effectively outweighed or negated.[10] This is at least the hypothesis of our example.

Modern times are not exempt from the blocking phenomenon just described. Most people in the secular West today would give precedence to the normative claims of logic, mathematics, natural science, and perhaps even social science and history in the sense that moral claims must be compatible with the claims of logic, science, and so forth, and would be blocked (set aside, revised, discounted) where they are not. And in some parts of our contemporary world, the claims of particular religions or world-shaping ideologies (like those of communism or capitalism) would have similar precedence and blocking power.

Imagine now a rather extreme case. Imagine an ideal foundational morality that no one was aware of. In all likelihood, it was not even reflectively available to persons in the society in question. Such a morality could not be normatively effective in that place and time. It could not normatively direct conduct there, and the grounds of good conduct and good judgment in moral matters, whatever these grounds were in that society, could not be connected to this ideal morality.

This is a matter about which one should not be dogmatic or too assured. But it does not seem implausible to believe that something like Nozick's libertarian individualism not only was not known but was not even reflectively available to our Neanderthal cousins (human though they were and, indeed, living in the state of nature). So the case we have imagined is not an impossible one and may even be a likely one.

This being so, no one would think such an ideal morality could justify rights (could justify ways of acting or being treated) there. It could not provide effective moral justification in such a case. It could not effectively underwrite claims and entitlements to given ways of acting or being treated, claims that could figure in the self-understanding of people. And, of course, it could not provide effective normative direction to the conduct of people in that society. It could not normatively justify duties to act in an appropriate manner toward these ways, duties that could figure in the self-understanding of people. The hypothetical ideal morality would be wholly normatively ineffective.

This is the big difference between the ideal morality hypothetical and the two earlier examples (concerning the free exercise of religion and the Aztec captive). These two earlier examples in fact exemplify cases that lie between two extremes, between two limiting cases. At one extreme is a hypothetical ideal morality, and at the other, its polar opposite, is a situation in which established ways of acting or being treated are fully connected with justifying standards. In the religious freedom case and in the Aztec-captive case, the required normative effectiveness is contingently unavailable rather than essentially unavailable (as it is in the ideal morality example). But the point is, nonetheless, that the required normative effectiveness is quite absent in both these cases, as absent in the religious freedom case as it is in the Aztec-captive case.

All these examples suggest, then, that there is an inexpungible element of social acceptance (of social recognition) in the idea of moral rights. It is built into them, at least if we regard these justified ways of acting or being treated as entities in a real social world, as more than the conclusions demanded or the practices enjoined in an ideal critical morality.

To put this basic point slightly differently, substantial or at least adequate moral justification is justification that is not blocked by competing normative considerations, and it is not justification that exists only in Plato's heaven. It is moral justification that is reflectively available to the people involved. But more than this is required for rights (be they moral rights or legal rights) to gain a grip. The people must take that justification on board and internalize it. When it is a right that they all have or when it involves duties that all (or many) of them have, then this business of taking on board must be widespread. It must affect the self-understanding of the people involved (a whole lot of people) in the appropriate ways.

We can take this analysis one step further, from mere social recognition to maintenance. Arguably, any right would be vitiated as a right if it were not protected or promoted at all. In such a case, the right would be a merely nominal one, a right that existed in name only but not in fact. Such rights do not, as some have suggested,[11] constitute a special class of full-fledged rights. Rather, they constitute a defective way of exemplifying any justified and recognized right; merely nominal rights are rights only on paper and nowhere else.

Now, to be sure, nominal rights are rights. The point is, though, that we regard the complete and continuing absence of promotion and maintenance as infirming a right, as rendering it totally (or almost totally) ineffective. A nominal right is a right in one sense only (that of formal acceptance or recognition and, presumably, that of sound moral justification), but it fails to function as a right; it fails to deliver the substance (the way of acting or the way of being treated) that the right is said to be *to*. Any right, when merely nominal, has failed in a crucial respect. It represents at best a marginal and precarious example of a right.

These, then, are the main arguments for the social recognition view that opposes the contention that rights are essentially justified or valid claims. The conclusion one comes to is that notions of acceptance or recognition (of some appropriate sort) and those of promotion and maintenance (usually on a variety of occasions) are themselves internal to the notion of any active right, be it legal, moral, or social.

THE ROLE OF GOVERNMENT IN HUMAN RIGHTS

Let us assume that any right under serious discussion is not merely nominal. Then, for any particular moral right (a human right included), there would have to be certain appropriate practices of identification, promotion, protection, enforcement, and so forth, in place on the part of society and at least forbearance by (other) private persons. The determination of what is appropriate for moral rights, and in particular for human rights (sometimes called natural rights), then becomes the exact point at issue.

It may be that some universal moral rights hold strictly between persons. Examples include the moral right to be told the truth (or at least not lied to), the moral right to gratitude for benefits provided, and perhaps the moral right to have promises kept. Such rights differ from the right not to be killed (for example) in being rights maintained exclusively, or almost exclusively, by conscience. They will, we can assume, have widespread acceptance. Such rights are socially recognized, but they are not institutionally embodied. They are moral rights merely and in no way claims against the government; the role of government is incidental or even nonexistent to them. Interestingly, however, it is often in these very cases that, while we are willing to call such rights moral rights, we would tend to withhold from them the name of human (or natural) rights. The great natural and human rights manifestos were intended to impose restraints upon governments. Individuals were involved as beneficiaries of these restraints but, for the most part, were not the parties to whom the manifestos were addressed. Or, at least, the class of all living individuals, taken one by one, was never the sole addressee of such manifestos, nor was it the primary one. The right to a fair trial, which is often given as an example of a human right (by Maurice Cranston and others), is a right that one has against governments in particular, especially one's own.[12]

The example is by no means atypical. The right to travel (found in the United Nations' Universal Declaration of Human Rights, article 13) certainly contemplates the absence of restraints imposed by governments; indeed, insofar as the issue is the liberty to travel, as distinct from the wherewithal to do so, it is primarily government that is addressed. And the right to freedom from the injury of torture is peculiarly held against governments; this is clear from the context (of court proceedings and, in particular, punishment) in which the right is set (article 5). The same pattern holds with rights to the provision of a service. The duty of providing social security is explicitly enjoined on governments (articles 22 and 25), and the duty to provide for elementary education, which shall be compulsory (article 26), is clearly addressed, in this crucial detail at least, to states in particular.

It seems, then, that the practice of treating governments as the primary addressees of human rights norms is too deeply embedded to be erased. Whether one looks at details of specific rights, as found in the great declarations of rights, or at the theory of human rights/natural rights (including its actual history), governments appear as an addressee, often the principal addressee.[13] So a consideration of the relevant governmental or social practices is never a dispensable or even a negligible matter as regards the human rights status of these moral norms.

This is not to deny, of course, that individuals are often addressed as well (the crucial prohibition invoked in the right not to be killed is addressed both to governments and to individual persons, for example). Even so, in such cases (unlike the case of merely moral rights maintained by conscience), the government is typically called upon to enforce compliance when individual conduct that should be supporting the right fails to do so.

Sometimes the primary addressee is neither individuals, taken one by one, nor governments per se. Rather, it is organized society that is being addressed, respecting the role and character of its social institutions and practices. A society might, for example, employ a complex set of economic and other institutions (such as privately owned firms, a competitive supply–demand market, nonpublic medical practices, and so on) as its main line of response. These institutions constitute the way that society has chosen to provide for its members (or most of them), for their needs (such as the need for medical care), for the availability of goods and services (including those involved in basic sustenance), and for their well-being (including the goods of cultural life). But, again, it is not to be expected that such a complex network could be put in place and maintained over time without the active support of government laws and regulation.[14]

There is a sound basis for saying, then, that human rights norms (that is, morally justifiable claims) are addressed to organized society, to governments in particular, often to governments primarily, and that natural or human rights can be distinguished from other universal moral rights in this very circumstance. Where human rights (as a special case of moral rights) are thought to be addressed to governments in particular (though not exclusively), either primarily (as in our earlier examples) or secondarily (as in the economic example just given), practices of governmental recognition and promotion are one of the main forms, if not the main one, for institutional recognition and maintenance to take.

A CONCEPTION OF HUMAN RIGHTS: SUMMARY AND APPLICATION

The overall account of rights developed here can be applied to human rights as these are understood today, as embodied in the Universal Declaration of Human Rights (1948) or in the European Convention on Human Rights (1954).

In this account, an active human right, understood simply as a moral right, is morally justified by accredited standards. More particularly, a human right is justified by the standard of mutual and general benefit (the benefit of each and all). There may be other standards of justification that are useful and that would be normatively sound, but the standard of mutual and general benefit is, nonetheless, perhaps worth singling out. It would be hard to say, convincingly, that something was a justified human right that quite clearly failed to meet the standard of mutual and general benefit. It would be hard, that is, if we adhered to the supposition that all rights are beneficial in some way to the right holder.

When the right in question is a human right, then the specific way of acting or being treated it identifies should be (at a minimum) a matter of benefit to each and all of a vast number of human beings alive now (and in the foreseeable future). A specific way of acting or being treated that did not meet even this somewhat-relaxed standard could not be justified as a human right.[15]

In short, sound or creditable moral justification is a necessary condition of any right's counting as a human right. The argument suggests that unless the standard of the benefit of each and all (perceived benefit) is satisfied (or can reasonably be expected to be satisfied), then there is not an adequate moral justification in the case at hand.

This standard could be met in the following way. Each person is presumed to be able to reflect and think reasonably carefully about important matters. Each is here presumed, then, to focus and reflect on a single consideration: whether this particular way of acting or being treated (if it were in effect for all) would, on the whole, be beneficial for that person (as beneficial in itself or as a reliable means to some other good thing) and for others as well, now and in the foreseeable future. If all could say, upon reflection, that this is so in their view, then the standard is satisfied. The standard is both minimal and abstract; it is similar in these respects to W. D. Ross's idea of a well-formed prima facie duty (or, in the case at hand, a prima facie right).

The test probably cannot be satisfied for all people. Some people simply cannot or will not think straight. And others do not seem able to get the hang of engaging in moral reasoning at any level. This is why the governing standard had to be specified somewhat more loosely, to say that the test could be satisfied if (arguably) the matter under consideration could be of benefit to each and all of a vast number of human beings alive now (and in the foreseeable future).

Also, there is some question whether the standard in question is a moral standard. Now, it clearly is a moral standard of conventional morality or, at least, a standard compatible with many different conventional moralities. Accordingly, even in the relaxed form just provided, it is a moral standard of sorts. But this may not be enough for some normative moral theorists. They may want to enlarge the scope of those who can be regarded as perceiving the matter as beneficial so as to make it truly universal and to connect that perception with some accredited critical moral principle or with some accredited standard of practical moral reasoning.

Thus, a utilitarian, assuming certain conditions and certain matters of fact, might come up with some ideal but followable moral rule (embracing all people, now and in the foreseeable future) that could itself be justified by the utilitarian general happiness principle. Or, a contractarian (or contractualist) theorist might specify that no reasonable person could deny or reject the prima facie standard in question (T. M. Scanlon) or specify that all reasonable people would accept or endorse it (Rawls).[16] The formulation used here requires neither of these two lines of attack, the utilitarian or the contractualist, to complete it. But it is compatible with both while being neutral between them.

In sum, then, the notion of a justified human right (understood as a kind of moral right) has three main features in the view here proposed. (1) It is a way of acting or being treated that is justified for all human beings by the standard of benefit for each and all and perhaps by other moral standards as well. (2) As an accredited way of acting or being treated, it has some sort of authoritative institutional recognition (in the typical case, through recognition in law and in the action of courts or through embodiment in legally supported and regulated social and economic institutions). (3) It is maintained by conforming conduct, and, where need be, it is enforced by governments.

These three features are linked elements in a procedure for constructing or constituting morally accredited human rights functioning at full capacity. A right could fail at some of these points and still have substance as a human right. Though, if it failed on the point of justification (by reference, for example, to the standard of the benefit of each and all), then it would most likely have reached the point of extinction.

Certainly, one can imagine a legal right that was morally neutral, that cannot be justified in any straightforward fashion by moral standards or by accredited forms of moral reasoning. In the account developed here, such a right would not be a human right. And if what a given right sustained, as one of its intended aims, was itself something wicked and contrary to morality (as was surely the case with the right to own slaves), then it would not be a human right at all but simply something morally wrong. (Though it might, we must add, still be a legal right.)

But a fully functioning human right (understood as a moral right) displays all three features: sound justification, effective recognition, maintenance. The fulfillment or realization, at a suitable level, of these three elements is essential to any robust and nondefective human right (understood as a moral right). Their realization allows human rights to be, as they have always been thought to be, both practical and critical.

THE UN'S UNIVERSAL DECLARATION OF HUMAN RIGHTS

The norms of the 1948 Universal Declaration of Human Rights, in order to be active human rights (as constitutional rights or as international basic rights) and to be morally justifiable as human rights, must satisfy these three points. Human rights, like all basic civil rights, require justification, effective recognition, and maintenance. Beyond that, all rights also require some specification of content, some setting of scope (with provision for making scope adjustments), some competitive weightings in cases of conflict, some institutional devices for the on-site resolution of conflicts, and so on. Otherwise, such rights will conflict with one another and collapse into an incoherent set.

If this is so, one cannot think adequately about human rights (where they are thought to be active rights, as distinct from mere norms) by dispensing with the institutional arrangements just emphasized (i.e., scope adjustment, competitive weighting, promotion, and maintenance). Features such as these are necessary to making moral norms into active human rights functioning at full capacity.

The proper focus here should not be on the manifesto element of the UN's declaration but rather on the embodiment of those norms as active civil rights within states, where such rights (presumably appropriately justified morally) could be and were authoritatively recognized, harmonized, and maintained.[17]

Some might argue that the account developed here relies too often on the great rights manifestos while disparaging another tradition in human rights discourse, one that sees moral rights as justified claims and standards for criticizing existing political or social arrangements, whether or not these claims are recognized and enforced at all.

It should be readily granted that others do regard such justified claims as human rights and that there is no problem in their doing so. There is no need to deny human rights status to such claims or to legislate how people should be talking about human rights. So long as the three-element procedure for constituting human rights is kept on the table as essential to the big picture, there is no need to attack the alternative view.[18]

The essentials of the three-element procedure for constituting human rights are present in the UN declaration. Thus, human rights can be regarded as constitutional rights within individual states. This is, in fact, the case primarily contemplated in the declaration[19] and in the two UN covenants (1966, entered into force 1976), on political and civil rights and on social and economic rights. Insofar as the emphasis is on this one type of case (the case of constitutional rights within individual states), the embodiment of human rights norms can be particularized (to a degree) to different cultural preferences and histories.

INTERNATIONAL HUMAN RIGHTS

A focus on constitutional rights within individual states is not the only option available to the resources of the present account. The human rights described here need not apply exclusively to so-called nation-states and their particular arrangements.

Others, of course, using arguments like some of the ones employed here, have alleged otherwise. Michael Walzer, for instance, says,

> Individual rights may well derive, as I am inclined to think, from our ideas about personality and moral agency, without reference to political processes and social circumstances. But the enforcement of rights is another matter. . . . Rights are only enforceable within political communities where they have been collectively recognized, and the process by which they come to be recognized is a political process which requires a political community. The globe is not, or not yet, such an arena.[20]

To the contrary, the account presented here can allow for the notion of basic rights in an emerging supranational entity or, better, a somewhat unified confederation of states, such as the nascent European Union (EU) and, within it, the European Convention on Human Rights. Indeed, to think clearly about human rights in the present day, one would have to allow for such cases.

One of the really difficult questions about human rights emerges, however, in contemplating even looser international federations or, sometimes, coalitions (even temporary coalitions) of states engaged in formulating or enforcing human rights norms (in a situation where such rights are not being recognized or maintained in some countries). These looser federations or coalitions pose a number of problems.

In the favored case (not always met, of course, in fact), such a federation (or such a coalition) would have to have the continuing support and cooperation of a wide variety of states; it would have to be, in effect, an agreed-upon international agency for identifying, formulating, and overseeing the understanding and the maintenance and enforcement of human rights. Such a federation, if it were international or cosmopolitan in the widest sense, would require the support of many states that were not democratic.

Perhaps only the UN or possibly the International Court of Justice (and within that framework the UN declaration, the two main covenants on human rights, and various other relevant international treaties, such as the treaty outlawing genocide) has that status worldwide, at present.[21] If it does, there is no barrier in principle to the United Nations becoming the kind of political entity described in this account of human rights.

Or, perhaps, a coalition of states acting under UN or EU auspices and authorization could become such an entity. In either of these two cases, there would be a confederation of nation-states, states working to a common purpose, to carry out the job of the international formulation and the maintenance and enforcement of certain basic rights.

Of course, one should not ignore the important (but still secondary) role played by nongovernmental organizations (NGOs), by various religious and charitable organizations, and by individuals. These too can be counted among the agencies (in both dimensions, the constitutional and the international) for identifying and contributing to the understanding and the promotion of human rights.

Another difficult question about human rights emerges from the diversity of justifying arguments offered for human rights, none of them currently universally (or even very widely) accepted. Not even the justification provided by mutual and general benefit, as it applies to specific cases or to specific lines of conduct, is uniformly accepted. Even it is not accepted in all concrete cases (for example, the case of freedom of conscience in matters of religion), and in that sense it is not accepted everywhere, not by all peoples or all governments. Moreover, whether any of these justifying arguments offer suitable grounds for intervention (and, in particular, for forcible intervention) against societies (against peoples) that do not accept these justifications remains a very difficult question.

The question becomes especially difficult when forcible intervention is contemplated against societies that regularly and unamendably engage in practices that are deeply unacceptable and violative of human rights in the light of the justifying arguments. Consider here (as examples of serious violations of human rights) genocide, slavery, and warlord-induced famine and starvation. Consensus might exist on the justifiability of forcible intervention in such cases. But there is far less consensus on such issues as the treatment of women, capital punishment, legal limitations on hate speech (much of which occurs under the heading of religious education), and the establishment of a democratic form of government.

The kind of justification at issue in all these cases would have to rely on standards considerably stronger than mutual and general benefit. The question goes beyond what justifies any given human right to the issue of when, if ever, a particular human right should be internationally enforced.[22]

Clearly, one of the most pressing problems for the international protection of human rights is that the UN lacks effective enforcement power. In enforcing its decisions, the United Nations must rely on the support of existing states. In many instances the international identification of the gravest threats to human rights and the protection of human rights against these threats can most effectively be dealt with regionally rather than globally.[23]

Perhaps, some time in the future, the world will be different. A genuinely universal international order or a family of strong but benign transnational regional orders may well emerge to recognize and maintain human rights. But this has not yet occurred.

In any event, human rights have come to play an increasingly important role in the domestic law and, in particular, the constitutional law of many countries today, for example, in Britain and other countries in Europe, in Canada, and in the United States. Moreover, the outlines of a new international order for human rights is emerging. The European convention and the evolution of the European Union point the direction toward a stronger institutional, though still regional, base for international human rights. And this may be replicated, to a degree, on a larger scale through the United Nations and the international courts. These are the structures through which human rights are recognized and maintained, to the extent that they exist in the world today.[24]

NOTES

1. For the point about the role of the checking devices (in particular, judicial review) as fundamentally democratic in character, see my paper "Constitutional Rights and Democracy in the U.S.A.: The Issue of Judicial Review," with Stephen M. Griffin (coauthor), *Ratio Juris* 8.2 (July 1995), 180–198. The point about the self-correcting character of democratic procedures is taken from Thorson, *The Logic of*

Democracy (New York: Holt, Rinehart, and Winston, 1962), esp. chap. 8; also pp. 120–124.

2. For the examples cited, see Bernard Mayo, Symposium on "Human Rights" II, *Proceedings of the Aristotelian Society Supplementary Volume* 39 (1965): 219–236; H. J. McCloskey, "Rights," *Philosophical Quarterly* 15 (1965): 115–127; McCloskey, "Rights—Some Conceptual Issues," *Australasian Journal of Philosophy* 54 (1976): 99–115; Joel Feinberg, *Social Philosophy* (Englewood Cliffs, NJ: Prentice-Hall, 1973), chaps. 4–6 ; Feinberg, *Rights, Justice, and the Bounds of Liberty* (Princeton, NJ: Princeton University Press, 1980), chaps. 7, 8, 11.

3. See L. Wayne Sumner, *The Moral Foundation of Rights* (Oxford: Oxford University Press, 1987).

4. See John Rawls, *A Theory of Justice* (Cambridge, MA: Harvard University Press, 1971). A second edition of *Theory of Justice*, with a new preface and a number of revisions, was published in 1999. A. I. Melden, *Rights in Moral Lives: A Historical-Philosophical Essay* (Berkeley, University of California, 1988).

5. See Mill, *Utilitarianism* (1863), chap. 5, para. 25. In para. 24, Mill makes a roughly similar analysis and characterizes rights there as "valid claims." This is not Mill's only way of characterizing rights in *Utilitarianism*, however; in chap. 2, para. 19, he calls them "legitimate and authorized expectations." I leave this complication aside (and stick to the two main cases). I have, it should nonetheless be noted, discussed the notion of legitimate expectations at greater length in *Rawls and Rights* (Lawrence: University Press of Kansas, 1985), at pp. 26, 28–29, 32–33, and 69. More interesting, for our purposes, is the account Mill gives of the justification of rights; he ascribes it to "general utility" (chap. 5, para. 25). Others, of course, give different accounts. Some turn to interests to justify rights and others to such considerations as agency or autonomy. These are all examples, then, of the criteria of validity or justification for human rights. Some might supplement any favored criterion with secondary nonmoral criteria such as (1) universality, (2) distributability among all individuals who are within the class of right holders, or (3) practicability under foreseeable real-world conditions.

6. See Joel Feinberg, *Social Philosophy*, p. 84, for the first quote, and Feinberg, *Doing and Deserving: Essays in the Theory of Responsibility* (Princeton, NJ: Princeton University Press, 1970), p. 85, n. 27, for the second.

7. Among thinkers working today, we might cite (besides Sumner) Derrick Darby and Gerald Gaus. For representative writings, see Darby, "Two Conceptions of Rights Possession," *Social Theory and Practice* 27 (2001): 387–417; Darby, "Unnatural Rights," *Canadian Journal of Philosophy* 33 (2003): 49–82; and Gaus, "The Rights Recognition Thesis: A Radical Defense," paper delivered at the Political Studies Association meeting, Aberdeen, and the T. H. Green Conference, Oxford (2002).

8. See Ronald Dworkin, *Taking Rights Seriously* (Cambridge, MA: Harvard University Press, 1977; reissued with an important appendix added in 1978), chap. 4, and Dworkin, *Law's Empire* (Cambridge, MA: Harvard University Press, 1986), chap. 11, also pp. 65–68; Joseph Raz, "Legal Rights," *Oxford Journal of Legal Studies* 4 (1984): 10–21, and Raz, *The Morality of Freedom* (Oxford: Oxford University Press, 1986), chap. 7.

9. See *The Works of Jeremy Bentham*, edited by John Bowring (Edinburgh: Tait; London: Simpkin, Marshall, 1843), vol. 2, p. 501. For elaboration of Bentham's

thinking here, see vol. 3, pp. 159, 181, 217–218, 221. For representative samples of Bentham's texts on this subject, coupled with helpful editorial commentary, see Jeremy Waldron, ed., *Nonsense upon Stilts: Bentham, Burke, and Marx on the Rights of Man* (London: Methuen, 1987), pp. 29–76. For another example of wholesale skepticism about human/natural rights, see Raymond Geuss, *History and Illusion in Politics* (Cambridge: Cambridge University Press, 2001), esp. chap. 3, §5, esp. pp. 143–144, 146; also pp. 137–138, 154, 156.

10. The relevant Aztec cosmological beliefs, besides a complicated theory of phases of cosmological history, include the idea that the perishing of the present cosmological order (and of the known human world within it) could be averted only by "nourishing" the cosmos through the shedding of human blood. For a brief discussion, see my article "The Problem of Other Cultures and Other Periods in Action Explanations," *Philosophy of the Social Sciences* 21 (1991), pp. 345–366, at pp. 355–363. For extended discussion see, for example, Miguel León-Portilla, *Aztec Thought and Culture: A Study of the Ancient Náhuatl Mind* (Norman: University of Oklahoma Press, 1963), chaps. 2–3. *La Filosofía Náhuatl* was originally published in 1956; a second edition was issued in 1959 by the National University of Mexico. See also, León-Portilla, "Philosophy in the Cultures of Ancient Mexico," in *Cross-Cultural Understanding: Epistemology in Anthropology*, edited by F. S. C. Northrop and Helen H. Livingston (New York: Harper and Row, 1964), pp. 35–54, at pp. 41–45.

11. For example, Maurice Cranston, "Human Rights, Real and Supposed," in *Political Theory and the Rights of Man*, edited by D. D. Raphael (Bloomington: Indiana University Press, 1967), pp. 43–53, at p. 48.

12. See Cranston, "Human Rights, Real and Supposed," p. 43.

13. The U.S. Declaration of Independence (1776) begins its famous second paragraph with the words "We hold these truths to be self-evident, that all men are created equal, that they are endowed by their Creator with certain unalienable rights, that among these are Life, Liberty, and the pursuit of happiness. That to secure these rights, Governments are instituted among Men."

14. For supporting argument and discussion, see *Rawls and Rights*, pp. 157–163, 169–173.

15. For the point made about rights as beneficial, see my book *System of Rights* (Oxford: Clarendon Press, 1993), chaps. 2, 5, and 10. The point about such rights being mutually and generally beneficial for all or almost all living human beings follows from our characterization of the rights in question as human rights. Just as civil rights are rights of all citizens, so human rights are rights of all human beings. But here we need to take care. It is important to distinguish between conditions of constitution or existence for moral rights and criteria for their possession. In the present account what justifies something as a right (be it a right to a way of acting or to a way of being treated) is that it is beneficial to the right holder and can be understood as beneficial and that others have a duty to sustain such ways. If different moral standards are brought to bear, and typically (in the case of a human right) many kinds of moral standards will be, then they too are a part of the justification. Putting the point crudely, what justifies a moral right is that it can be understood as following from or being compatible with accredited moral principles or practices (or with accredited forms of practical moral reasoning). Most of the things in the UN's Universal Declaration of Human Rights can be regarded as

justifiable in these ways. Interestingly, many of them would be beneficial only to adult human beings, within a certain range of capabilities and interests: freedom of political speech, the right to vote, liberty of conscience, right to a fair trial or to a job, and so on. The point is that since all or almost all adult human beings are within this range, all are eligible to possess the rights in question; no such adult should be excluded.

16. See T. M. Scanlon, *What We Owe to Each Other* (Cambridge, MA: Harvard University Press, 1998), p. 4 (and throughout his book), for this first formulation and for elaborations on it. See John Rawls, *Political Liberalism* (New York: Columbia University Press, 1996), p. 217, also pp. l (Roman numeral L), 137, 226, 241, 393, for the second formulation here. (Rawls's book was originally published in 1993 and revised in 1996; both versions contain, unrevised, Rawls's important 1982 essay "The Basic Liberties and Their Priority.") Later Rawls adds yet another possible line of formulating the contractarian rubric when he says that those proposing a principle of cooperation or mutual relations "must think not only that it is reasonable for them to propose it, but also that it is reasonable for [others] to accept it"; see Rawls, *The Law of Peoples with "The Idea of Public Reason Revisited"* (Cambridge, MA: Harvard University Press, 1999), p. 57; also pp. 14 and 69.

17. The universal declaration avowedly has a "manifesto" element: it speaks in its preamble of "proclaiming" a "common standard" and calls itself a "declaration." Clearly, then, it lays out a set of aspirations, but it does not stop there. The idea of the recognition of the rights proclaimed and their observation is repeatedly invoked.

18. What might we call a human right that had only the one element, the element of morally valid claim (that and nothing else)? Perhaps it might be called a *human rights norm*. This seems apt because the italicized phrase recognizes that we do not have a fully constituted right here (do not have a full capacity right) while at the same time affirming that a mere morally valid claim does have status as a human right even when only the first of the constituting conditions, the condition of sound normative justification, is fully satisfied. A good example of this alternative way of talking, with which no quarrel is being raised, is provided by Henry Shue, in his book *Basic Rights: Subsistence, Affluence, and U.S. Foreign Policy*, 2d ed. (Princeton, NJ: Princeton University Press, 1996). The first edition was published in 1980; the second edition eliminates chap. 7 of the first edition and adds a new afterword, pp. 153–180. In his book, Shue begins by characterizing human rights as morally justified demands (pp. 13–15), but he immediately goes on to emphasize the importance of such rights being "socially guaranteed" (pp. 15–18). In later chapters, this particular feature is emphasized, and it becomes clear that such guarantees necessarily involve the elements of social recognition and maintenance by both private persons and governments (see esp. chaps. 2 and 5 and the afterword). For a good summary of his views, in which all the components just identified figure, see Shue's chapter "Solidarity among Strangers and the Right to Food," in *World Hunger and Morality*, edited by William Aiken and Hugh LaFollette, 2d ed. (Upper Saddle River, NJ: Prentice-Hall, 1996), pp. 113–132.

19. The preamble to the UN declaration begins with the assertion that the "Member States" are intent on achieving not only the "promotion of universal respect" for human rights and "fundamental freedoms" but also their "observance."

The preamble ends with a commitment to secure for these rights and liberties "their universal and effective recognition and observance, both among the peoples of the Member States themselves and among the peoples or territories under their jurisdiction."

20. Michael Walzer, "The Moral Standing of States: A Response to Four Critics," *Philosophy and Public Affairs* 9 (1980): 209–229, at p. 226; see also, pp. 227–228.

21. It could plausibly be argued that democratic institutions—universal eligibility to vote (on a one-person, one-vote basis), regular and contested voting operating at two distinct levels (the level of parliament and the level of general elections), and majority rule—can, acting as a set (and on a majority electoral base), effectively perform the job of creating and maintaining basic civil rights. This could be claimed because democratic procedures are a stable and relatively reliable way of identifying and then implementing laws and policies that serve interests common to the voters or to a large number of them, presumably at least a majority. At least they are a reliable way of doing so under the conditions outlined in the introductory paragraph of this chapter. Accordingly, when certain rights, the same rights, can be found in a number of contemporary democratic polities and when these rights more or less overlap with those found in the UN's universal declaration and in the two main UN-sponsored covenants on rights, then we have a benchmark for saying that these rights are good candidates for human rights status. This argument does not imply that the operation of democratic institutions and norms is a necessary condition for the creation of basic civil rights. Thus, the UN, which is made up of a good many nondemocratic (even antidemocratic) states and is not itself a democratic body, is not ruled out as a venue for the formulation and maintenance of rights that can be justified by the standard of the benefit of each and all individuals.

22. Criteria of the sort John Rawls urges (just to cite one instance) might prove useful here. Rawls argues, first, that cases such as genocide, slavery, or warlord-induced famine and starvation are violations of rights that would be found on a short list of the most urgent rights (basic liberties and noninjuries) that we, as individuals, have and should have against the greatest evils (see Rawls, *Law of Peoples*, p. 79; also see p. 67). He argues, second, that these ways of acting (liberties) and ways of being treated (noninjuries) are necessary conditions of social cooperation (see *Law of Peoples*, p. 81). These two justifying considerations go well beyond the merely conventional: they have a normative dimension (one that could be endorsed in a critical moral theory), and they have a universal reach (in that they could apply in any society). Other examples of appropriate justifying standards for forcible international intervention could be cited as well. It should be noted that the standard of perceived benefit would probably hold in the three severe and urgent cases (genocide, slavery, etc.). All persons (including those in the affected country) could reflectively decide that the avoidance of these particular injuries was beneficial to them. It is not so clear that it could be met in the second-tier cases (treatment of women, soul-curdling religious intolerance and invective, etc.) in every single case. It might be, but again it might not be. It is the latter cases (cases where it is not met) that forcible international intervention becomes especially problematic.

23. Some, indeed, have argued the virtues, in extreme cases, of unilateral intervention (of forcible intervention by one nation in another to prevent or stop grave violations of human rights). Examples usually cited (from the last thirty years or so) are India in East Pakistan (now Bangladesh), Vietnam in Cambodia, Tanzania in Uganda, and (most recently) Nigeria in Sierra Leone. For the advocacy of unilateral intervention, see Michael Walzer, *Just and Unjust Wars: A Moral Argument with Historical Illustrations*, 3d ed. (New York: Basic Books, 2000), preface to the third edition, esp. pp. xiii–xvi, and chap. 6, esp. pp. 105–108 (1st ed. of *Just and Unjust Wars*, 1977; 2d ed., 1992.) See also, Walzer, "The Argument about Humanitarian Intervention," *Dissent* (Winter 2002): 29–37, esp. pp. 31–33.

24. My first serious attempt at developing a theory of human rights was an article called "Human Rights and Civil Rights," *Philosophical Studies* 37 (1980): 391–403. I quickly became dissatisfied with its argument, but it took me some time to rework it into a more satisfactory form. This I did in chap. 4 of *A System of Rights* (1993), wherein my main account (before now) of human rights can be found. The argument of this book, however, has two serious deficiencies. (1) It does not develop a constructive theory of the justification of human rights; indeed, it seems sometimes not to take the crucial issue of justification seriously: it does not keep a firm grip on the idea that moral justification is essential to human rights. (2) It leaves human rights at the constitutional stage and does not develop the crucial international dimension of human rights at all. The present chapter tries to set things right at both these points of serious deficiency. Perhaps the simplest way to view it is to see the present chapter as an attempt to improve upon, to clarify and correct and then extend, the *System of Rights* argument. In the writing of the present chapter, I have drawn on my article on the concept of rights, with Jim Nickel (coauthor), in the *American Philosophical Quarterly* 17 (1980): 165–180; on my article on rights in the *Routledge Encyclopedia of Philosophy* (London, Routledge, 1998), vol. 8, pp. 325–331; and on two of my books, *Rawls and Rights* and *System of Rights*. For elaboration on the notion of basic rights (in paragraph 1 of the present chapter), see my chapter "Rights and Human Rights" in *Multiculturalism, Identity, and Rights*, edited by Bruce Haddock and Peter Sutch (London: Routledge, 2003), pp. 175–194, at 175–179. Earlier versions of this chapter were presented at the University of Tennessee and at conferences in Pittsburgh, Cardiff, and Washington, D.C. (all in 2002). For their helpful comments, I am indebted to Will Aiken, John Arthur, Richard Brook, David Duquette, Mark Evans, Bruce Haddock, John Haldane, Mikael Karlsson, David Lyons, Alistair Macleod, David Reidy, Peri Roberts, Peter Sutch, Anton Tupa, and Carl Wellman. An earlier and shorter version of the present chapter was published in *Philosophy and Its Public Role*, edited by William Aiken and John Haldane, *St. Andrews Studies in Philosophy and Public Affairs* (Exeter: Imprint Academic, 2004), pp. 181–196.

4

Universalism and Relativism in Human Rights

David Duquette

Asserting the universality of human rights raises two problems. First is the problem of relativism insofar as relativism presents a challenge to the very idea of universal rights. I argue that any coherent relativism does not present a serious threat to the universality of human rights. Second is the problem of a viable universalism, which involves the issues of how to establish whether there are universal moral norms supporting human rights and of how to identify their content. I hope to present a plausible general conception of the universalism of human rights that recognizes the place of cultural relativism, avoids foundational appeals in the argument for universalism, and thus allows for the implementation of human rights in culturally diverse contexts while both recognizing the importance of cultural differences and preserving the universality of human rights. Before I move to the task at hand, I think it may be helpful if I lay out some of the analytical assumptions underlying this approach.

PART 1

First, although it is natural to think of any truly universal human right as (in some sense) a most fundamental right, as distinct from human rights that might be thought of as in some way less fundamental or derivative from "basic rights," my argument for universal human rights does not assume that universality hangs essentially on some such notion of fundamentality. The question whether human rights can be prioritized according to a hierarchic scheme need not enter into the defense of universal human rights against certain relativistic and epistemic challenges.

Second, universal human rights are viewed here as essentially "valid moral claims" regarding the recognition and protection of individuals in respect to particularly important dimensions of human dignity. What makes a moral claim to a human right "valid" is precisely that which explains the importance of what is at stake, the "substance" of the right. Whether or not a particular valid moral claim to a human right receives legal recognition, as in the form of a constitutional provision for a civil right within a nation-state, does not in my view determine the authenticity of the human right in question,[1] although lack of legal recognition—whether in civil or international law—will likely weaken the implementation and protection of the right. Legal recognition and enforcement, while a practical goal for the implementation of human rights, are not part of the "existence conditions" for human rights. There is, however, need for an understanding of rights in a context of recognition, since purely abstract arguments for rights are not sufficient to capture the social significance of moral rights. Given appropriate social recognition, a valid human right constitutes a moral entitlement for an individual to make a *claim to* the enjoyment of a moral good, such as liberty or security, and a *claim against* whoever, given the circumstances, is obligated either to avoid preventing access to the good or to actively provide access to the good, depending on the level and strength of obligation of the addressee of the right in question. While human rights as high-priority norms do involve a number of dimensions, such as those articulated in the Hohfeldian classification of liberties, claims, powers, and immunities, there is an implicit (and very often an explicit) claim to recognition at the heart of every human right, since rights do not exist as mere entitlements without regard to the normative burdens they impose on their addressees. In a deep and generic sense, all human rights are inherently claims for social and legal recognition of the moral status of the individual, but they also presuppose that, in a significant way, social recognition already obtains for the basic norms that support human rights.

Third, there is the question of whether, or to what extent, normative consensus about what constitutes a right, or which rights actually exist, is relevant to the existence of a human right. The observations made at the outset of this discussion about the irrelevance of legal recognition might suggest that such consensus is unimportant; however, consensus remains important because human rights are not held solipsistically by isolated Leibnizian monads but by socially situated individuals, in virtue of their shared humanity and social consciousness of the moral significance of human dignity. This requires further discussion, but it must be recognized at the outset that "normative consensus" about human rights is constructed in the course of experience, discussion, and debate within the human community. Normative consensus is expressed most broadly in international law and in the various institutions and practices of international human rights, but mere de facto agreement (acceptance) cannot in itself constitute moral validity (justification), which also requires good reasons supporting agreement about human rights. These reasons need not appeal to metaphysical givens, as if, for example, human rights were somehow deducible from natural law. Rather, moral justification involves practical reasoning about objective moral norms, understood nonfoundationally in reference to our experiences and expectations regarding what is intrinsic to human dignity. The position advocated here stands in the middle ground between moral foundationalism on the one hand and positivism on the other.

Finally, while the opposition between universalism and relativism in human rights can be taken as a simple either-or proposition, in fact this is rarely done either by universalists or by relativists. The great universalist thinker Thomas Aquinas, in his discussion in the *Summa Theologica* of whether the natural law is the same in all people, distinguishes between the necessary truths of speculative reason, such as that the three angles of a triangle are equal to two right angles, and the contingent matters that are the concern of practical reason, such as the repaying of debts to a creditor. If repaying a debt would lead to a significant harm due to the particularity of the situation, then it would be contrary to reason, at least without certain qualifications or precautions, "for as the limiting particular conditions become more numerous, so do the possibilities that render the principle normally applicable, with the result that neither the restitution nor the failure to do so can be rigorously presented as right."[2] Furthermore, Aquinas holds that while the natural law is in essence the same in everyone and while human law is derivable from natural law, human law is not always derivable as a conclusion from premises but rather varies when it is derived "by way of determination of certain generalities," such as the determination of the manner of punishment of an evildoer (punishment itself in some form being mandated by the law of nature). "The general principles of natural law cannot be applied to all men in the same way, on account of the great variety of human affairs, and hence arises the diversity of positive laws among various peoples."[3]

The ways in which principles of natural law can be qualified in application does not, of course, make Aquinas a relativist, but it does show that to a certain extent relativity is built into his conception of universal law, the most fundamental precept of which is to do good and avoid evil. Conversely, rather clearly "derived" precepts of natural law, such as those affirming the preservation of life and proscribing murder, might be challenged by a moral cynic or nihilist but not by a defender of moral relativism per se. Moral relativists do not necessarily challenge the existence of any or all universal principles but rather challenge whether there is (1) a way of definitively stating moral principles such as to be universally understood or accepted and/or (2) a way of definitively translating principles into common practice. Indeed, those who advocate relativism in the context of human rights often argue for a universal but "thin" conception of human rights that is maximally compatible with multicultural diversity. Hence, the "Statement on Human Rights" by the American Anthropological Association in 1947,[4] crafted by some well-known cultural relativists, argues not against universal human rights per se but against an ethnocentric universalization that promotes the values of a particular (i.e., Western) culture at the expense of respect for cultural differences. The anthropologists' conception of an appropriate universalization would recognize that standards and values are relative to the cultures from which they derive and, accordingly, that conceptions of human freedom and justice for the whole world must be nonabsolute and must accommodate particular cultures' different realizations of freedom, justice, and rights for their members. Clearly, the appeal to universality is still present for such cultural relativists, although there remains a question as to what sort of meaningful universals can be salvaged under such cultural constraints and whether anything more is implied than the tolerance of cultural differences.

PART 2

Cultural and ethical relativism also can be considered in a more analytical way, examining the premises and inferences. First, there is that conception of cultural relativism that is essentially a theory about how members of any given culture perceive and evaluate their surroundings based upon cultural conditioning. According to this view, for members of any given culture, thoughts, values, and actions tend to follow an "inner cultural logic," which causes them to form patterns according to the dominant mores of society. The standards of morality and normalcy to which people appeal when either praising or blaming others are themselves culture bound so that their intelligibility and normative force exist only in the context of already established patterns of behavior and conditioned expectations. The essential point is that members of a given culture are effectively "enculturated" into their understanding of and allegiance to normative principles and that those principles are themselves not objective truths ascertained impartially by reason but, on the contrary, are highly contingent matters that arise out of complex constellations of sociological, historical, and other causal elements.

The empirical basis for cultural relativism is the recognition of significant diversity of practices among cultures and fundamental differences regarding norms and principles of behavior. The step from the fact of cultural diversity to normative relativity relies upon the hypothesis of enculturation, which claims that culture—the totality of norms, institutions, and forms of behavior within a society—stipulates the values that form the individual's ethical self-perception and perception of others. Cultural diversity in combination with the theory of enculturation suggests that all norms are not only cultural in origin but also particular in their very nature and, therefore, that any claim by any particular culture to the superiority or universality of its norms would be arbitrary, at least if the claim were based on nothing more than the assertion of privilege arising out of the strength of felt commitment to those norms.

If cultural relativism meant no more than this, then it would not be logically objectionable. However, cultural relativism becomes ethical relativism only when it adds the meta-ethical claim that, because of enculturation, there can be no value judgments or norms that are valid objectively or independently of specific cultures or that there is no normative justification that can claim privilege in transcending cultural particularities to get at ethical truth (leaving aside the alternative appeal to functionalism as a way of blunting moral criticism of indigenous cultural practices).

The fallacious inference here is obvious. Even if one were to accept enculturation as a universally established fact, and not merely as an hypothesis or heuristic device or as an established feature of some but not all cultures, the conclusion that there are no objective norms independent of cultural particularities does not follow. The hasty generalization, in which characteristics found to be true of some are claimed to be true of all cultures (especially in cases where the cultures under consideration are highly integrated or traditional in character), leads to the unsupported assumption that since none of the candidates for objective norms thus far examined meet the test of cultural independence, then none can or ever will. The supposed ubiquity of enculturation makes impossible the existence of objective norms of which we may be ignorant, since all such norms are assumed to have a cultural origin, which begs the question whether the hypothesis of universal enculturation is valid in the first place.

Hence, the first non sequitur of cultural relativism is meta-ethical relativism and its accompanying skepticism regarding the existence of rationally justified universal norms. Of course, cultural relativists do not expect members of various cultures to view their own cultural norms as merely particular, and certainly not as arbitrary, because enculturation, like indoctrination, makes true believers of its members, if not with regard to all cultural norms, then at least for those that are most significant or fundamental. (However, for those who espouse cultural and ethical relativism, science and "reason" apparently overcome enculturation.) There is a certain degree of ethnocentrism, a sense of the inherent superiority of the norms of one's own culture, in every society, and, again, this is to be expected, given the thesis of enculturation. What is not to be expected, at least not logically, is the further meta-ethical thesis that since normative standards are essentially culturally defined, then what is morally right or correct is stipulated precisely by a particular culture, thus constituting a move away from skeptical relativism—the rejection of any justified universal morality—to a kind of radical ethical pluralism, which affirms the validity of the many different cultural normative systems (as opposed to an ethical nihilism, which denies the validity of all norms). In particular, such relativism prescribes (1) that individuals adhere to the norms of their culture rather than to pseudo-universalist norms and (2) that if there is any essentially universal norm, it would be, minimally, tolerance of cultural differences in light of the equal validity of their different norms. Here we have what appears to be a version of the naturalistic fallacy, the derivation of an *ought* from an *is* or, in this case, deriving a theory of the equal validity of norms and prescribed tolerance and respect for diversity from the empirical facts of diversity. (Or, to put it in a critical and rhetorical way that is consistent with the theory of enculturation, cultural relativists are here espousing values fundamental to the liberal, pluralist societies in which they themselves have been educated.)

Some cultural relativists recognize the logical problems with what can be called "prescriptive," or normative, relativism (which is what seems to underlie the American Anthropological Association's statement on human rights mentioned earlier) and have correctly concluded that no normative claims follow from the fact of cultural diversity, neither the claim that the rightness of an act is determined by what is considered right in a culture nor the claim that tolerance of cultural differences is entailed by cultural relativism.[5] Moreover, prescriptive relativism is self-refuting in claiming that all norms and the prescriptions that follow from them are culturally particularistic and that tolerance of cultural differences is to be universally prescribed. Cultural relativism as a theory about the source of value judgments is not itself a value theory and cannot properly prescribe tolerance or moral objectivity as a universal value. Rather, the implication of cultural relativism is that, in light of the diverse inner logics of cultures, all claims to universality of standards can be challenged and that this challenge is an appropriate response to the ethnocentric assumption of the superiority of Western norms and values.

For cultural relativism that stops short of such prescriptivism, whether there are universal norms that serve as a basis for universal human rights is not a matter of inferring tolerance from diversity or of making a moral or rational argument but of determining empirically the extent to which there is overlap between cultures with regard to norms, which is not ruled out by the theory of enculturation. If there are values or norms shared by all or almost all cultures, then this could indicate universal agreement supporting universal human rights, but it would be a de facto circumstance only, that is, a matter of the mere correspondence or overlap of norms—what are called "cross-cultural universals"[6]—and not a result of rational argument or moral justification. Empirical investigation into the possibility of cross-cultural norms could be valuable and could serve to strengthen claims for universal human rights in those cases where the norms support such rights. However, what anthropologists discover about the differences between cultures due to enculturation, or the serendipitous overlap of cultural norms, cannot in itself support normative claims regarding cross-cultural interaction. For example, showing that all or almost all cultures adhere to a conception of retribution tied to proportionality does not establish a justified norm for a universal human right not to be killed or harmed arbitrarily. Describing patterns of behavior and intersections of such patterns does not provide a normative reason for sustaining or enhancing them but only indicates commonality of practices that may suggest an underlying rationally justified moral conception. Rational justification requires a philosophical account that explains in normative terms the importance of the moral ideals associated with human rights.

In any case, when cultural relativism embraces the skeptical implications of meta-ethical relativism, moral justification becomes a moot issue, for such relativism is skeptical of the existence of objectively true value judgments that could be justified outside specific cultural frames of reference. Such skepticism is a logical non sequitur of the theory of enculturation. Nonetheless, if the theory of enculturation could be confirmed with a high degree of confidence, then it would provide at least some uncertainty about the possibility of objectively justified norms or a rationally defensible ethics. Lack of universal agreement about norms and their justification has always been a source of doubt among the more skeptically minded. But, there remains a significant difference between dogmatic skepticism and a milder or more "mitigated" doubting that weighs the evidence (both empirical and logical) critically but also realizes the likely uncertainty of any given conclusion. Presupposing such a perspective, the essential question is, what would it take to convince one to give up altogether the project of providing an objectively justified ethics that could serve as the basis for universal human rights? Cultural relativism does not discredit the universalist project and force one to dispense with objectivity in ethics, with all the psychological and moral consequences that would entail.

PART 3

Traditionally, universal human rights have been founded upon one or more versions of moral objectivism, "the doctrine that even though different societies hold different moral codes, an objective core morality exists, made up of universally valid moral principles."[7] Of course, one can easily raise difficulties that make moral objectivism problematic, such as proving that an objective core morality does exist and how a person can be confident that one has truly identified the core principles in question. Given the fallibilistic sensibility that modern epistemology has in one way or another engendered in many of us, along with the heightened sensitivity to cultural-normative differences that cultural relativism engenders when we assess its claims fairly (and when it does not fall into an incoherent moral skepticism), there may be a reluctance to defend moral objectivism straight out for fear of falling into dogmatic absolutism. But it would clearly violate our strongest human intuitions (whether enculturated originally or emergent from the philosophical search for understanding) to deny moral objectivism and thereby weaken the basis of any attempt to exert moral criticism of other cultural practices. Moral arguments cannot rest on simple assertions of cultural prejudice or frank ethnocentricity. They require appeals to our shared humanity and common moral human nature.

Human beings generally recognize a distinction between right and wrong and accept that good should be preferred to evil in constructing human society. Despite disagreements in identifying good and evil, people recognize the existence of universal values that individuals can advance (or not) in their social relations. This is the most fundamental sense of the meaning of morality that Aquinas captures in his generic principle of natural law: to do good and avoid evil (which even the moral cynic understands but against which he or she rebels). Aquinas also asserts other first practical principles that relate to the various basic goods that are the objects of our natural inclinations and which he claims to be ultimately indemonstrable and self-evident.[8] Perhaps this "self-evidence" is largely a matter of experience in the range of things that humans typically desire, such as friendship, justice, harmony, and happiness. There is nothing inherently fallacious in generalizing from experience when experience is appropriately broadened, but greater specification of the meanings of the goods or virtues said to be universal will also heighten cultural differences and even apparent normative incommensurability. Taking cultural differences seriously need not defeat the universality of norms as long as their truth is evaluated in terms of their value, which means appealing to their practical human significance without ontologizing first principles.

Some might say that such principles of practical reason seem based subjectively in human desire and thus lose their status as objective moral truths, but objectivity need not be understood in terms of some sort of external metaphysical grounding, such as God as the source and cause of all existence, goodness, and rationality. While neither moral ontology nor philosophical anthropology are sufficient to ground moral universals, experience shows that the sense of the moral is itself universal and that the relativity of human experience and of interpretations of the human good(s) does not eliminate or make arbitrary reasonable conjectures about commonalities in human moral life.

This leads to a pragmatic view of universal human rights, arising out of practical experience, focusing specifically on human moral concerns and the ways that they are expressed, but without reducing human value to pure instrumentalities of expedience and efficiency so that a universal norm will have the character of the "pragmatic a priori."[9] This approach is also "historicist" in that it evaluates experience and knowledge in the context of historical change and development.[10] This combined pragmatic and historicist position supports a coherent humanistic orientation in which discussion and debate about human rights are viewed as part of the practical and historical evolution of human rights. As Morton Winston has put it, "the human rights we now recognize have evolved in response to perceived threats to basic human values and interests as they have arisen in definite historical, political, and economic circumstances."[11] So, for example, the natural rights that John Locke enunciates were responses to tyranny and religious persecution in sixteenth- and seventeenth-century Europe; the rights proclaimed in the French Declaration of the Rights of Man were a response to the political and social inequities and class conflicts of the time; and many of the rights that have become important in the twentieth century are responses to the effects of the Industrial Revolution, colonialism, world wars, and various atrocities and acts of genocide, such as the Holocaust.[12]

From this perspective human rights are grounded in our moral nature, are understood as an evolving phenomenon, and give expression to "a social choice of a particular vision of human potentiality, which rests on a particular substantive account of the minimum requirements of a life of dignity."[13] From a range of human possibilities of becoming, people select those to which they have given special importance for realization in society, whether at the national or global level. Central to the concept of human rights is an idea of individual human dignity, which denotes those aspects of human potential to which we attribute intrinsic value. Human rights are forms of recognition intended to protect human dignity; conceived of in a particular way, against prevailing threats to it; posed either by individuals, groups, or states. Threats to human rights are moral dangers or liabilities, due either to active oppression, subtle intimidation, or simple neglect by others, not by the severities of the natural world. Therefore, implementation and protection of human rights will focus on the actions and inactions of human agents. Moreover, the practical approach must be systematic since "human rights are a social practice that aims to realize a particular vision of human dignity and potential by institutionalizing basic rights."[14]

If human rights are considered as being social practices, as distinct from commodities that are possessed in a literal sense (the language of "possession" of rights being common but misleading), they can be understood dialectically as a "constructive interaction between moral vision and political reality."[15] On the one hand, through strategies of both justification and critique, human rights articulate an evolving moral vision of human dignity, serving as an ideal for how to institutionalize social life. On the other hand, only through appropriate forms of recognition in the social and political sphere can that evolving moral vision be realized. Indeed, the conceptual ability to articulate a moral vision of human nature that ascribes human rights to individuals presupposes an existing political reality already shaped in a manner that makes the moral vision itself possible, intelligible, and persuasive. Accordingly, human rights reflect current practices of recognition, where moral consciousness about human rights has been shaped by existing social conditions, including the contemplation of future possibilities of moral self-realization.[16] What Hegel said about freedom is equally true of human rights: their real development coincides with the development of the consciousness of their importance.

Both human nature and human rights should be understood not as a fixed essence emanating from the Divine, from natural Reason, or from instinctive inclinations or needs but as the product of social conventions arising out of the exigencies of human experience. Human rights are an evolving social project constructed for human purposes and under particular conditions, not eternal unchanging Truths fixed in the scheme of the cosmos. Appeal to such Truths is not necessary to recognize the nonreducibility of the ideal to the real, thus avoiding positivism. However, the ideal and the real, though distinct, cannot be completely separated since these two dimensions are internally, or dialectically, related in that each plays an important role in developing the other. The real and the ideal constitute a circle of dependencies in which conceptually there is no ultimate first foothold. There is no need for dogmatic skepticism regarding the "ultimate" foundations of human rights since there can be no definitive proof of the absence of ontological status—the existence of eternal unchanging Truths cannot categorically be denied. Nor can such truths be dogmatically asserted in the face of widely different perceptions and interpretations of their content. Instead, it will be prudent to suspend judgment regarding metaphysical and foundational claims. Foundational claims do little to explain the concrete characteristics of human rights, despite a usefulness for expressing the nonarbitrary nature of rights.

How then are human rights "objective" moral norms? What are the necessary conditions for legitimate claims to human rights? What are the sufficient conditions for their realization? Can we appeal to a system of international law that, without universally accepted sanctions for violations, at least offers a fabric of institutions that give expression to an international consensus on human rights? Must it be the case that, prior to such institutionalization, human rights have no reality at all? Are the fundamental moral rights claimed for all people in the American Declaration of Independence or the French Declaration of the Rights of Man merely "manifesto" rights—that is, mere recommendations that claims recognized as civil rights in a particular society be made into civil rights universally for all societies?

Such questions suggest the positivism that a pragmatic-historicist account seeks to avoid. The positivist position, associated with Jeremy Bentham's idea that rights are essentially legal artifacts of positive law, holds that human rights have reality only if they are part of practices already widely accepted, where for a right to exist is for it to be recognized. This view, at bottom, appeals to the common-sense idea that a rights claim that, for example, was unintelligible or unimaginable would not likely have any significance or reality. However, it is not clear that moral concreteness and intelligibility requires a legal or even quasi-legal standard of measure. An "all or nothing" approach to human rights will set the standard quite high so that something can legitimately qualify as a right only if it can easily be identified as a possession, like the possession of property. However, in spite of the language of "possession" used in ascribing rights to individuals, it is misleading to think of human rights as being analogous to ordinary possessions such as tables and chairs. The existence conditions for moral "possessions" such as human rights are indeed a matter of their recognition, but this recognition is a complex affair involving the matter of how moral ideals, and the language expressing those ideals, relate to social and political reality through the act of interpretation. Morality itself is a social phenomenon, but it cannot be reified in particular sets of rules, regulations, or practices.[17] Both moral norms and their social recognition are embedded in social practices that cannot be reduced to a social status quo, for moral consciousness maintains a critical stance in relation to all practices. Social morality is dynamic and adaptive.

Moreover, consensus regarding a moral issue does not establish the validity of a moral norm, nor does it logically add moral force to already recognized norms. The moral views of the majority are not necessarily correct. For example, the ubiquity of racism and chauvinism does not make racism and chauvinism morally acceptable. Consensus does confer legitimacy when it has normative backing, which is provided by critical discussion and debate, including the provisions of explicit justification. On the pragmatic-historicist view, custom and consensus enter into the constitution of morality but not exclusively. Human rights are a function of humanity's moral self-understanding, rooted in linguistic, cultural, political, social, and economic practices. In the twentieth century, particularly since the Second World War, and in the aftermath of the creation of the United Nations and the Universal Declaration of Human Rights in 1948, there has been a strengthening normative consensus regarding the existence of universal human rights, including their nature and their content. Normative consensus is reflected in international law, in the significant number of nations that have ratified the successive international covenants on human rights, and in the array of human rights organizations. While a moral obligation to respect human rights follows from such formal commitments, it also precedes them in already reflecting an international normative consensus regarding the minimum necessary requirements for a dignified human life.[18]

What then of the clearly divergent cultural conceptions of human rights that were not reconciled when the Universal Declaration was drafted and that to some extent remain: for example, the objection of the Arab states to the right to change religion or the old Soviet and Chinese opposition to civil and political rights? Some Asian politicians have criticized the concept of human rights as being essentially a Western idea, or at least they have claimed that the rights enumerated in the Universal Declaration reflect a Western bias. The conceptual universalization of human rights internationally might seem to conflict with the reality of moral diversity when values are proclaimed that are not shared on a worldwide basis, such as private ownership of property, democratic free elections, and the freedom of religion or marriage. Asserting universal rights might seem to threaten minority values or offer a cover for ethnocentrism and cultural imperialism.

Cultural imperialism must be carefully avoided because it subordinates the weak to the strong and threatens human dignity; but ethnocentrism is a natural product of a human community and is therefore unavoidable due to enculturation. All people are culturally situated and tend to prefer their own cultures. What Jean-Paul Sartre said of each individual holds for peoples as well, that in choosing for ourselves we choose for all humankind and intend that our fundamental value commitments be accepted by all others. The universalization of values is an expression of the seriousness of commitment to an image of humanity as we think it ought to be, with the underlying recognition that the other, though different, is not alien. "We always choose the good, and nothing can be good for us without being good for all."[19] Moreover, the universalization of values, without appeal to an a priori good, means greater, not less, responsibility, which is expressed in the anguish of choosing exemplary actions.

When cultures come into contact with each other, they must decide how they will interact. Ethnocentrism has encouraged interaction by conquest and cultural transformation by force. There is a qualitative difference, however, between ethnocentrism driven by a sense of cultural superiority and desire to dominate and the ethnocentricity that results from the fact that a culture simply cannot treat its own mores as being no more important than those of others, as if it were somehow inherently obvious that one's own possessed no more truth than another's. Participants in cultures typically do not take a relativistic view of their own cultural norms, but nonetheless they are capable of tolerating cultural differences while promoting their own cherished norms. Moreover, not only is tolerance of different cultural values in the spirit of universality, but it also serves enlightened self-interest in the long run.

However, when a culture seeks the aggrandizement of its own power through the brutal domination of other peoples, toleration is not what is called for but rather resistance, rebellion, and perhaps warfare. Warfare is preeminently ethnocentric, whether waged according to principles of just war or not, and can seem at odds with notions of equal respect for cultural differences and the rights of cultural self-determination. The limits of toleration emerge when cultures are so at odds with each other that it is a matter of survival to resist or overcome the other and where appeals to universal norms are substituted by a resort to force.

PART 4

According to the pragmatic-historicist account, the objectivity of universal human rights is based on practical reasons for accepting these rights within a context of social recognition. "Practical reason" in this context is not intended to evoke Immanuel Kant's formalistic and ahistorical attempt to capture the absolute and ultimate transhistorical principles of morality. Practical reason is more properly conceived as being practical reasoning that is engaged critically in providing justification for norms, with emphasis on the process of argumentation, experimental thinking, and discovery, presupposing various intellectual traditions, whether or not these are explicitly or thematically recovered.[20]

Practical reasoning in relation to universal human rights requires moving from considerations of self-interest or social utility to the specifically moral concern with living life as a moral being, with moral dignity. Human rights articulate minimum standards for a decent life in the world we inhabit, not in a utopia or a kingdom of ends. The moral point of view recognizes the importance of a life of dignity for all moral beings, which remains an ideal to be realized and that the necessary conditions for this must be articulated in terms of secure claims to life, liberty, and fairness in rights trade-offs and in the distribution of costs and burdens in upholding rights claims.[21] Practical reasoning about the basic conditions for life as a moral being will appeal not only to philosophical conceptions about what it means to be a moral being but also to human psychology and to human practices. Articulating what constitutes the "moral point of view" may well be difficult when considering international rights that apply cross-culturally, but the process is in principle no different than when debate occurs within a specific culture, whether between competing traditions or competing interpretations of traditions and norms.

Clearly, one of the more difficult areas of consideration is how the concept of equal concern and respect can gain purchase in societies that are highly stratified and where the principle of equality comes into conflict with conceptions of status. Since practical reasoning is not about the perfect society, even though it aims at a moral ideal, there will be qualifications and limitations on meeting the minimal standards of a life of dignity, with constraints of feasibility and the costs of implementing human rights.[22] Moreover, the weight, rank, or importance of a right in relation to other norms is not absolute—sometimes other normative considerations will take precedence. For these reasons, universal human rights are prima facie rights, authentic because they give expression to fundamentally important values but nonabsolute in that their weight in relation to other normative concerns and to competing rights is initially indeterminate and will be clarified only at the stage of implementation.[23] Practical reasoning about human rights is a posteriori both in the articulation of the principles of human rights, which requires appeal to a shared moral vision, and in their application in particular circumstances.

Aside from these sorts of practical considerations, there are metanormative problems that relate to the historicist approach. If it is the case that one exists as a moral being only as a member of some sort of community and that theoretical justification of moral norms must itself be a culturally situated practice, then if one wishes to offer moral justification for all communities, one must engage in the construction of moral ideology.[24] This is "ideology" in the sense that the legitimation of a universal norm comes from a particular perspective, with its partisan concerns, but at the same time is presented as though it were the view of some thoroughly disinterested party and as if the principles espoused were objectively necessary. However, if reason and objectivity are historically constituted, there can be no neutral standpoint from which moral universality can be enunciated, for it is itself a historical result.[25] This means "*there are no demonstra-*

tively valid moral principles, if by a principle one means an exceptionless normative rule (that is not tautological) legitimated by reference to some modal invariance or necessity of reason or reality."[26] This palpably skeptical conclusion, nonetheless, is not quite the same as that of meta-ethical relativism, which draws solely from the facts of enculturation and cultural difference, for historicism posits not the existential impossibility of valid moral principles constituting objective norms independent of particular cultures but rather the phenomenological failure to make the case without appealing to a privileged standpoint, a failure that seems reflexively endemic to historical consciousness for which the real and the ideal are dialectically related. For such consciousness, "whatever we offer in the way of principles or laws or rules are artifactual posits formed within a changing *praxis*. It is the modal claim that fails, *not* the sense of the 'indicative' regularities. . . . 'Principles' are no more than the idealized 'necessities' of the observed *sittlich* regularities of our world (or invented 'improvements' of the same)."[27]

This does not mean that moral objectivity is totally lost to us but only that it must be viewed as being socially and historically constructed. This construction, without the presumption of privileged access to unchanging moral truths, allows for a "second best" moral vision—that is, a vision that is self-conscious of the historical situatedness of its positing and thus does not pretend to make claims for the "best" in a categorical or unqualified way but rather draws upon widespread sensibilities, moral intuitions, and political and social developments.[28] Objectivity of moral norms is a function not of demonstrating moral absolutes but rather of discerning their practical universality (which is perhaps closer to Kant's conception of objectivity in his *Critique of Pure Reason*, as opposed to the *Critique of Practical Reason*). Moreover, historically this universality emerges as the concept of human rights is progressively articulated in documents given wide international acceptance, in the increasing adherence to these rights in customary law, as well as the widespread incorporation of human rights in state constitutions and the continuous demand for inclusion of human rights with constitutional guarantees where they have not been incorporated. Even mere rhetorical or hypocritical acceptance of respect for human rights, "the homage that vice pays to virtue," implies in principle commitment and accountability.[29]

PART 5

The universalism and relativism of human rights should not be viewed as being entirely antithetical conceptions but rather as being on a spectrum, with the radical extremes at each end.[30] Radical universalism, with its dogmatic appeals to a priori principles, might understate the importance of cultural diversity and contribute to moral imperialism, whereas too radical a relativism might understate the similarities of human experience and the commensurability of human cultures and promote skepticism about the objectivity of moral norms. Neither of these extremes are morally attractive or practically viable, and they usually appear in public discourse in the insincere justification or rationalization of imperialist or protectionist policies.

Between these extremes stands a variety of positions that emphasize either universalism or relativism but with some degree of mutual accommodation. The stronger the universalism, the weaker the relativity, and vice versa. These distinctions are somewhat abstract but provide a useful organizing principle in differentiating actual positions taken in debates about universal human rights.

The strongest type of relativism argues for the superiority of indigenous standards and makes primary the value of cultural diversity. Since "the folkways are always right," universal human rights are largely considered barriers to cultural development, except perhaps for the right to cultural self-determination and other similar rights, the recognition of which would help to protect cultural integrity. Respect for cultural differences means high tolerance of those differences and a policy of noninterference, with little or no cultural criticism being morally justified.[31] Other relativistic positions are more supportive of universal human rights. While accepting that the argument from cultural difference proves that there are no objective moral norms or truths, some relativists still endorse human rights as being a moral "least common denominator" based on a cross-cultural overlap of norms. To the extent that there are empirically verifiable common norms, tolerance of cultural differences is not required categorically, and moral criticism of a culture is not ruled out.[32] While accommodating a stronger universality than the strongest form of relativism, this viewpoint is not likely to support anything close to the full array of human rights articulated in international rights manifestos. A more moderate prescriptive relativism recognizes a greater depth and wider scope to universal rights while holding that they must be supported through cultural legitimation. This may require some alteration of the cultural status quo, leading to enlightened interpretations of cultural norms through internal discussion and cross-cultural dialogue based on a presumption of reciprocity.[33] This position can admit the possibility of some objective moral norms but still denies that moral knowledge can be placed beyond culture.

Beyond the midpoint of the spectrum are positions that put their primary emphasis on universalism. These universalisms recognize a full array of universal human rights and generally accept (with relatively minor criticisms) the lists of rights presented in the international rights documents. They differ in their accommodation of relativity of human rights norms. The most moderate universalism recognizes optimal flexibility in respecting diversity in the implementation of human rights so that, for example, latitude can be given to local interpretations of the rather broad statements of rights found in rights documents and that some human rights can be overridden in emergency situations, recognizing that "the duty to comply with human rights standards is conditional on the ability to do so."[34] Perhaps a stronger universalism will emphasize greater cross-cultural consensus and the normative universality of human rights, holding that a comprehensive set of prima facie universal human rights should be uncontroversial but recognizing that the relativity of rights can serve as a check on any tendency toward excessive universalism.

The relativity of human rights can be thought of in terms of variation at the levels of substance, interpretation, and form.[35] The level of substance considers the basic norm or value that the right designates, and if a stated right is indeed based on universal normative consensus, then there should be little, if any, variation in its definition. The level of interpretation considers the conceptual variability at issue in the implementation of a right, such as what the right to political participation can mean in a particular context. The level of form considers the specific mechanisms that actuate the exercise or provision of the concretely conceptualized right. Generally, the stronger the universalism, the more emphasis on the invariance of morality and universal human rights across cultures, with variation from stated norms being more limited and exceptional. Differences among universalists are perhaps most significant in their conceptions of the foundations of human rights, but a foundationalist need not reject relativity altogether, although accommodating relativity may be conceptually more difficult.

A pragmatic-historicist account of universal human rights will by its very philosophical orientation tend toward a moderate universalist position that gives generous consideration to relativity, recognizing the constructive and nonfoundational nature of its claims. However, it can never be a matter simply of adhering to a position as if it were definitive and nonrevisable. The tension between the universality and relativity of human rights is practically and historically necessary, serving dialectically to advance the evolution of human rights, with all of the attendant conceptual and existential challenges. Because the nature and extent of universal human rights is always in the process of realization, clarity can be achieved only to the extent that an appeal to ideal principles is adjusted to the realities of a diverse world.

NOTES

1. See my article "The Basis for Recognition of Human Rights," in *Southwest Philosophy Review* (January 1992) V. 8, No. 1:40–56. In this essay I give a critique of Rex Martin's thesis that human rights are civil rights.

2. Thomas Aquinas, "Summa Theologica," part II, q. 94, art. 4, in *The Political Ideas of St. Thomas Aquinas*, ed. Dino Bigongiari (Hafner Press, 1981), 49–51.

3. *Ibid.*, 59.

4. Morton E. Winston, *The Philosophy of Human Rights* (Belmont, CA: Wadsworth Publishing Co., 1989), 116–120.

5. Alison Dundes Renteln, *International Human Rights: Universalism versus Relativism* (Newbury Park, CA: Sage Publications, 1990), 70–76.

6. *Ibid.*, 13.

7. Louis Pojman, *Global Political Philosophy* (New York: McGraw-Hill, 2003), 7.

8. John Finnis, *Aquinas: Moral, Political and Legal Theory* (Oxford: Oxford University Press, 1998), 86–88.

9. H. S. Thayer, "Pragmatism," *Encyclopedia of Philosophy*, ed. Paul Edwards (New York: Macmillan Publishing Co., 1967), Vol. 5, 435.

10. Maurice Mandelbaum, "Historicism," *Encyclopedia of Philosophy*, ed. Paul Edwards (New York: Macmillan Publishing Co., 1967), Vol. 3, 22–24.

11. Winston, 37.

12. *Ibid.*

13. Jack Donnelly, *Universal Human Rights in Theory and Practice* (Ithaca, NY: Cornell University Press, 1991), 17.

14. *Ibid.*, 18.

15. *Ibid.*

16. *Ibid.*, 18–19.

17. For this reason, Rex Martin's distinction between rights as morally justified (valid) claims and rights as socially recognized practices is not likely to serve his purpose—that is, to distinguish rights as being merely formally established and, on that basis alone, merely nominal from rights that are fully accredited because they include, in addition, practices of recognition and maintenance. The problem is that moral justification itself presupposes some context of social recognition; otherwise, it would be so formal and abstract as to be virtually meaningless to the people of society or culture. Hence, rather than say that a justified moral principle is effectively "blocked" by opposed practices of recognition, as if in this circumstance the moral principle would actually be viewed as being justified, it is more plausible to view this as a case of competing norms due to internal moral dissonance in the practices of recognition. Of course, if social practices of recognition are held up against a moral principle justified from an external standpoint, a discrepancy would be due not to a blocking effect but simply to lack of acceptance of the proposed or purported justified principle.

18. *Ibid.*, 27.

19. Jean-Paul Sartre, "Existentialism Is a Humanism," in *Satre and Human Emotions*, ed. Hazel Barnes (New York: Philosophical Library, 1957), 17.

20. Michael Walzer, "Philosophy, History, and the Recovery of Tradition," *Chronicle of Higher Education* (June 16, 2000): A56.

21. James Nickel, *Making Sense of Human Rights* (Berkeley: University of California Press, 1987), 93–95.

22. *Ibid.*, 96–98.

23. *Ibid.*, 14–15; cf. chap. 7.

24. Joseph Margolis, *Life without Principles: Reconciling Theory and Practice* (Cambridge, MA: Blackwell Publishers Inc., 1996), 175.

25. *Ibid.*, 182–183.
26. *Ibid.*, 201.
27. *Ibid.*, 206.
28. *Ibid.*, 208–210.
29. Louis Henkin, "The Universality of the Concept of Human Rights," ANNALS, AAPSS 506 (November 1989 (13)).
30. Donnelly, 109–110.
31. William Graham Sumner, *Folkways* (Boston, Ginn and Company, 1906).
32. Renteln, 73–82.
33. Abdullahi Ahmed An-Naim, "Toward a Cross-Cultural Approach to Defining International Standards of Human Rights," in *Human Rights in Cross-Cultural Perspectives: A Quest for Consensus* (Philadelphia: University of Pennsylvania Press, 1992), 26–29.
34. Nickel, 76.
35. Donnelly, 116–118.

II

THE PARTICULAR IN UNIVERSAL HUMAN RIGHTS

5

Are Women Human? Feminist Reflections on "Women's Rights as Human Rights"

Lucinda Joy Peach

For more than a decade, feminist scholars and human rights organizations have worked to incorporate women's rights as human rights within international human rights law.[1] They have done so in the belief that incorporating women's rights into human rights represents the best available path to the end of patriarchal oppression of women around the world. Whether or not they have succeeded in materially improving the conditions of women around the world, they have at the very least generated a significant consensus in favor of "women's rights as human rights."

At first glance, this consensus around the campaign for "women's rights as human rights" is surprising. Much familiar feminist theory expresses deep skepticism about social ideals dominated by legalistic commitments to individual rights, whether domestically or internationally, and of law-based approaches to women's emancipation. And many feminists openly reject the idea that all women share or ought to share, simply by virtue of being women, certain "women's human rights." Such thinking, they claim, is inextricably bound up and ought to be rejected with discredited Enlightenment notions of and ambitions for universalism, impartiality, and related values.

These apparent inconsistencies have surfaced within recent debates over the development and implementation of women's human rights. One way in which they have surfaced is in the posing of the question "Are women human?" This question is partly tongue-in-cheek, of course. But within the context of international human rights law, it is meant seriously to raise some basic feminist concerns. One is whether women have been so excluded from the creation of and debate over law and legal rights, including international human rights law, that whatever "human" may mean within the domestic or international legal contexts, its meaning is not likely to incorporate women as women and is thus not likely to range over basic women's interests. Another is whether it is not unreasonable, given the vexed place of women in the processes of both law creation and law justification, to suppose that women might best be empowered and their interests advanced through strategies other than "women's rights as human rights."

For the most part, feminist analyses of human rights have directly paralleled the evolution of feminist theory more generally. They begin—at least in the United States—with typically "liberal" rights-based approaches to women's emancipation, moving then into "cultural" or "gender" critiques, and finally splintering more recently into a range of diverse theoretical approaches, including liberal defenses of a rights-based approach against the criticisms of cultural and other feminists. In this chapter, I trace the development of feminist reactions to the women's-rights-as-human-rights movement, focusing especially on the apparently entrenched and polarized positions taken by contemporary liberal and cultural feminists. I begin with a brief introduction to the movement for women's rights as human rights and an overview of some of the standard worries any feminist might have about such a movement. I then sketch the liberal feminist defense of women's rights as human rights against such generically feminist worries and the cultural feminist critique of the liberal feminist defense. I conclude by pointing a way past this apparently intractable conflict between liberal and cultural feminists, arguing that a more self-consciously pragmatist feminism offers a more fruitful way of thinking about the place of any movement for women's rights as human rights within the larger feminist struggle to end patriarchy.

More specifically, I argue that the diversity of cultural and institutional contexts within which women and child-age girls are oppressed, as well as the diversity of interests affirmed by women and girls around the world, demands a pragmatic, flexible approach to women's rights as human rights. Such an approach, I argue, is better suited to promoting feminist goals while respecting the agency of women to determine the course of their own lives than is either a liberal legalistic approach based solely in and on the global demands of international human rights law or a culturally relativist or pluralist approach committed to the emancipation of women through only a plurality of diverse and bounded efforts at immanent cultural critique.

WOMEN'S RIGHTS AS HUMAN RIGHTS AND SOME INITIAL FEMINIST WORRIES

Although the campaign for women's rights as human rights is fairly recent, the United Nations rejected discrimination based on sex in 1945, when the UN Charter was ratified.[2] Since then prohibitions on sex discrimination have gained focus and achieved the status of law through a number of international treaties and agreements, including, most notably, the Universal Declaration of Human Rights in 1948[3] and the Convention to Eliminate Discrimination against Women (CEDAW) in 1979.[4] In 1995, years of campaigning by women's rights and human rights activists to identify women's rights as human rights finally bore fruit at the United Nations' Fourth World Conference on Women held in Beijing, China. At both the official UN's conference on women as well as the parallel nongovernmental organizations conference, women's rights as human rights was a central theme. The platform for action drafted at the UN's conference on women frames women's rights "as indivisible, universal, and inalienable human rights."[5] Since the Fourth World Conference on Women, the platform has been reproduced in large numbers and widely disseminated, becoming the foundation for a range of different movements, organizations, and strategies to empower and promote the status of women around the world.

The movement to promote women's rights as human rights has gained visibility and has even achieved mainstream status, notwithstanding the fact that the central idea, that the emancipation of women is well-served by women's rights as human rights, is in tension, if not in outright contradiction, with several aspects of well-established feminist critiques of the law and individual rights. What these critiques share is a commitment to the idea that the law is inherently oppressive of women and that, accordingly, law-based approaches to the emancipation of women and the promotion of their interests are of limited value. This commitment is supported by several feminist claims and arguments.

One key claim is that in several respects the law is inherently "male." It was designed by men to serve predominantly male interests; has functioned historically to maintain patriarchy and male domination; and notwithstanding various reforms, continues to reflect a bias toward men's interests and concerns.[6] A second and related claim is that the vehicle through which the law historically has been placed in the service of men and men's interests was the exclusion of women as legal subjects or right holders and that recent inclusions of women as legal subjects and right holders fail to serve women's emancipation and interests since they assimilate women to an already male-oriented conception of the legal subject as right holder. This inherent bias against women in the law is said to be evident in international law as well as domestic law. As Hilary Charlesworth points out, "human rights documents use men's rights and male standards of equality as the model for the inclusion of women's rights, making it more accurate to characterize it as international men's rights law."[7] This male bias within the women's-rights-as-human-rights movement reveals itself through a persistent emphasis on individual rights at the expense of group rights or other non-rights-based claims and through the pervasive legal division between public and private domains within international law.

Feminist critiques of legal rights as being inherently male range over several claims. One is that legal rights attach only to a male-gendered conception of the legal subject as an independent, autonomous, rationally self-interested individual. Another is that the privileging of civil and political rights over social and economic rights, as well as negative rights over positive rights more generally, reflects a male-gendered understanding of human interests and needs and ignores those of women. This, of course, should not surprise, feminists argue, since women were neither participants nor considerations when these rights were formulated. In light of these features of legal rights, many feminists ask whether women are in fact "human" in the male-biased senses that are assumed by international human rights law.

In addition to the foregoing, some feminist theorists (whom I refer to here as "culture feminists") have drawn on Carol Gilligan's work to argue that men tend to resolve conflicts on the basis of an "ethic of justice," which is framed in terms of individual rights and abstract legalistic principles of fairness and justice, whereas women tend to resolve conflicts more on the basis of an "ethic of care," which is less adversarial and embodies principles of nurturing, maintaining relationships, and community.[8] According to these theorists, the law epitomizes an ethic of justice and excludes an ethic of care, thereby making it inhospitable to women's forms of moral reasoning and moral concerns. This critique has been extended to international as well as domestic law. Kathleen Mahoney, for example, draws on this critique and concludes that "international human rights law is largely meaningless to women because the definitions and development of rights are built on the male experience and have not responded to women's needs or realities."[9]

Feminist critics have objected not just to the law's privileging of individual rights over other sorts of claims, whether group rights or non-rights-based claims, but also to its deep commitment to the gendered boundaries between the so-called public sphere of governmental, political, and commercial activities traditionally dominated by men and the so-called private sphere of familial and domestic life to which women have traditionally been confined. The law's greater concern with protecting individual rights in the "public sphere" than with doing so in the "private sphere" reflects a bias against women, these critics argue.[10] This bias manifests in the law's general blindness to the crimes that disproportionately affect females—domestic violence, marital rape, and child sexual abuse—crimes perpetrated behind closed doors in the "private" sphere of marriage and family, where male power is allowed to reign unchecked.[11]

This bias appears in international human rights law as well as domestic law. The focus of international human rights law has been on the public sphere. Individuals are attended to only to the extent that they interact with governments and state actors. And governments and state actors are regarded as the primary parties upon whom human rights impose duties. In most instances, international human rights law does not impose obligations on private individuals in their relations with one another.[12] Thus, in the absence of overt state action, international human rights law offers little help to women attempting to seek redress for so-called private acts such as domestic violence and rape, even if the relevant state has systematically failed to institute legal protections for women.[13]

Feminist theorists have also pointed to the great practical difficulties in effectively enforcing international human rights law, especially on behalf of women victims. All procedures permitting individuals (rather than states) to complain directly to UN agencies of human rights violations are optional under UN human rights treaties. Further, compliance with UN human rights treaties is largely voluntary. The practical reality is that states are not and cannot be sanctioned for their failure to protect women's rights under international law.[14]

In addition to the lack of explicit enforcement mechanisms, numerous states attempt to avoid compliance with various aspects of the human rights treaties they sign and ratify. This has been an especially vexed problem with respect to UN conventions and treaties relating to women's rights. A conspicuous example is the practice of many UN member states to issue "reservations" (qualifications or objections) to certain provisions in the treaties to which they become signatories and parties. More states have entered reservations to CEDAW than to any other human rights convention. And many of these are "framed in very wide and general terms . . . relating to women's rights to legal capacity or equality within the family."[15]

Another practical compliance problem is that the procedures for enforcing international human rights instruments are generally slow, in part because national remedies must usually be exhausted before recourse is made to international remedies, which often takes years. And when a complaint finally makes it to an international tribunal, it will most likely be heard by jurists who are predominantly male. So there are good reasons, feminist critics maintain, not to put too much hope in international human rights law when it comes to emancipating women and advancing their interests. When complainants do not win in international forums, the states against which they asserted their claims may insist that their failure to win just shows that their rights were not violated in the first place.[16] While this is unjustified as an inference from the mere failure to win relief from an international tribunal, it may be attractive as part of a political backlash against women.

The problems of backlash ought not go unmentioned. International law is perceived by many states as being an external, foreign, and sometimes hostile force. Thus, appeals to international law to protect and advance the interests of women may make some governments more resistant to women's claims than appeals framed in terms of local or indigenous norms and values. As Andrew Byrnes admits, "recourse to international bodies and procedures may provide some additional leverage to a campaign at the national level, but will only infrequently do more than that. Indeed, in some circumstances the appeal to an international forum and international standards may be counter-productive."[17]

The risk of this kind of backlash is especially pronounced with respect to members of those Muslim societies who see themselves to be unjustly besieged by Western values coercively imposed upon them. Evidence may be found, for example, in the Sudan, where "Muslim women are being told that patriarchy is not what is hindering them, but [rather] international law as part of Western ideas."[18] Elsewhere in Africa, "women's groups working to reform discriminatory laws and practices are dismissed by some governments 'as misguided elite women aping Western concepts.'"[19]

In light of all the foregoing feminist criticisms of international law and human rights as a mechanism for advancing the status of women, it seems rather odd that the campaign for women's rights as human rights has been as popular and well supported as it has been. Nevertheless, those who advance women's rights as human rights as the key to the emancipation of women and the promotion of their interests remain optimistic, at least relatively so, that international human rights law should be, and with some reform can be, placed in the service of women's interests as well as men's.

WOMEN'S RIGHTS AS HUMAN RIGHTS: A LIBERAL FEMINIST DEFENSE

Feminists who promote the use of international law and women's rights as human rights to secure the emancipation of women and advance women's interests typically use "liberal theory" to support their position. They claim that what women need first and foremost, and thus what feminists and others ought to work for, are equality and justice for women enforced through government regulation and sanction. Accordingly, they favor a law- and rights-based approach, both domestically and internationally, to advance the feminist agenda. And they do so while remaining generally aware of the more generic feminist worries about any law- or rights-based approach to women's emancipation. In support of their endorsement of women's rights as human rights, these feminists offer several lines of argument.

The first is that international human rights agreements already impose significant obligations on states to end discrimination against women and that it would be foolish not to press first to ensure that those obligations are met. For example, CEDAW requires that "state parties condemn discrimination against women in all its forms [and] agree to pursue, by all means and without delay, a policy of eliminating discrimination against women."[20] Article 2(f) of that convention requires state parties "to take all appropriate measures, including legislation, to modify or abolish existing laws, regulations, customs and practices that constitute discrimination against women." This duty is further elaborated in Article 5(a), where state parties agree "to modify the social and cultural patterns of conduct of men and women, with a view to achieving the elimination of prejudices and customary and all other practices which are based on the idea of the inferiority or the superiority of either of the sexes or in stereotyped roles for men and women." The task at hand is not to figure out how to obligate states by law to end discrimination against women. That has been done. It is, rather, to force states to honor their legal obligations.

Advocates of women's emancipation through international human rights law also argue that, where needed, human rights law can be reformed to better include and protect women's rights. They point out, for example, that domestic violence has been added to the international human rights agenda, as have other gendered human rights violations, such as trafficking in women and using rape as a weapon in war.[21]

Of course, all this would be beside the point if effective enforcement of international human rights law was not possible. But proponents of women's rights as human rights insist that it is possible. They note that international human rights agreements protecting women's rights are supported by committees established to oversee the rights' implementation and enforcement.[22] In this regard, Rebecca Cook claims that "the duty to report to CEDAW keeps states parties conscious of their legal accountability for violations of the Women's Convention, and of their legal obligation to eliminate private discriminatory behavior."[23] As one instance of this, Maria Isabel Plata observes that when women's groups in Colombia used the women's convention to advance women's equality and reproductive health, "the moment we used an international treaty, the government saw that our claims were legitimate and began to take us seriously."[24]

In an effort to bolster the effectiveness of such enforcement efforts, women's human rights advocates have proposed an optional protocol to CEDAW.[25] In contrast to most of international human rights law, which typically restricts victims of human rights violations to state-sought and state-sanctioned remedies, the optional protocol would provide a private right of action to enable victims of violations of the convention to file complaints directly with the CEDAW committee. The optional protocol was opened for signature by any state that had signed, ratified, or acceded to the women's convention and to ratification and accession by any state that had ratified or acceded to the convention on 22 December 2000. Its status as of 15 October 2004 was seventy-six signatories, sixty-seven contracting parties.[26]

Proponents of the women's-rights-as-human-rights movement claim that an important advantage of such a law-based approach to overcoming the oppression of and discrimination against women is that it empowers women, especially those in socially or economically disadvantaged positions. In particular, the proponents contend that a "women's rights" strategy is likely to be more compelling, persuasive, and uplifting than one appealing to "women's needs."[27]

This may be true even where there is no indigenous tradition of women's rights that can be appealed to in framing claims against the state. Indeed, in such circumstances, many feminists argue that it may be especially important and helpful to take a "women's rights" approach. For example, Berta Hernandez-Truyol argues that "local and regional networks are often inadequate to effect change in national and/or international policies that are inhospitable to women."[28]

A signal advantage of the women's-rights-as-human-rights movement is that it offers an international standard for women's rights that can inform the reform of domestic law and practice. And "applying the international equality norm to inform the content of constitutional and legislative provisions in domestic courts remains the most effective mechanism for protecting women's rights," according to Sara Hossain.[29] There is no reason why the application of this norm may not extend to legislation (or the lack thereof) governing the conduct of private nonstate actors or areas traditionally regarded as within the domain of the domestic. In *Attorney General v. Unity Dow,* the court of appeals of Botswana appealed to international human rights law in order to strike down a provision of the Botswana Citizenship Act of 1984, which recognized the right of male, but not female, citizens who marry foreigners to convey their citizenship statuses to their children.[30] As human rights, women's rights establish global standards of great value to women around the world struggling against governments hostile or indifferent to the legitimate claims of women. The international publicity and attendant political capital gained by treating women's rights issues as human rights issues is no small part of this value.[31]

The foregoing considerations have led many feminists, including many who would identify as liberal feminists, to defend vigorously the law-based women's-rights-as-human-rights approach to overcoming the evils of patriarchy around the world. The fundamental idea is that the basic structure and content of international human rights law are sound and that the task at hand is to expand or revise that law so that its benefits extend fully to women.[32] For those taking this view, there is no question that women are "human" for the purposes of international human rights law, and there are no real worries about a normatively undesirable male bias to the notion of the "human" in human rights law. Further, for those taking this view, notwithstanding the diverse cultural, social, and economic locations of women, women's basic interests are sufficiently alike for women to be protected and advanced through a universal international human rights legal regime.

International human rights laws may be largely the products of Western cultures and male authors, but proponents of women's rights as human rights insist that the Universal Declaration of Human Rights and CEDAW and other human rights documents relevant to women either are or ought to be at home in all cultural traditions.[33] It is not that they do not recognize the important cultural differences between women. It is rather that they limit the relevances of these differences within human rights discourse and practice. So, for example, Rebecca Cook acknowledges that "the experiences of women within their own countries and cultures [must inform our] understanding and application of uniform principles of respect for human rights." But she also insists that "asking the woman question" will result in making human rights laws appropriate for women in all cultural contexts.[34]

Notwithstanding the visibility and the apparent widespread appeal of women's rights as human rights, the mainstream consensus in support of such a law-based approach to the liberation of women from patriarchy has not been endorsed by all feminists. Indeed, many of the initial feminist concerns about law-based approaches to the emancipation of women and the advancement of women's interests have resurfaced in more recent feminist critiques of women's rights as human rights.

WOMEN'S RIGHTS AS HUMAN RIGHTS: RECENT FEMINIST OPPOSITION

In contrast to the prevailing liberal feminism, other strands of feminist theory have been far less positive about the possibilities of international human rights law to alleviate women's oppression. Despite the considerable differences among feminist theorists in this group, I discuss them together as "cultural" feminists to contrast their views with those of the liberal feminists described earlier. Cultural feminist criticisms of international human rights law, which both draw on and go beyond more familiar generically feminist worries about law and rights generally, cast a shadow of doubt on the optimistic views of liberal feminists just discussed.

Cultural feminists generally stress the significance of differences both between men and women and among women. And since cultural feminists regard the law as being both inherently male gendered and incapable by virtue of its universalism of addressing the particularities and differences that distinguish women from one another, they are generally pessimistic about the potential of law to empower women and child-age girls. More concretely, they are openly skeptical about the ability of international legal norms originating and designed in Western European cultures to adequately address the needs of women in non-Western cultures. The problems and needs of so-called Third World women, they maintain, are unlikely to prove amenable to international legal solutions, especially those based on individual rights.

A central premise in cultural feminist arguments is that the conception of personal identity assumed by international law is inextricably bound up with Western masculinist assumptions based on what Hernandez-Truyol describes as "a white, Western/Northern European, Judeo-Christian, heterosexual, propertied, educated, male ideology."[35] Feminists drawing from a cultural studies perspective contend that this definition fails to accurately reflect the relational, interdependent character of female identity, either generally (establishing a difference between men and women) or at least within non-Western cultures (establishing a difference among women). This conception of the human, which was developed primarily by representatives of Western nations with little regard for the identity of peoples from non-Western cultural traditions, ought not simply be assumed to be universally applicable. As Leslye Obiora argues persuasively, "the individual's formation of a sense of humanity, self, and identity is invariably contingent on a cultural context, [and so] respect for the totality of individual human rights necessarily entails some degree of respect for the variability and specificity of culture."[36] Cultural feminists are, then, skeptical about the value of subsuming all "women" under the concept of "human" as the latter has been defined in international human rights law. At most, the concept of "human" as it functions in international law may extend without distortion or loss to the self-conception of some women (though that may even be doubted) but certainly not to all.

Because international human rights law frames prohibitions on sexual discrimination in terms of principles of abstract equality, cultural feminists argue that such law cannot adequately address the harms done to women. Women are, they insist, different from men and from one another. Because the antidiscrimination provisions of international human rights law continue to view men as the standard by which discrimination against women is evaluated, women's distinctive interests and needs, either as a single group or as a plurality of distinct groups, continue to be ignored. For example, interests and needs related to reproduction and childbearing and to women's health are rendered invisible within a nondiscrimination regime organized around male interests and needs. Although by their participation in drafting processes, women have remedied some of these defects in more recent international human rights documents (e.g., CEDAW and the platform for action), the bias still exists within international law, according to cultural feminist critics, especially in the older documents.

Cultural feminists reject nondiscrimination norms grounded in abstract ideals of equality not just because of differences between men and women but because of differences among women as well. Existing international human rights law is, they argue, "essentialist" in that it presumes rather than demonstrates morally and legally significant commonalities among all women. The trouble with such essentialism is that the differences among women are often more significant, morally and legally, than the commonalities. Given the intersectionality of gender with race, class, ethnicity, religion, sexual orientation, and other primary determinants of identity, these feminist theorists contend that the differences among women make it inappropriate to assume the universality required to characterize women as a monolithic group, even if a group distinct from men, for purposes of human rights laws.[37]

Because of its abstractness and aspiration for universality, international human rights law is, according to cultural feminists, ill-equipped to take seriously cultural diversity. Indeed, the problem is even worse, since international law generally accords little value to the integrity of local cultures. As Leslye Obiora describes it, "because 'human rights' rest on a view of the individual person as a 'human' separate from any particular society and endowed with inalienable rights against his or her state, . . . the integrity and basic rights of individuals [requires] that coercive cultural measures be constrained by rigorous standards."[38] The normative priority given to individuals as abstract equals within international human rights law functions to undermine and devalue the integrity of local cultures. And it may lead to too quick and easy a condemnation of various cultural practices. With respect to female circumcision, for example, Obiora suggests that "since circumcision cannot be understood in isolation from its complex socio-cultural, moral, ethical, and religious matrix, an effective eradication campaign must locate it in relation to patterns and values relevant to these contexts."[39]

Apart from worries about the ability of international human rights law to emancipate all women from oppression—given its male-gendered conception of the legal subject, or "human"; the relationship between its nondiscrimination norms and abstract equality; and its privileging of abstract individuals over the integrity of particular cultures—cultural feminists also worry about the ability of international law to penetrate the social and psychological domains within and through which so much patriarchal oppression is generated and reproduced. The focus of international human rights law is on public acts and actors. It is, as a result, poorly designed to reach the psychological and social space where "private" attitudes and values about women function to perpetuate women's oppression. Even if women's legal rights were established and protected effectively just as the liberal feminist wishes, the law would remain unable to change underlying attitudes toward and values about women; thus, sexism, patriarchy, and misogyny, indeed the oppression of women, would likely continue.

Against those who insist that the legal realization of women's rights as human rights will bring about the necessary social and psychological changes, cultural feminists insist that in fact the efficacy of the legal reforms presupposes such changes. As Ronald Krotoszynski observes, "one cannot rewrite by legislative fiat the content of people's hearts and minds."[40] Krotoszynski explains that "as a general proposition, changing people's minds and beliefs is a necessary prerequisite to altering their attitudes and behaviors through modifications in the legal order."[41] And as Leslye Obiora notes, "law alone seldom changes behavior. Although it is certainly a key determinant of change, it is not a panacea nor is it a brooding omnipresence in the sky. It is instead a mechanism that is integral to, and contingent on, a broader societal scheme. Against this backdrop, it is reasonable to infer that law can wield considerable influence over actions and attitudes [only] where it is accepted as legitimate authority."[42] Thus, given its inability to alter the stereotyped, sexist, patriarchal, and sometimes misogynist views of women, which must ultimately be transformed in order to create through law any fundamental or stable change in women's status, international human rights law can be, at best, of only limited value for women's empowerment.

For better or worse, international law has developed around the assumption that social and political power resides primarily in a centralized state authority. This makes international law, including the women's-rights-as-human-rights movement, a blunt instrument for bringing about the end of women's oppression, especially since so many of the denials of women's humanity take place in the so-called private realm by nonstate actors. According to cultural feminists, then, women's empowerment must come primarily from alternative, perhaps subaltern, social and psychological strategies that recognize and respect sexual difference, cultural diversity, and the radically different social locations that women in various parts of the world occupy. Rather than propose a universalist and legalistic strategy that ignores the differences between men and women or among women, cultural feminists advocate a diverse range of locally tailored and wide-ranging strategies that take account of such differences as they affect the full scope of women's lives.

Finally, it should be noted that cultural feminists insist that international human rights law is not simply generically "male." It is "male" in a very particular sense, one associated with privileged European male interests. Cultural feminists share with many others the view that international human rights law was developed on the basis of specifically European, Enlightenment, male-centered conceptions of persons, a conception of maleness not universally shared around the world.[43] This explains, they maintain, why the Universal Declaration of Human Rights focuses more on civil and political rights than it does on social and economic rights. The former are simply more important to the privileged elites of the First (or "developed") World, for whom social and economic rights are taken for granted.[44] Since few women share such a privileged social location, international human rights law is unlikely to be of much, if any, use to the majority of women in the world, according to cultural feminists. These women need first and foremost to improve the basic material (as well as social and psychological) conditions of their lives before they can take advantage of those civil and political rights taken as being paradigmatic within international human rights law.[45]

To sum up, cultural feminists reject the arguments offered by liberal feminists in favor of the women's-rights-as-human-rights movement. Both drawing on and going beyond more familiar and generic feminist worries about social ideals that give too central a place to law and individual rights, they claim that the liberal arguments in favor of women's rights as human rights are insufficient to justify placing much hope in, and thus working hard to implement, that strategy as a primary vehicle for ending the oppression of women globally.

What I want to explore now is whether there may be a reasoned path beyond this apparently intractable opposition between two dominant streams of feminist thought over the merits of the women's-rights-as-human-rights movement.

TOWARD A PRAGMATIST FEMINIST APPROACH

Given the present discussion, should we conclude that international human rights laws in general, and the movement for women's rights as human rights in particular, are or are not effective ways to promote the interests and statuses of women? I want to suggest that it is not necessary to choose between the two diametrically opposed alternatives suggested by the feminist theories discussed here. Rather, I want to offer feminist pragmatist theory as an alternative perspective on the debate within feminism over women's rights as human rights.

There have been a few feminist theorists who have explored the potential of pragmatism for feminist theorizing but none, to my knowledge, who have addressed human rights in particular.[46] Those who have explored the relations between pragmatist and feminist thought have noted striking similarities. Both reject traditional rationalist and empiricist approaches to philosophy. Both regard theory and practice as being inseparable. Both sail by the North Star of the lived experience of everyday life, including its communal, particularist, affective, and emotive aspects. Indeed, both reject theories of knowledge or truth that do not take seriously these aspects of human experience. And both accordingly offer theories of knowledge or truth as being contextual and relative to particular concrete interests and lived experience (what is also known as "standpoint epistemology"), as opposed to the universal, abstract, or necessarily generalizable.[47]

A pragmatist feminist approach to the issue of women's rights as human rights would draw on elements from both liberal and cultural feminism but would also break new theoretical ground and open the way to new areas of inquiry. It would ask whether there are good reasons for thinking that affirming women's rights as human rights might be an effective tool toward advancing women's interests in some contexts or circumstances. And if the answer to that question were affirmative, it would support appeals to women's rights as human rights just to that extent. It would reject any wholesale abandonment of the campaign for women's rights as human rights grounded in primarily theoretical or philosophical concerns.

From the pragmatist feminist point of view, it is neither "essentialist" nor necessarily problematic to recognize that there are some morally and legally significant commonalities within human experience that cut across sex and gender and cultural differences. As a matter of lived experience, at least in the present historical context, humans universally share certain basic interests that cut across sex or gender differences. All human beings have physical bodies. In almost all cases after birth, these bodies are individuated from all others. And in all cases, they are subject to illness, decay, pain, and deprivations of various sorts. And nearly all human beings (and certainly all human beings possessed of minimally adequate neurological function) are conscious at least some time and thus possessed of mental states. And, of course, nearly all human beings are psychologically aware of their own mental states. In light of the foregoing, it should hardly strike us as being problematic to accept the idea that all human beings have an interest in being protected from physical and psychological harm or suffering and that, accordingly, there are good reasons to affirm universal proscriptions against torture, sexual and other physical violence and abuse, starvation, the most serious of psychological assaults, and so forth.

Nor should it strike us as being problematic to accept the root idea of the right to nondiscrimination. Notwithstanding the facts of cultural diversity, women, like men, share an interest in not being thrust into a permanently subordinate social status simply by virtue of their sex. For women, this underwrites a shared interest in eliminating fundamental forms of discrimination in access to basic social resources, the devaluation of women's labor, the feminization of poverty, and the tolerance of violence against women.[48]

The foregoing are among the interests that international human rights were designed to protect. They are interests universally or nearly universally shared by all women. Thus, arguments against women's rights as human rights that rest upon a radical cultural relativism would seem unsound. Women universally share a basic interest in material and economic security, and where they are denied equal or nearly equal access to paid work, where the kinds of work available to women and men is thoroughly determined by sex, where women are overwhelmingly held responsible for the unpaid work of the household, and where men hold disproportionate power within the family, women are denied the social conditions needed to satisfy their basic interests in material and economic security. In such circumstances, their human rights are violated.[49]

Of course, from a pragmatist feminist point of view, whether any particular case presents a violation of one or another of the women's rights taken up as a human right is a question that cannot be answered in the abstract or upon a bare recitation of a few isolated facts. It is a question, as are all human rights questions, the answer to which will turn on a particularized, concrete, contextualized analysis of the relevant claims, all with an eye toward the relevant social goal—namely, the emancipation of women from oppression and the advancing of their fundamental interests. Moreover, the issue of how to remedy a human rights violation is likewise an issue calling, from the feminist pragmatist perspective, for a particularized, concrete, contextualized analysis with an eye toward what is most likely to advance the relevant social goal. What may be justified as a remedy in one context may not be justified in another.

The pragmatist feminist point here is not just that all prescriptions, even those made in light of universal values or norms, must be justified in full awareness of the concrete facts of the particular circumstance with respect to which the prescription is being made. The point is not just that culture is relevant. The pragmatist feminist point is also that the concrete facts against which any prescription applying universal values is to be justified must themselves be understood as being fluid. Cultures are dynamic and changing, not static and monolithic. As Arati Rao explains, "culture is a series of constantly contested and negotiated social practices whose meanings are influenced by the power and status of their interpreters and participants."[50] And so pragmatist feminists will attend to the ways in which legal judgments regarding women's rights as human rights will alter the relevant cultural backdrop against which those judgments are made and enforced. They will recognize that even within cultures currently lacking a human rights tradition, there may be room for one to develop and that pressing for women's rights as human rights may be an effective strategy toward that end. But they will also recognize the need to monitor regularly the ways in which legal judgments and interventions alter the background cultural landscape so as to be sure not to sacrifice an end to a means.

A pragmatist feminist can allow that a social constructionist conception of identity may be more accurate descriptively than the universalist liberal conception of the autonomous self existing apart from any particular social or cultural context. What is important for the pragmatist feminist is whether this conception entails any normative conclusions. And while it surely entails the conclusion that facts about social and cultural context will matter to any politics of emancipation, it does not entail the conclusion that persons are or ought to be inescapably bound by their social or cultural contexts to the dominant self-understandings offered by them. Of course, there are virtually no cultures left on Earth immune to various international or global influences. And so even from a constructivist point of view, all identities are shaped as a matter of descriptive fact by forces both local and global. As a descriptive matter, there is no reason not to acknowledge here the important effects of the global discourse of human rights on individual self-understandings around the world. More to the point, feminists have no reason not to welcome—or, at least, cultural feminists provide no across-the-board reasons not to welcome—this development from a normative point of view.

A pragmatist feminist, then, can acknowledge and approve of the introduction of the global discourse of universal human rights within any culture. Of course, within any particular culture, the perceived legitimacy or effectiveness of such a discourse and the legal practices it supports may turn on whether universal human rights can be seen as being justified from the normative point of view characteristic of that culture. But this point of view is itself something that is dynamic and changing, and claims made by self-declared official arbiters of any particular culture about the relationship between human rights norms and cultural norms do not in themselves determine the actual validity of the relevant human rights norms. Pragmatist feminists can acknowledge that there may be in many cases good moral reasons for being patient and accommodating with respect to women's rights as human rights or the human rights agenda more broadly. But they can do so without taking on board the range of cultural feminist commitments.

Importantly, though, pragmatist feminists can, without contradiction, agree with cultural feminists that there may be good reasons in some cases not just to be patient and accommodating with respect to women's rights as human rights but, even more dramatically, not to place much emphasis on that strategy at all when it comes to acting for the sake of women's interests. Pragmatist feminists do not privilege human rights or women's rights as human rights in some absolute sense above the goal of securing for women the social conditions within which women may flourish and advance their interests on their own terms and in their own way. Cultural differences in women's experience may lead women to understand their own interests and their own flourishing differently and thus to take different attitudes toward particular women's rights as human rights. This need not trouble the pragmatist feminist. Of course, pragmatist feminists will want to be sure that women enjoy those social conditions minimally necessary to have and express their own views with respect to their interests and flourishing. But those views need not line up neatly with some conception of the true or essential interests of women sometimes thought to be implicit in the women's-rights-as-human-rights agenda.

In this respect, a pragmatist feminism does not regard the subject and thus the woman as being essentially either an abstract universal rights holder or a particularized socially constructed self. It rejects this dichotomy. For the purposes of international human rights law, it rejects both the liberal feminist conception of women as first and foremost, always and everywhere, "human" in the sense of being male-gendered, abstract universal rights holders and the cultural or gender feminist conception of women as never "human" in that sense and first and foremost, always and everywhere, particular, embodied, diverse, socially constituted beings. Rather, a pragmatist feminist approach begins with the premise that the "human" is itself fundamentally socially constructed but with an eye toward certain ends and may therefore differ in different situations.[51] This makes the efficacy and appropriateness of women's rights as human rights contingent upon the specificities of particular subject positions rather than predetermined theoretical presuppositions.

Given this broadened conception of female identity, a pragmatist feminist approach begins with the premise that just as women's identities are varied and diverse, so too must be approaches to ending women's oppression. The movement for women's rights as human rights can then be viewed as but one of a number of potentially applicable strategies for advancing women's interests, which may or may not be appropriate or efficacious in a particular case. In determining which strategy or combination of strategies is likely to be most effective for empowering women and improving their social statuses in particular circumstances, a number of factors need to be considered.

The first is, what is the specific cultural, religious, geographical, political, and socioeconomic context in which the women in question are located? All of these factors need to be assessed in light of the potential for an international women's human rights strategy to be effective. In particular, it is important to know whether cultural conditions exist, such as religious or other gender ideologies, that would either subvert or facilitate the recognition and enforcement of women's human rights, and whether, if they do exist, those conditions are deeply and firmly entrenched and likely to change only slowly or are less fixed and perhaps more easily changed. For example, under some circumstances, long-standing and culturally grounded hostility by the relevant government to "the West," to international legal pressure, or to rights talk generally may make the success of a women's-rights-as-human-rights strategy for empowering women locally somewhat dubious. In general, the women's-rights-as-human-rights strategy is more likely to empower women in cultures at least not hostile to the idea of "the West" and with some history or tradition of recognizing and enforcing individual rights and responding to the demands of international law.

Pragmatist feminists can allow that where a women's-rights-as-human-rights strategy generates direct and deep conflict with local religion, culture, and tradition, it may be more appropriate for feminists and others eager to empower women in that context to pursue a more subversive, nonlegalistic strategy rather than one grounded primarily in international human rights law. Pragmatist feminists will search for resources internal to the religion, culture, and tradition upon which women might draw effectively in their struggle to end patriarchal oppression. This sort of flexibility in strategy without losing sight of the goal sought is a singular advantage of the pragmatist feminist approach over that of either the liberal or cultural feminist. No approach to ending women's oppression can succeed if it lacks the resources to respond to women in all their diversity, taking seriously differences of culture, religion, class, race, ethnicity, geography, sexual orientation, economic location, and the like. It is the flexibility inherent in the pragmatist approach that enables the pragmatist feminist to guide feminist work across all these differences. And it is this same flexibility that enables the pragmatist feminist to address, importantly, those situations within which the power oppressing women is not centralized or deployed primarily by state actors, situations with respect to which the liberal feminist approach offers little. Under such circumstances, pragmatist feminists will want to explore the possibilities of decentralized, grassroots, local, and psychological strategies for empowering women.

A second factor pragmatist feminists will consider with respect to the use of a women's-rights-as-human-rights strategy in any particular case is whether the relevant population, including and especially the women, possesses, a "legal" or "rights" consciousness, whether self-understandings are responsive to public, political, and legal institutions and practices. Where such institutions and practices play little or no role in the constitution of self-understandings, the pragmatist feminist will have reason to hesitate before endorsing an unmediated imposition through international law of women's rights as human rights. In such circumstances, such a framework is likely to be poorly received, if it is accepted at all, both by the intended female beneficiaries as well as the larger communities within which they live. Absent some active or latent space for a legal or rights consciousness within the self-understandings of members of a particular culture, a women's-rights-as-human-rights strategy will inevitably be, and be perceived to be, determined and imposed from the outside as an alien force. And this may make it a poor choice as a dominant strategy for empowering women.[52] Of course, pragmatist feminists will insist that it does not follow from the fact that a people presently does not possess a legal or rights consciousness that they might not eventually develop one. Their point is simply that if the goal is empowering women and ending patriarchal oppression and if women's agency is to be taken seriously in that process as it must be, then there may be good reasons in certain contexts not to place immediate and great weight on the women's-rights-as-human-rights strategy.

To cite just one example, it is frequently argued that Asian societies are more communitarian than individualistic and that both institutional and cultural forces in such societies generate in their members self-understandings within which legal or rights consciousness is either absent or more strongly disfavored.[53] Consequently, using a rights-based strategy in response to women's oppression in at least some of these societies may be inappropriate, ineffectual, or even harmful, all things considered.

To be sure, many Asian societies have well-developed political and legal institutions and have agreed to various international human rights protocols, including some addressing women's rights as human rights. But because "legal norms do not exist free and clear of cultural expectations," what these societies understand themselves to be agreeing to and what Western states understand them to be agreeing to may be very different things.[54] Given the powerful and typically communitarian pull of the background culture of such societies on their political and legal institutions, it is not likely that an exclusively legalistic women's-rights-as-human-rights strategy will be very effective at significantly advancing the interests of the women in such societies.

A third factor pragmatist feminists will consider when evaluating any proposed application of a women's-rights-as-human-rights strategy is the historical experience of success and failure by other groups using legalist or rights-based strategies to forward their claims against the state. Pragmatist feminists take their cues from human experience, what works and what does not. If legalist and rights-based strategies for advancing the interests of labor, of gays and lesbians, or of racial minorities or political dissidents have all failed while nonlegalist and non-rights-based strategies (perhaps religious, for example) have had some success, the pragmatist feminist will have reason to be skeptical about whether a women's-rights-as-human-rights strategy will offer much success.

Further, since legal and rights-based reforms are rarely a complete and comprehensive solution to group-based oppression, feminist pragmatists will want to know how successful they have been in broad terms, even when they have been institutionalized and thus successful on their own terms.[55] In states where legal and rights-based reforms have unleashed larger social processes aimed at ending oppression, pragmatist feminists will have reason to be optimistic about a women's-rights-as-human-rights strategy. In states where such reforms have not unleashed such larger social forces, they will have reason to be skeptical or at least to inquire further into whether there are good reasons to expect a different outcome with respect to women's rights and the end of women's oppression. The very real risks of social and cultural backlash that an international human rights strategy presents heighten the importance of considering whether implementing this approach in this or that context may disadvantage the women there more than it empowers them.

Finally, before endorsing a women's-rights-as-human-rights strategy in any particular context, pragmatist feminists will want to know which rights the women in question think are in need of legal recognition. While women more or less universally agree on the need for the legal recognition of a right to be free from unchecked domestic violence, women are divided over the need to secure legal recognition for a right to be free from female circumcision or to abortion. Given that dissensus, efforts to secure the latter through a women's-rights-as-human-rights undertaking are likely to be far more problematic than efforts to secure the former. As Karen Engle points out, both women's rights and human rights organizations have not been able to successfully incorporate the "Exotic Other Female" into their analyses.[56] Without doing so, however, women's human rights jurisprudence will remain either essentialist—assuming all women are alike—or exclusionary, refusing to include women who do not agree with "our values." The pragmatist feminist seeks a way beyond this impasse by focusing on and self-consciously and strategically working within the longer-term dialectical processes through which women's and human interests and self-understandings are shaped.

Where the preconditions for effective recognition and enforcement of a particular right are lacking in a particular locale, alternative nonlegal strategies are likely to be more effective, at least in the short run. These may include literacy and reading campaigns, economic initiatives such as small bank loans or redistribution of land ownership, or various forms of cultural reinterpretation. Suwanna Satha-Anand, for instance, has argued that a general cultural effort aimed at reinterpreting sacred Buddhist texts would be a more effective strategy than the pursuit of women's rights as human rights through international law when it comes to ending the enormous trafficking of Thai and Burmese women for the sex trade in Thailand.[57] Similarly, Norani Othman has noted that Muslim women's organizations in Malaysia are advancing a reinterpretation of foundational Islamic texts in order to reveal the discursive space within the Islamic tradition for significantly advancing the status of women.[58] Indeed, "the experience of many women's groups operating in Muslim countries these past two decades demonstrates that in their daily battles, a great deal more progress is achieved by working within their respective religious and cultural paradigm" than through pressures for reform rooted in international human rights law.[59] Othman is led, sensibly, to suggest that efforts to end women's oppression globally must mediate between a legalist women's-rights-as-human-rights strategy that seeks to bring change from the outside and a culturally relativist, immanent critique strategy that seeks to secure all change from the inside.

Othman is surely correct that the most effective global approach to women's oppression will be a multifaceted one with particular approaches being shaped in light of the particular context to which they are responding. Saba Bahar shares this view. While she criticizes Amnesty International's recent work for women's rights as human rights on the grounds that it is rooted in gendered assumptions about the relationship between the state and families and images of women as being naturally weak and dependent upon a strong paternal state for protection, she also urges feminists to continue to strive to expand Amnesty's understanding of women's rights but to do so while taking "their cues from . . . grassroots movements, allowing them to define the agenda for the movement in a manner relevant to their local, cultural, and national contexts."[60]

Satha-Anand, Othman, and Bahar reflect well the feminist pragmatist approach suggested here. These more contextualized, gender-sensitive, and culturally specific and nuanced approaches to securing women's needs and interests globally can undoubtedly be more effective than pursuing an overly legalistic international human rights strategy alone. Of course, the appropriate strategy for promoting the status of women cannot be determined in the abstract but only in a particular context.

CONCLUSION

Many feminists and women's groups have advocated the use of international human rights law to end women's oppression and to empower women to determine and advance their own interests. Notwithstanding the obvious attractions of the women's-rights-as-human-rights strategy, critics have argued that this approach is unlikely to empower women and improve their statuses in many parts of the world. I have surveyed the arguments for and against giving pride of place to this strategy within the feminist agenda, but rather than ally myself with either side in this theoretical battle, I have proposed a pragmatist feminist alternative. On this alternative view, international human rights law in general and the women's-rights-as-human-rights strategy in particular may provide an effective approach for promoting the status of women's rights in some contexts, but it ought not be supposed to do so in all. (And, of course, even if it were to work well in all contexts, the fact would remain that legal reforms are always no more than partial and incomplete strategies for ending significant and long-standing oppression.)

Applied unreflectively and without regard to social and cultural context, the women's-rights-as-human-rights strategy is likely at least sometimes, if not often, to be ineffective, if not positively damaging, to the interests and well-being of the women it purports to assist. A pragmatist feminist approach urges a more cautious use of the women's-rights-as-human-rights approach, one that attends to a wide range of factors relevant to determining how best to secure the social conditions needed for particular populations of women to enjoy greater freedom, security, and capacities, resources, and opportunities for self-realization.

NOTES

1. The literature addressing human rights from feminist perspectives is fairly recent but burgeoning rapidly. See, e.g., Rebecca Cook, "Women's International Human Rights Law: The Way Forward," in Rebecca Cook, ed., *Human Rights of Women: National and International Perspectives* (Philadelphia: University of Pennsylvania Press, 1994), pp. 3–38; Julie Peters and Andrea Wolper, eds., *Women's Rights, Human Rights: International Feminist Perspectives* (New York: Routledge, 1995); Noleen Heyzer, ed., *A Commitment to the World's Women: Perspectives on De-*

velopment for Beijing and Beyond (New York: UNIFEM, 1995); Janice Wood Wentzel, *The World of Women: In Pursuit of Human Rights* (Houndsmill, N.J.: Macmillan Press 1993); Case Western Reserve Law Review Editorial Staff, "Colloquium: Bridging Society, Culture, and Law," *Case Western Reserve Law Review*, Vol. 47, pp. 275–444 (1997); Human Rights Watch Women's Rights Project, *The Human Rights Watch Global Report on Women's Human Rights* (New York: Human Rights Watch, 1995); Amnesty International, *Its about Time! Human Rights Are Women's Right* (New York: Amnesty International, 1995).

2. United Nations, "United Nations Charter," in *The United Nations and Human Rights* (New York: United Nations), pp. 143–46. The most relevant charter provisions regarding sex discrimination are Articles 1(3), 13(1)(b), 55(c), and 76(c), all of which state as a goal that of "promoting and encouraging respect for human rights and for fundamental freedoms for all without distinction as to race, sex, language, or religion."

3. See *The United Nations and Human Rights* , *supra* note 2, at p. 153.

4. See *The United Nations and Human Rights, supra* note 2, at p. 277. In addition, the International Covenant on Economic, Social, and Cultural Rights and the International Covenant on Civil and Political Rights, both ratified in 1966, which make binding on states many of the principles contained in the Universal Declaration of Human Rights, also prohibit discrimination on the basis of sex. See *United Nations and Human Rights, id.* at pp. 229, 235.

5. United Nations, *Beijing Declaration and Draft Platform for Action*, UN Doc. A/CONF.177/20 (1995). Charlotte Bunch characterizes the platform as being "a positive affirmation of women's human rights in many areas." Charlotte Bunch and Susana Fried, "Beijing '95: Moving Women's Human Rights from Margin to Center," *Signs: Journal of Women and Culture*, Vol. 22(1) (1996), pp. 200–204, at 201.

6. Judith Baer, "How Is Law Male?" in Leslie Friedman Goldstein, ed., *Feminist Jurisprudence: The Difference Debate* (Lanham, MD: Rowman & Littlefield, 1992), pp. 147–72; see also, Joan Hoff, *Law, Gender, and Injustice* (New York: New York University Press, 1991).

7. Hilary Charlesworth, "Human Rights as Men's Rights," in Julie Peters and Andrea Wolper, eds., *Women's Rights, Human Rights, supra* note 1, pp. 103–113; see Hilary Charlesworth, "What Are 'Women's International Human Rights'?" in Rebecca Cook, ed., *Human Rights of Women, supra* note 1, pp. 58–84, at 64.

8. Carol Gilligan, *In a Different Voice: Psychological Theory and Women's Development* (Cambridge, MA: Harvard University Press, 1982). After studying how adolescents and others responded to a number of hypothetical moral dilemmas, Gilligan observed a gender difference. Whereas the males in her study tended to resolve moral problems in accordance with an "ethics of justice," characterized by a concern with individual rights, abstract principles of justice, and adversarial relations, Gilligan found that the females tended to rely on "an ethic of care," one that (1) assumes that persons are socially interdependent rather than independent and (2) is centrally concerned with caring for and nurturing others and with preserving relationships rather than individual rights.

9. Kathleen Mahoney, "Theoretical Perspectives on Women's Human Rights and Strategies for Their Implementation," *Brooklyn Journal of International Law*, Vol. 21 (1996), pp. 799–856, at 838.

10. See, e.g., Cecilia Romany, "State Responsibility Goes Private: A Feminist Critique of the Public/Private Distinction in International Human Rights Law," in Rebecca Cook, ed., *Human Rights of Women, supra* note 1, pp. 85–115.

11. See, e.g., Catharine MacKinnon, "Crimes of War, Crimes of Peace," in Stephen Shute and Susan Hurley, eds., *On Human Rights: The Oxford Amnesty Lectures* (New York: Basic Books, 1993), pp. 83–110; Berta Hernandez-Truyol, "Concluding Remarks—Making Women Visible: Setting an Agenda for the Twenty-first Century," *St. John's Law Review*, Vol. 69 (1995), pp. 231–54, at 231.

12. See Rebecca Cook, "State Accountability under the Convention on the Elimination of All Forms of Discrimination against Women," in Rebecca Cook, ed., *Human Rights of Women: National and International Perspectives* (Philadelphia: University of Pennsylvania Press, 1994), pp. 228–256, at 247; Cecilia Romany, "State Responsibility Goes Private," *supra* note 10, at 85.

13. See MacKinnon in Shute and Hurley, *supra* note 11; Kathleen Mahoney, "Theoretical Perspectives on Women's Human Rights," *supra* note 8, at 843, 851; Andrew Byrnes, "Toward More Effective Enforcement of Women's Human Rights through the Use of International Human Rights Law and Procedures," in Rebecca Cook, ed., *Human Rights of Women, supra* note 1, pp. 189–227, at 203–4; Dorothy Thomas, "Conclusion," in Julie Peters and Andrea Wolper, eds., *Women's Rights, Human Rights, supra* note 1, pp. 356–59, at 358; Cecilia Romany, *supra* note 10, at 85–86. This circumstance has led some feminist legal scholars to argue that the state should be held responsible for acts of private violence when it has failed to provide women with the same degree of protection that it regularly provides to men for similar crimes committed against them. See Catharine MacKinnon, "Crimes of War, Crimes of Peace," *supra* note 11; Kathleen Mahoney, *supra* note 9.

14. Andrew Byrnes, "Towards More Effective Enforcement," *supra* note 13, at 198–99, Rebecca Cook, *supra* note 12, at 228.

15. Sara Hossain, "Equality in the Home: Women's Rights and Personal Laws in South Asia," in Rebecca Cook, ed., *Human Rights of Women, supra* note 1, pp. 465–494, 470; see Radhika Coomaraswamy, *Report of the Special Rapporteur on Violence against Women: Its Causes and Consequences*, submitted in accordance with Commission on Human Rights Resolution 1995/85, United Nations Commission on Human Rights, 52nd Session, Item 9a, E/CN.4/1996/53, 1996, at p. 16. According to Kathleen Mahoney, "the widespread practice of states opting out of fundamental provisions of the Women's Convention, have rendered it ineffective where its provisions are needed the most." Kathleen Mahoney, *supra* note 9, at 841. As another example, nineteen states entered reservations to text in the UN conference on women's platform that did not conform to Islamic law or traditional religious interpretations (*id.*).

16. Andrew Byrnes, "Towards More Effective Enforcement," *supra* note 13, at pp. 199–202.

17. Andrew Byrnes, "Towards More Effective Enforcement," *supra* note 13, at p. 192.

18. Asthma Mohamed Abdel Halim, "Challenges to the Application of International Women's Human Rights in the Sudan," in Rebecca Cook, ed., *Human Rights of Women, supra* note 1, pp. 397–421, at 406.

19. Rebecca Cook, "Women's International Human Rights Law," *supra* note 1, at 18.

20. United Nations, *Convention to Eliminate Discrimination against Women*, 18 Dec. 1979, UN GAOR Supp. 34th Sess., No. 21 (A/34/46) at 193, UN Doc. /RES.34/ 180 (entry into force 3 Sept. 1981).

21. These two gender-distinctive provisions are contained in the United Nations Convention for the Suppression of the Traffic in Persons and of the Exploitation of the Prostitution of Others of 1949 (see United Nations, *The United Nations and Human Rights*, *supra* note 2, at 147), and the *Declaration on the Elimination of Violence against Women of 1993* (G.A. Res. 104, UN GAOR, 48th Sess., Supp. No. 49, at 217, UN Doc. A/RES/48/104 [1994]); see Charlotte Bunch, "The Global Campaign for Women's Human Rights: Where Next After Vienna?" *St. John's Law Review*, Vol. 69 (1995), pp. 171–78 , at 174; Berta Hernandez-Truyol, "Concluding Remarks," *supra* note 11, at pp. 245–46.

22. For example, the committee established to oversee CEDAW has interpreted Article 2 of the women's convention to make states responsible for violations of the enumerated rights of women by private actors if they fail to "act with due diligence to prevent violations of rights, or to investigate and punish acts of violence." See Joan Fitzpatrick, "The Use of International Human Rights Norms to Combat Violence against Women," in Rebecca Cook, ed., *Human Rights of Women*, *supra* note 1, pp. 532–71, at 535. In addition, Article 4 of the Declaration on the Elimination of Violence against Women exhorts states to condemn violence against women and not to "invoke any custom, tradition, or religion or other consideration to avoid their obligation with respect to its elimination." United Nations, *Declaration on the Elimination of Violence against Women*, *supra* note 20.

23. Rebecca Cook, "State Accountability," *supra* note 11, at p. 252.

24. Maria Isabel Plata, "Reproductive Rights as Human Rights: The Colombian Case," in Rebecca Cook, *Human Rights of Women*, *supra* note 1, pp. 515–31, at 519.

25. United Nations, *Optional Protocol to the Convention on the Elimination of All Forms of Discrimination against Women* (New York, 6 October 1999), http:// untreaty.un.org/English/TreatyEvent2001/index.htm.

26. United Nations website, Division for the Advancement of Women, "Signatories to and Ratifications of the Optional Protocol," http://untreaty.un.org/ English/Index/Alphabet38.pdf (2004).

27. For instance, Hilary Charlesworth argues that "rights discourse offers a significant vocabulary to formulate political and social grievances which is recognized by the powerful." Rebecca Cook, "Women's International Human Rights Law," *supra* note 1, at 4; see Hilary Charlesworth, "What Are 'Women's International Human Rights'?" *supra* note 7, at 61. Philosopher Martha Nussbaum and law professor Patricia Williams make similar arguments about the empowering character of rights language. See, e.g., Martha Nussbaum, "Capabilities and Human Rights," in Patrick Hayden, ed., *The Philosophy of Human Rights* (St. Paul, MN: Paragon House, 2001), pp. 212–40, at 231–32; Patricia Williams, *The Alchemy of Race and Rights: Diary of a Law Professor* (Cambridge, MA: Harvard University Press, 1991), pp. 149.

28. Berta Hernandez-Truyol, "Concluding Remarks," *supra* note 11, at p. 250.

29. Sara Hossain, "Equality in the Home, " *supra* note 15, at 485.

30. See Rebecca Cook, "Women's International Human Rights Law: The Way Forward," *supra* note 1, at 14–15.

31. Wang Zheng, one of the participants in the UN's conference on women, suggests that because the platform document was affirmed by the Chinese government,

it has legitimated the campaign to expand women's rights in China, which in turn is "creating legitimacy for expanding Chinese women's activism under the guidance of the official international document. In other words, the document will serve as the measure of Chinese women's achievements from now on." Wang Zheng, "A Historic Turning Point for the Women's Movement in China," *Signs*, Vol. 22, No. 1 (1996), pp. 192–99, at 198.

32. See, e.g. Berta Hernandez-Truyol, "Concluding Remarks," *supra* note 11, at 232.

33. See Berta Hernandez-Truyol, "Women's Rights as Human Rights—Rules, Realities, and the Role of Culture: A Formula for Reform," *Brooklyn Journal of International Law* Vol. 21 (1966), pp. 605–678, at 651; see, e.g., Radhika Coomaraswamy, *Report of the Special Rapporteur on Violence against Women*, *supra* note 15, at 17; Abdullahi An-Na'im, "The Cultural Mediation of Human Rights Implementation: Al-Arqam Case in Malaysia," in Joanne Bauer and Daniel Bell, eds., *The East Asian Challenge for Human Rights* (New York: Cambridge University Press, 1999), pp. 147–68.

34. Rebecca Cook, "State Accountability," *supra* note 11, at p. 241.

35. Berta Hernandez-Truyol, "Women's Rights as Human Rights," *supra* note 33, at 651.

36. Leslye Obiora, "Bridges and Barricades: Rethinking Polemics and Intransigence in the Campaign against Female Circumcision," *Case Western Reserve Law Review*, Vol. 47 (1977), pp. 275–378, at 279. Yet Abdullahi An-Na'im observes that "the impact of culture on human behavior is often underestimated precisely because it is so powerful and deeply embedded in our self-identity and consciousness. Our culture is so much a part of our personality that we take for granted that our behavior patterns and relationships to other persons and to society become the ideal norm. . . . Culture influences, first, the way we see the world and, further, how we interpret and react to the information we receive." Abdullahi An-Na'im, "Toward a Cross-Cultural Approach to Defining International Standards of Human Rights," in Abdullahi An-Na'im, ed., *Human Rights in Cross-Cultural Perspective: A Quest for Consensus* (Philadelphia: University of Pennsylvania Press, 1992), pp. 19–43, at 23.

37. See, e.g., Elizabeth Spelman, *Inessential Woman: Problems of Exclusion in Feminist Thought* (Boston: Beacon Press, 1988); Patricia Williams, *Alchemy of Race and Rights*, *supra* note 27.

38. Leslye Obiora, "Bridges and Barricades," *supra* note 36, at 332.

39. *Id.* at 360.

40. Ronald Krotoszynski, "Building Bridges and Overcoming Barricades: Exploring the Limits of Law as an Agent of Transformational Social Change," *Case Western Reserve Law Review*, Vol. 47 (1997), pp. 423–444, at 436.

41. Krotoszynski, *id.*, at 424.

42. Leslye Obiora, "Bridges and Barricades," *supra* note 36, at 358.

43. See, e.g., Jack Donnelly, *Universal Human Rights in Theory and Practice* (Ithaca, NY: Cornell University Press, 1989), pp. 9–14.

44. Civil and political rights are understood to be valid claims that individuals have to protect them against interference by the state, such as freedom of speech, religion, press, due process, and so forth. Socioeconomic goods are generally

viewed as being "entitlements" rather than "rights," which the state is not obligated to provide. This is certainly the case in the United States, where the rights enumerated in the U.S. Constitution and Bill of Rights have largely been interpreted as being restricted only to the so-called negative rights, which individuals have against state interference with their civil and political liberties, rather than extending to encompass also "positive" rights, which would require the state to provide individuals with social and economic goods.

45. To some extent, the force of this critique of international human rights is diminished by the establishment of the Covenant on Social, Economic, and Cultural Rights, which provides for the equal protection of women in the provision of such basic rights as a minimum standard of living. However, many nations, including the United States, do not accept an obligation to provide social, economic, and cultural rights and have refused to ratify the economic covenant, even though they did ratify the Covenant on Civil and Political Rights. In fact, the very decision by the UN to establish an economic covenant separate from the civil covenant was in part the result of objections by a number of states to recognizing social and economic benefits as being legal "rights" that states are affirmatively obligated by positive law to provide. See Boutros Boutros-Ghali, "Introduction," *The United Nations and Human Rights, 1954–1995* (New York: United Nations, 1995), at 43.

46. See, e.g., Charlotte Haddock Seigfried, *Pragmatism and Feminism: Reweaving the Social Fabric* (Chicago, IL: University of Chicago Press, 1996); Haddock Seigfried, ed., "Special Issue: Feminism and Pragmatism," *Hypatia*, Vol. 8, No. 2 (1993); Haddock Seigfried, "Where Are All the Feminist Pragmatists?" *Hypatia*, Vol. 6, No. 1 (Summer, 1991), pp. 1–19; Margaret Jane Radin, "The Pragmatist and the Feminist," *Southern California Law Review*, Vol. 63 (1990), pp. 1699–1726; Richard Rorty, "Feminism and Pragmatism," *Michigan Quarterly Review*, Vol. 30, No. 2 (Spring 1991), pp. 231–58; Nancy Fraser, "From Irony to Prophecy to Politics: A Response to Richard Rorty," *Michigan Quarterly Review*, Vol. 30, No. 2 (Spring 1991), pp. 259–66; Charlotte Haddock Siegfried, *William James's Radical Reconstruction of Philosophy* (Albany: State University of New York Press, 1990).

47. See Margaret Jane Radin, "The Pragmatist and the Feminist," *id.*, at 1707; Charlotte Haddock Seigfried, "Where Are All the Feminist Pragmatists?" *supra* note 47, at 2, 16.

48. See Moira McConnell, "Violence against Women: Beyond the Limits of the Law," *Brooklyn Journal of International Law*, Vol. 21 (1996), pp. 899–913, at 906.

49. Susan Moller Okin, "Gender Inequality and Cultural Differences," *Political Theory*, Vol. 22, No. 1 (1994), pp. 5–24.

50. Arati Rao, "The Politics of Gender and Culture in International Human Rights Discourse," in Julie Peters and Andrea Wolper, eds., *Women's Rights, Human Rights*, *supra* note 1, pp. 167–75, at 173.

51. This view is akin to some strands of feminist theory in its understanding that personal identity is multiple or plural rather than unitary, heterogenous rather than homogenous, composed of a number of aspects or components, and constantly shifting and changing rather than remaining fixed. See Marilyn Friedman, *What Are Friends For? Feminist Perspectives on Personal Relationships and Moral Theory* (Ithaca, NY: Cornell University Press, 1993), pp. 76–77; Judith Butler, "Contingent Foundations: Feminism and the Question of 'Postmodernism,'" in Judith

Butler and Joan Scott, eds., *Feminists Theorize the Political* (New York: Routledge, 1992), pp. 3–21, at 8–9, 13; Iris Marion Young, *Justice and the Politics of Difference* (Princeton, N.J.: Princeton University Press, 1990), p. 148; Chris Weedon, *Feminist Practice and Poststructuralist Theory* (Oxford: Basil Blackwell, 1987); Lois McNay, *Foucault and Feminism: Power, Gender, and the Self* (Boston: Northeastern University Press, 1992), pp. 12–13.

52. See Rebecca Cook, "Women's International Human Rights Law," *supra* note 1, at pp. 4–5; Radhika Coomaraswamy, "To Bellow Like a Cow: Women, Ethnicity, and the Discourse of Rights," in Rebecca Cook, ed., *Human Rights of Women," supra* note 1, pp. 39–57, at 65.

53. See, e.g., Lucinda Peach, "Are Women Human? The Promise and Perils of 'Women's Rights as Human Rights,'" in Lynda Bell, Andrew Nathan, and Ilan Peleg, eds., *Negotiating Culture and Human Rights* (New York: Columbia University Press, 2001), pp. 153–96, at 169–70; Sharon Hom, "Re-positioning Human Rights Discourse on 'Asian' Perspectives," in Lynda Bell et al., *Negotiating Culture and Human Rights, id.*, pp. 197–213, at 198–203; Bauer and Bell, *The East Asian Challenge for Human Rights, supra* note 33.

54. Ronald Krotozynski, "Building Bridges and Overcoming Barricades," *supra* note 38, at 442.

55. See, e.g., Ratna Kapur and Brenda Cossman, *Subversive Sites: Feminist Engagements with Law in India* (New Delhi: Sage Publications, 1996).

56. Karen Engle, "Female Subjects of Public International Law: Human Rights and the Exotic Other Female," in Dan Danielson and Karen Engle, eds., *After Identity: A Reader in Law and Culture* (New York: Routledge, 1995), pp. 210–28.

57. Suwanna Satha-Anand, "Thai Prostitution, Buddhism and 'New Rights' in Southeast Asia," in Joanne Bauer and Daniel Bell, eds., *The East Asian Challenge for Human Rights, supra* note 33, pp. 193–211, at 204–11.

58. Norani Othman, "Grounding Human Rights Arguments in Non-Western Culture: Shari'a and the Citizenship Rights of Women in a Modern Islamic Nation-State," in Joanne Bauer and Daniel Bell, eds., *The East Asian Challenge for Human Rights, supra* note 33, pp. 169–92.

59. Othman, *id.*, at 42.

60. Saba Bahar, "Human Rights Are Women's Right: Amnesty International and the Family," *Hypatia*, Vol. 11, No. 1 (Winter 1996), pp. 105–34, at 123.

6

Human Rights and the Ethic of Listening

Helen Stacy

There can be only one winner to a legal contest, and the figure of the judge embodies all the authority of the nation-state in determining who that winner is. In both civil and criminal cases, judicial determinations stand as authoritative pronouncements of whose story is credible. The stakes are always high. And the judicial task is always difficult. Judges must pay close attention to evidence and credibility and to the relationship between general legal rules and concrete and particular facts. These are difficult tasks even in a relatively homogeneous society or context where a judge shares with the litigants a common sense of the self and thus understands the point of view from which the complainant seeks, and from which the law provides, legal redress. But these are vastly more difficult tasks in a profoundly heterogenous society or context where such shared understandings often will not exist. Within such heterogenous contexts, the work of judges is especially difficult when complainants draw, more or less explicitly, on particularist and culturally specific self-understandings to ground their claims for legal redress.

While this sort of especially difficult work can arise in any adjudicatory context, it arises perhaps most often and most clearly within the human rights context, where such claims are often adjudicated within both national and international tribunals. There, judges are often called upon to authoritatively settle legal contests where at least one party is drawing on a self-understanding, a culturally and historically determined frame or point of view, that the judge may neither share nor easily understand. For example, British or French judges are not likely to share or easily understand the self-understandings of the African Muslim women who practice female genital cutting. And this constitutes a serious challenge to their abilities to adjudicate, in morally acceptable ways, whether such cuttings or a state's failure to prosecute those who commit them violate human rights. Similarly, American or Australian judges are not likely to share or easily understand the self-understandings of those who regard the primary harm of rape to be constituted by a violation not of the bodily integrity and autonomy of the individual victim but rather of the honor of the community to which she belongs. Again, this constitutes a serious challenge to a judge's ability to adjudicate and, in this case, to identify appropriate punishments. How are such judges to determine whether the practice in some central Asian state of punishing rapists by requiring financial restitution to the family and village of the victim constitutes a prosecution for rape sufficient to secure the right to bodily integrity?

In this chapter, I argue that the adjudication of human rights claims must be understood as involving more than a scientific search for the legal truth performed by judges acting impartially, objectively, and always exclusively from a professional and legal self-understanding. More specifically, I argue that the adjudication of human rights claims requires judges to adhere to an "ethic of listening," within which they are sensitive to and critical of the ways in which their own culturally and historically shaped self-understandings may get in the way of their understanding of the claims they are called upon to adjudicate. Judges, I argue, must practice an open-ended, critically self-aware, and never finally complete sort of empathetic listening, where neither their own self-understandings nor their understandings of others are ever finally fixed or static or beyond amending. At the same time, of course, judges must still resolve the cases before them with finality. And naturally, they must also draw on their best judgment as to the true facts and the true content of the law when so doing. Judging is, then, a double process: one that aims, on the one hand, at a fixed, determinate, and sound authoritative judgment and that temporarily freezes the identities of the parties in the articulation of that judgment but one that, on the other hand, also takes seriously the moral demand to be always critically engaged in the endless mediation between Self and Other through which our always fluid and increasingly complicated and fragmented identities are constructed and reconstructed over time. In other words, the process through which the authoritative legal judgment is reached is itself genuinely dialogic.

A sound theory of adjudication, especially one adequate to human rights conflicts within a rapidly globalizing yet profoundly pluralist world, must acknowledge and respond to the destructive potential that dwells at the very core of rationalist modernity and its legal religion of truth and objectivity. But it must do so without sacrificing the ideal of justice under law. The judicial ethic of listening I argue for here belongs, I think, to such a sound theory of adjudication. My argument proceeds as follows. First, I survey a number of the reasons why in recent years human rights adjudication has grown increasingly complex, making the need for a theory of adjudication adequate to the human rights challenge increasingly evident. Second, using as exemplars the work of Tom Campbell and Ronald Dworkin, I argue that the currently dominant approach to adjudication is incomplete or in any case inadequate to the human rights challenge. Third, I develop and offer my own ethic of listening as a corrective or necessary supplement to the dominant approach to adjudication. Finally, I introduce Judge Athena, perhaps a cousin of Dworkin's Hercules, and sketch how she might approach the adjudication of some especially difficult and novel human rights claims from her bench in San Francisco, Arusha, or The Hague. In conclusion, I briefly note the implications of my view for our understanding of the relationship between law and morality.

THE CHALLENGE OF HUMAN RIGHTS ADJUDICATION

Human rights claims have grown increasingly complex in a variety of ways in recent decades, and this complexity constitutes much of the challenge to be met by any theory of adjudication adequate to the legal discourse and practice of human rights. Here I want to set out a number of the ways in which human rights claims have become ever more complex.

Human rights claims are not simply legal claims under international law. They are also often political and procedural claims. And they are not limited to claims made upon governments. Increasingly they are also made upon nongovernmental organizations (NGOs), as, for example, in the cases brought in the United States against multinational corporations under the Alien Torts Claims Act for alleged human rights violations in other jurisdictions.[1] Nor are they limited to claims made by other governments or by victims of alleged human rights violations. NGOs and various community groups often bring charges before the United Nations Commissioner for Human Rights alleging that nations have failed to implement their international human rights treaty obligations.[2] Indeed, human rights claims now seem capable of arising in virtually any context. They may arise even in everyday domestic criminal or civil cases where a party claims a cultural defense—for example, where a husband claims that his culture commends physical chastisement of his wife. Here the husband claims that a straightforward application of the law of assault would run roughshod over his human right to freedom of cultural expression. Human rights claims are, simply put, proliferating at an exponential rate in many venues, and increasingly, the language of human rights is the international language not just of law but also the language of politics, resistance, and struggle.

Human rights claims have proliferated especially in the area of minority rights. Indeed, within human rights discourse and practice, minority and group rights claims have claimed center stage, with the more familiar claims of universal individual rights rooted in ideals of liberal equality. These newer rights claims not only challenge the racial and ethnic hierarchies of old but also claim a special status for the victims of colonialism and redress for the failures of liberal equality. One aspect of this proliferation of minority and group rights claims is that new claims to unique cultural identity or special group status are made regularly in various legal, political, and civic forums by NGOs, advocacy groups, individuals, and states. Many minority and group rights claims have now become part of the official international human rights agenda through incorporation into international treaties.[3]

This attention to minority and group rights issues has additionally generated another sort of proliferation within human rights discourse and practice. Increasingly, the language of human rights is being appropriated by different groups to give expression to distinctive intellectual, religious, and cultural traditions and paradigms, traditions and paradigms perhaps antithetical to more familiar Western understandings of human rights. For example, the Cairo Declaration of Human Rights in Islam put forward in 1990 by the Organization of the Islamic Conference offers a distinctively Islamic understanding of human rights discourse, an understanding that affirms both a common humanity shared by all peoples as well as the distinctiveness of particular Islamic human communities to which distinctive rights might attach.[4] In another example of multicultural proliferation within human rights discourse and practice, the Bangkok Declaration of 1993 asserts that human rights mean something different in Asian cultures than they do in the individualistic West.[5] "Asian values," it claims, place the group over the individual, harmony and consensus over adversariness and debate, and deference to authority over individual self-expression and freedom. "Asian values" emphasize economic development and political stability (both domestic and regional) at the expense of individual civil and political rights. Human rights as understood and enforced in the West, it argues, run contrary to Asian political and cultural sensibilities and threaten to undermine Asian economic and political ambitions.

The Cairo and Bangkok declarations highlight an important philosophical problem inherent in the very use of liberal human rights discourse itself—namely, that a too ambitious insistence on a certain understanding of human rights, one rooted in ideals of liberal equality among individuals, may eradicate certain cultures by radically transforming certain group-based differences. Of course, it is possible that these declarations may be no more than examples of governments using human rights language cynically and opportunistically to assist their shifting political strategies and goals.[6] Nevertheless, that they exist and enjoy widespread support in many parts of the world demonstrates the extent to which human rights claims are no longer necessarily tethered to the universalist liberal individualism so familiar in the West.

Perhaps paradoxically, along with the growing legal, political, and philosophical recognition of cultural diversity and minority identities within human rights discourse and practice, a certain skepticism about minority and group rights has emerged as a sort of counterforce. And this further complicates many human rights claims. This skepticism would appear to be rooted in recent post–Cold War experiences of genocide and ethnic cleansing, such as what occurred in Rwanda and Bosnia in the 1990s and what sadly continues today in the Sudan.

Until the mid-1990s, there was a confident sense in law, politics, and philosophy that respect for cultural pluralism and minority identities would continue to improve. History seemed to support this confidence. For example, the rights of indigenous and colonized peoples in postcolonial countries had gained recognition through international economic sanctions[7] and international human rights treaties.[8] In the global North and West, civil rights for blacks and women were followed by the children's rights movement. The movements for gay rights and for immigrant and refugee rights were gaining ground. The political tide seemed to favor increasing respect for cultural differences and minority identities.

But then came the genocides in Rwanda and Bosnia. Indeed, these are just two pronounced examples of post–Cold War claims to cultural identity and independence that have involved violent, even genocidal, repression of other cultural groups. Why things have taken this turn is a matter of dispute, though there seems to be a growing sense that cultural and collective identities are under assault, not least from the homogenizing forces of a global economy. These forces may encourage cultural and ethnic conflict. Thus, as one commentator has noted, "India and Turkey, among the earliest and oldest democracies of the Third World, are in the throes of religious struggle and ethnic strife that at times calls into question the very project of a secular representative democracy. [And then there is, of course,] the civil war in the former Yugoslavia and the simmering nationality conflicts in Chechnya, Azerbaijan, Macedonia, and Rwanda."[9]

The veritable tidal wave of human rights claims rooted in cultural difference or minority identity, when taken together with the emergence of new and exceptionally violent ethnic conflicts, has produced in recent years a growing suspicion that the recognition of cultural difference within human rights discourse and practice may produce harmful, perhaps even violent, consequences. Reminiscent almost of colonial times, human rights claims either grounded in particularist cultural differences or otherwise taking the form of group rights are once again seen as being difficult, even dangerous. Naomi Schor writes, in "what may pass for the repetition of Auschwitz, the ongoing ethnic cleansing in Bosnia-Herzegovina, has if not revived universalism, then called into question the celebration of particularisms, at least in their regressive ethnic form."[10]

But, of course, it is too late (and it would be wrongheaded) to turn back the clock completely with respect to human rights claims rooted in cultural difference or minority identity. And this is what renders so many human rights claims increasingly complex. It is simply unclear how to treat cultural difference and minority identity along with other group-based differences within a sound theory and practice of human rights.[11]

This lack of clarity is present not just in the legal and political aspects of human rights discourse and practice but also in its philosophical aspects. Human rights traditionally were justified philosophically by drawing out the political implications of a common human identity or nature. But within philosophical circles, there is a growing sense that the notion of a common human identity or nature is a Western intellectual myth. For many years now the mood in philosophy, as well as political theory and cultural studies, has been to emphasize alternatives to the individualist and universalist account of human identity or human nature central to familiar Western justifications of human rights. Increasingly, philosophers and others have sought to justify rights from within a diverse range of particular local narratives, cultural practices, and traditions rather than within a universalist account of human identity or human nature. As Slavoj Zizek puts it, "For the last two decades, multitude has been in, unity out; contingency in, necessity out; difference in, universality out; antinomy in, noncontradiction out; resistance in, revolution out."[12]

This philosophical complexity within human rights discourse and practice is itself exacerbated by psychoanalytic and linguistic critiques of the individual as the sovereign agent. The psychoanalytic critique proposes that our identity is always the temporary and fluid result of both external contexts and our internal subconscious and that, accordingly, "the sovereignty of the 'I' is never unlimited but always dependent on contexts, conscious and unconscious."[13] The linguistic critique, on the other hand, insists that every speech act not only iterates the old linguistic codes but also revises or alters them so that the limits of human speech, thought, and emotion are never fixed but always being transformed by the very activity of human speech, thought, and feeling.[14] The upshot here is that various postmodern critiques have cast doubt over conceptions of the individual subject being the essentially stable, unified, rational agent presupposed by traditional philosophical justifications and theories of human rights.[15]

New pressures at the international level have only served to reinforce these contradictory pulls in the law, politics, and philosophy of human rights. A new global civilization is spreading at breakneck speed via increasingly sophisticated technologies. Regional identities continue to cement with the expansion of the European Union, the consolidation of the Inter-American and African systems, and through trading pacts like the North American Free Trade Agreement (NAFTA) and the Association of South East Asian Nations (ASEAN). Human rights claims to a distinctive history and a unique culture are erupting at precisely the moment when economic and technological forces appear to be creating a "world" culture. The court of world opinion, and not just arcane religious and legal scholars, now debates the right of Muslim states to amputate the hands of convicted thieves. The international media routinely debates the right of mothers of eight-year-old girls to subject their daughters to procedures of genital cutting. There is a growing worldwide public political discourse, and human rights issues are among its core concerns.

The increased stakes in many state-to-state relations, including securing the goods associated with membership in regional federations and in various alliances, have also rendered human rights issues more complex. It is commonplace for member states in various federations and alliances to make compliance with human rights norms a condition of membership. The European Union requires nondiscriminatory religious practice and good human rights performance. The United States continues to debate the extent to which the human rights performance of a country ought to affect trade relations between it and the United States. And, of course, in all these contexts, NGOs and other interested and vocal parties engage in aggressive surveillance and reporting with respect to human rights issues. The result is that the line between respect for human rights, including the human right to be culturally different and to belong to a cultural minority on the one hand, and xenophobia and isolationism, on the other, seems more difficult to dance than ever.

For all the foregoing reasons, human rights claims are today more complex than ever. The question is, how ought those adjudicating human rights claims approach and understand their task? Consider an international criminal tribunal adjudicating a case involving rape. How should the court understand the wrongness or harm of an act of rape? From the point of view of the dominant individualistic Western jurisprudence, the wrongness of rape lies in the violation of or harm to the individual victim's agency or autonomy. Courts are to punish perpetrators accordingly. But some non-Western jurists argue that the wrongness or harm of a rape should be understood in terms of a violation of or damage to the honor of a community rather than to the individual victim. And this view suggests very different sorts of punishment, such as economic restitution from the offender's family directed to an entire village. Which approach should be adopted in an emerging international criminal jurisprudence, within which at least some rapes in some contexts may be prosecuted as war crimes or international crimes violating basic human rights?

Or consider a judge in California or Wisconsin faced with a Muslim mother from Africa charged under a U.S. state law with the crime of causing her daughter to have a procedure of female genital modification.[16] One view might be that a suspended sentence is appropriate where, for instance, a seventeen-year-old daughter has requested the procedure so that she might enter adulthood within her community's norms. Does it then follow that a term of imprisonment is more appropriate in a case of a daughter who seems more socialized as an American teenager and who seems less involved in her minority culture's norms? Should the mothers of these young women be able to assert a cultural defense in such circumstances, and how ought the moral valence of a minority cultural identity affect the ethics of legal adjudication? And flowing from this, how should a judge navigate her own identity and her own responses to the facts adduced in her court when she is confronted with radically different forms of human existence that proceed from starkly different paradigms of human values to her own?

One approach to these issues might be to assert even more strongly the universalism of Western individualism and identity. In some ways, it seems the least complicated way out of the legal, political, and philosophical quagmire, at least, when one is comfortably speaking from the West. But the trouble is that the old twentieth-century assumptions of universal identity are simply now passé. It seems clear that claims to culturally differentiated identities are likely to increase and find philosophical and political support and that no amount of cautious warnings about the new possibilities of isolationism and aggression raised by such claims will prove sufficient to subordinate them fully to a universalist individualist liberal conception of the human subject. The complex contemporary forces present in the adjudication of human rights claims where there are radically different cultural identities in play means that judges confronted by such claims must adjudicate across radically different self-understandings and worldviews. The complexity of human rights adjudication requires a self-conscious reexamination of judicial ethics—one that looks again at the issue of objectivity.

THE DOMINANT ADJUDICATION STORY

The dominant view of adjudication is one that emphasizes the objectivity, or the aspiration to objectivity, of legal judgment. Here I take the recent work of Tom Campbell and Ronald Dworkin as, notwithstanding their differences, being illustrative of this dominant view. What I want to suggest in rough outline is that what is missing from this dominant view, if it is to prove adequate to the demands of adjudicating human rights claims, is an ethic of listening.

In *The Legal Theory of Ethical Positivism*, Tom Campbell emphasizes the ethical prerequisites that make the separation between law and morality feasible and that make such a separation in itself an ethical undertaking.[17] Campbell argues that the role of judges is to act impartially by setting aside their own moral beliefs and applying the will of the people as articulated through legislative enactments. Adamant that judges must not be influenced by their own subjective values, Campbell urges judges to read statutes "in terms of their literal or evident meanings, as understood by participants in the relevant social situations."[18] These meanings "rely upon intersubjective agreement sustained by shared cultural understandings."[19] For Campbell, judges ought to "read . . . the [legislative] rules in some appropriate register of the ordinary natural language of the society in which they . . . apply."[20] For Campbell, it is only by judges' so doing that the law can have an objective existence apart from morality and allow citizens to subordinate the law to their collective will.

Ronald Dworkin takes in his writings a slightly different approach but one that still emphasizes the importance of objective legal judgment. Dworkin argues that moral philosophy is an integral part of legal judgment. Whenever a judge makes a legal judgment, she gives an interpretation of the law. Her interpretive judgment will inevitably and properly reflect her own convictions as to the political and moral theory in terms of which the legal system is best understood. It does not follow that her judgment is a mere, though perhaps camouflaged, statement of what might be called *subjective* or *personal* morality. While her judgment is always her judgment, it is also always, if properly judicial, a judgment made in light of the political and moral theory in terms of which the legal system, objectively speaking, is understood best or seen in its best light. When faced with conflicting claims, the judge seeks resolution by appealing to the right or correct political and moral narrative about the community within which the conflicting claims arise. In this sense, the judge seeks to objectively identify the law and its demands for the case at hand. Dworkin's aim here is to square the rule of law and legal determinacy with the reality of hard cases and reasonable judicial disagreement in any mature legal system.

Neither Campbell nor Dworkin deal adequately with cultural differences as they affect legal conflicts. Both require judges to identify the law through which any legal conflict is to be resolved by appealing to some broad objective consensus underlying the legal system. For Campbell, this consensus exists as a matter of descriptive fact, to be discerned through the shared cultural and linguistic understandings against and through which the law is made. For Dworkin it exists as a matter of interpretive judgment, to be discerned through the political and moral theory in light of which a shared legal practice is revealed as the best it can be. The trouble with both of these approaches is that at the concrete level of daily life, where so much adjudication must take place, it is virtually impossible to identify, whether through description or interpretation, the relevant sort of consensus. Both domestic societies and the international society as a whole are divided along so many axes of race, gender, class, and culture that the very idea of a broad consensus underlying the legal system seems increasingly implausible.

Both Campbell and Dworkin fail to take seriously cultural difference and minority identity in their theories of adjudication. Both aim to ground adjudication in an objective and autonomous normative discourse called law. But both underestimate the extent to which the deep and radical group-based divisions characteristic of any pluralist domestic order render the aspiration to such an understanding of law problematic. What both theories need is a supplement sufficient to take account of cultural difference and minority identity but without totally throwing overboard the aspiration to objectivity in legal judgment.

There are two accounts of truth that circulate in post-Kantian philosophy that may provide the resources of such a supplement. The first of these accounts is the transcendental-hermeneutic notion of truth associated with the work of Gadamer. The second is the self-reflexive conception of truth associated with Hegel.[21] Both draw on the relationship between truth and identity formation; together they provide the philosophical resources from which a much-needed supplement to contemporary adjudication theory may be developed. Among contemporary thinkers, Charles Taylor and Seyla Benhabib have both drawn on these approaches to truth in their own meditations on identity formation.

In *Truth and Method*, Gadamer redefines the philosophical enterprise. Philosophy is not about gradually approaching the truth of life but rather about formulating the preunderstanding that already and always guides us. He wants each of us to appreciate our own particular horizon of understanding. For Gadamer, truth is best understood not as a scientific notion or as a representation of an objective mind and independent reality but rather as an articulation of our preunderstanding of life and reality implicit in our dealings with other people and the world. Charles Taylor characterizes Gadamer's notion like this: "A horizon provides the frame . . . within which I can try to determine from case to case what is good, or valuable, or what ought to be done, or what I endorse or oppose."[22] This horizon defines or constitutes our identity because it gives us the vantage point from which we can identify our commitments and values.[23]

The Hegelian notion of truth as self-reflexivity suggests, however, that this identity is never stable, complete, or self-sufficient unto itself. In Hegel's conception of truth, he couples our abstract notion of phenomena with our actual practices of dealing with them. He does not have in mind phenomena as they "really are," being somehow independent of our partial opinions and surmises, but instead he sees the phenomena and our practices of dealing with them as those dialectically informing each other.[24] Taylor describes this Hegelian dialectic as that involving "webs of interlocution" such that "one cannot be a self on one's own . . . [but] only in relation to certain interlocutors."[25] Thus, on this view, there is no stable or complete self or identity until we make a decision or form a view, always in relation to other interlocutors, in response to a particular phenomenon.

Seyla Benhabib seizes on this conception of the self, arguing that to be, and to become, a self is to insert oneself into webs of interlocution. It is to know how to answer competently when one is addressed and, in turn, how to address others competently. Benhabib's point in that, as interlocutors we are each born into many narrative webs, such as narratives of family, gender, class, linguistic narratives, and macronarratives of collective identity. We achieve our identities by learning to be competent conversation partners within each of these narratives.

What I want to suggest here is that Taylor and Benhabib point us toward the supplement needed for a theory of adjudication fully adequate to human rights law within a culturally pluralist context and in the face of diverse and minority identity claims. This supplement is a conception of judicial identity constituted and reconstituted through an ongoing process of interlocution with various and sometimes conflicting narratives, coupled with what I shall call an *ethic of listening*.

AN ETHIC OF LISTENING: SUPPLEMENTING THE STORY

To be a judge is to inhabit a distinctive identity that differs from individual identity. As an officer of the court, a judge acts on behalf of the judicial arm of government, independent from both the executive and legislature on the one hand and the citizenry on the other. When negotiating the cross-currents of communication in the courtroom, a judge assumes a professional identity more tightly scripted than that available to her as a citizen outside the courtroom. She is supposed to put aside her sentiments as a citizen and approach the matters before her by drawing only on her legal training. She relies on rules of evidence and procedure and on norms of legal reasoning, all of which she assumes as being essential to arriving at a sound, objective legal judgment. But regarding her narrowly particularized identity as a judge, it will prove most difficult to see and hear all of the intersubjective rationalities circulating between the parties to the dispute or to engage fully the conflicting narratives offered by them. If she neither tries to nor is able to place herself in conversation with these narratives, if she takes her own professional self-understanding as given, fixed, and always already objective prior to engaging others, her professional judgment will, like the adjudicative theories of Campbell and Dworkin, inevitably fail to take seriously cultural differences and minority identities. Her adjudication will thereby constitute something less than amorally defensible legal judgment as to the merits of the cultural claims before her.

The challenge judges face when hearing and adjudicating issues involving radical cultural difference and minority identity is to understand how in the process of judgment they create categories and make sense of difference. Judges must try to make sense of the stories told to them by the parties to any conflict before them. And they must try to do so from a legal point of view, from the point of view of their legal rationality. But that point of view, that of their own legal and professional identity, exists alongside, within, and around their point of view as citizens and persons, as well as the points of view of the parties to the conflict before them. A sound legal judgment from a judicial point of view must engage, in a self-conscious and self-reflective way, these other points of view and the narratives associated with them. Judges must bring to the surface as they adjudicate the cases before them the intersubjective processes through which their own judicial identity is constituted and reconstituted.

To do so, judges must self-consciously listen to the intersubjective rationalities circulating between the parties and within themselves. And they must listen in a way that draws on the full range of their affective, empathic sensibilities and capacities. Only by so listening can they put their own professional identity into dialogue with that of the parties to the dispute before them and with their own nonprofessional identities and thereby render a professional judgment from a point of view both objective and dialogic, a point of view located in the interplay between Self and Other. Judging, then, requires a very demanding sort of listening.

From within a judicial ethic of listening, a judge properly attaches weight to her own subjective experience; her personal experience is relevant to her assessment of any claim that human rights have been violated. Her own understanding of her personal experience will inevitably and properly draw on the emotive and affective aspects of her identity. These aspects of her identity, whether as citizen or judge, may properly be put in play as she seeks to listen to the human rights claims before her. In the end, her professional identity will be constituted through a complex process within which legal findings and pronouncements, as to both the content of the law and the moral force of claims grounded in cultural difference and minority identity, are arrived at through a genuine dialogue between various points of view, within herself and between herself and others, empathetically engaged with one another.

Of course, judges must not forsake their traditional professional duties to the demands of this struggle. They must still undertake to identify and enforce the communal will, the law, as expressed in legislation, case law, and elsewhere. Ultimately, they must judge and must do so as judges, as authoritative voices for the body politic capable of resolving disputes with finality. It is, however, precisely the great weight of this responsibility—and the inevitability of freezing in the moment of judgment the identities of all the parties, including their own—that demands the struggle for a judgment predicated on genuine listening.

One objection to this ethic of listening as a corrective supplement to more familiar theories of adjudication is that it appears to permit discriminatory predispositions or stereotypes to influence legal judgment.[26] This objection might be met, however, by developing the ethic of listening in two different ways. The first is to incorporate into it an account of the serious and complex difficulties involved in genuinely hearing an Other speak. A wide range of cognitive biases may inhibit listening, and they must be identified and overcome. The second is to develop more fully what is involved in empathetic listening. Empathy may be said to come in two distinct forms. First, a person displays *incident-specific empathy* when she is able to relate to another because of familiarity with a specific shared predicament or circumstance. Second, a person displays *broad empathy* when she is able to relate to another because of a holistic appreciation of the other person's life, history, and worldview rather than any particular shared predicament or circumstance. Both sorts of empathy are necessary to a proper ethic of listening. Incident-specific empathy often enables a judge to overcome one or another bias or stereotype and engage the narrative of a claimant. But broad empathy is what is needed to call such biases and stereotypes into question in a more general way.

The need for and value of broad empathy can be seen in the work of feminists engaged in challenging female genital modification (FGM) in Islamic states. These women activists employ broad empathy with the aim of making a respectful intervention. Rather than suppose that those who have experienced FGM share the activists' Western conception of subjectivity and their sense of the harms involved in FGM, the activists instead patiently try to take stock of the lived experience of these individuals, engaging them in dialogue and empowering them to arrive at and articulate their own understanding of FGM. This approach has been very successful in advancing human rights concerns, all with a proper reverence for cultural difference.

But how can this approach be integrated into the deliberations of judges without putting at risk the objectivity, validity, and authority of the law as its own normative discourse? Here, legal proceduralism provides an important resource. A great deal of recent scholarship has emphasized the importance of proceduralism in a range of legal and political contexts. The idea is that the legitimacy or validity of a legal or political judgment depends crucially on the moral quality of the deliberations from which it proceeds. Jürgen Habermas relies on an ideal of legal proceduralism to preserve the relative autonomy of law, maintaining that legal validity is not a function of the certainty of the outcome in a legal conflict but rather of the moral quality of the distinctive legal procedures followed, procedures designed to ensure that judicial judgments will turn only on relevant reasons.[27] Fidelity to an ethic of listening that is framed by or located within a distinctive and determinate set of legal procedures need not compromise the objectivity, validity, or authority of legal judgments.

Of course, the demands of the courtroom will remain. Even judges faithful to a revised judicial ethics and constrained by a morally informed legal proceduralism have to render a judgment that effectively vindicates one party's story at the expense of the other's. The ethical supplement to adjudication I am offering here cannot remove, and is not intended to remove, the Kantian and Weberian overtones of adjudication entirely. The moment of legal judgment remains, and every legal judgment still carries with it the authority of the state to hear, to judge, and to construct or identify out of the competing narratives an official narrative, an official truth. It follows that legal contests over human rights will, indeed ought, to have a different texture to them than political contests over human rights. Political contests are often ongoing and, even when conducted within morally sound deliberative procedures, are typically less structured than legal contests. Participants in political contests over human rights can keep various claims of cultural difference and minority identity in play. But not so with participants in legal contests over human rights. Judges, at least, must issue a final authoritative judgment, and that judgment will temporarily freeze a particular pattern of difference and identity as definitive.

An ethic of listening places, then, two basic requirements on judges: Judges must listen to all parties before them empathetically; they must be willing to put their own professional identity into self-reflective dialogue with the identities of the parties and with their own identity as citizen and person. With respect to human rights claims based on cultural difference or minority identity, it would seem to follow that judges must at the least engage such claims and resist the temptation to negate them prior to engaging in any genuine dialogue. Not all human rights claims based on cultural difference or minority identity will or should gain legal recognition. But all or nearly all should be heard.

JUDGE ATHENA

What consequences might an ethic of listening have for Judge Athena? Judge Athena might be hearing a charge against a Muslim American mother charged in a U.S. court with aiding genital surgery on her marriage-age daughter. Or she could be a judge sitting on the International Criminal Tribunal for Rwanda in Arusha, Africa, hearing a charge of rape as genocide. Or she could be sitting on the many internationalized courts—East Timor, Cambodia, or Sierra Leone—where the question may be whether a particular type of warfare is "traditional" may affect a sentencing outcome. Or Judge Athena may be called upon to evaluate a claim to the human right to carry out a particular cultural practice that has no analogue in standard Western practices. In any of these cases, she may be called upon to award a remedy to a human rights transgression that lies outside the armory of Anglo-American jurisprudence. Each situation calls upon the judge to listen empathetically, not just as a judge, but as a citizen and person, to the claimant's evidence and arguments. To rigidly maintain judicial objectivity and detachment in such circumstances would amount to negating completely the identity of the claimant before the court. But after listening in this way, the judge must judge, arriving at a determinate and definitive legal decision. In doing so, though, she must carry forward her own subjective reception of the claimant's allegations and arguments into the realm of the public sphere, within which she judges in her professional identity. The more radical the identity claim before the court, the more unknown the cultural practice or the harm alleged, the greater the extent to which judges must draw on both their subjective reactions as citizens or persons and their objective evaluations within the relevant legal procedures to arrive at a sound legal judgment.

While this ethic of listening moderates or tempers judicial objectivity, it also validates the authority and reinforces the moment of legal judgment. Cultural differences and minority identities call for greater creativity and imagination from courts, but the adjudication of claims rooted in cultural differences and minority identities also emphasizes the authority and autonomy of the law and of judicial power specifically. In some cases, it is impossible to avoid directly engaging conflicting moral schemas or cultural systems. Some cultural groups may have a value or practice that is irreducible, that has its own distinctive ethical valence, and that conflicts fundamentally with important commitments of another cultural group. For example, the different emphasis upon bodily integrity and the capacity of individuals to exit their cultural group makes it unlikely that the practice of female genital modification will be legally accepted in the United States or Europe. In this case, it may be that judges can do no better than to recognize the minority identity claims of orthodox Muslims while holding that female genital modification is legally impermissible. Even here, though, it is important to highlight the moral gains an ethic of listening brings. The agency of Muslim women and the social and political conditions essential to civility and nonviolence in political struggle are both strengthened when courts and judges genuinely listen to and hear the claims of Muslims regarding their own self-understandings and the values and practices central to their cultural identity, even if fidelity to legal procedures requires that they do not rule in favor of those claims.

It is important, then, that struggles and disputations over the content of human rights outside the sphere of law, in political fora and civic associations of various sorts, continue. For a number of reasons, only a tiny percentage of human rights conflicts go before courts. And the law is not necessarily best equipped to resolve adequately all conflicts that do reach the courts, even when judges practice an ethic of listening. Thus, it is crucial that the politics of human rights continue to play out center stage within the political and cultural sphere—in the media, in the workplace and shopping center, and before the U.S. Congress. Lawyers tend to have an unrealistic view of the centrality of adjudication to the resolution of conflict and tension. Adjudication, and the law more generally, play a part. But it is only a part of a far broader repertoire of other means, formal and informal, through which social conflicts are resolved. Nothing in my argument for including an ethic of listening in a theory of adjudication adequate to human rights conflicts replaces the urgent need to continue to engage one another over human rights claims in a wide range of settings. Judge Athena need not regard herself and her court as the only venue within which claimants may profitably advance their human rights claims.

CONCLUSION

Contested human rights claims call for new forms of judicial listening, especially under conditions of globalization. To fully hear human rights claims, especially when they are rooted in claims of cultural difference or minority identity, judges must approach adjudication as a double process. In their professional role, judges must reach definitive judgments in the cases before them by enforcing the community's values and beliefs within the constraints of settled legal procedures. But in so doing, judges must also enter into a critical and self-reflective dialogue with their professional selves, a dialogue within which the other participants are the judge's core self as citizen and person and the selves of the parties to the dispute before the court. Within this dialogue, judges must listen empathetically, in both their professional and personal capacities, to what the other parties are saying.

The judicial ethic of listening argued for here occupies a middle ground between, on the one hand, cynicism about the capacity of law and legal institutions to mediate conflicts across seemingly antithetical intellectual and cultural lines and, on the other, naive optimism about the intrinsic superiority of any one position in all legal conflicts and the infallibility of law and legal institutions to negotiate disagreements about it. In an era of globalization, when our awareness of cultural variety and diverse identities is growing rapidly, we need an approach to adjudication that is able to steer us between these two unattractive alternatives. I have argued that a judicial ethic of listening must figure in any such approach.

From the point of view of the theory of adjudication sketched here, human rights inhabit the space between contingency and certainty. Contingency—in any event, part of life—is formalized as the recognition of cultural difference and minority identity and of the demand to listen in a way that calls one's self, one's own identity, into question. Certainty—at least enough for peaceable living in a culturally diverse world—arises out of the legal procedural framework within which cultural differences, minority identities, and human rights claims are articulated, heard, and judged.

NOTES

1. *Doe v. UNOCAL Corp.*, 248 F.3d 915 (9th Cir. 2001)(en banc); *Bigio v. Coca-Cola Co.*, 239 F.3d 440 (2d Cir. 2000); *Presbyterian Church of Sudan v. Talisman Energy, Inc.*, 244 F.Supp.2d 289 (S.D.N.Y. 2003).

2. www.unhchr.ch.

3. For example, UN General Assembly, *Declaration on the Rights of Persons Belonging to National or Ethnic, Religious, and Linguistic Minorities*, New York, Dec. 18, 1992; Committee of Ministers, *European Charter for Regional or Minority Languages*, June 22, 1992; [European] *Framework Convention for the Protection of National Minorities*, Strasbourg, Feb. 1, 1995.

4. www1.umn.edu/humanrts/instree/cairodeclaration.html.

5. See ministers and representatives of Asian states, *Bangkok NGO Declaration on Human Rights*, 2 April 1993.

6. See Ann E. Mayer, *Islam and Human Rights*, Westview Press, 1998.

7. Amid international pressures including the exclusion of the South African seat from the United Nations, West Germany limited export guarantees for South Africa in 1977. See Kenneth Grundy, *South Africa: Domestic Crisis and Global Challenge*, Westview Press, 1991, pg. 78. Other nations, including the United States and the European community, eventually followed suit with the passage of the *Anti-apartheid Act of 1986* and the Commonwealth and European Community actions of 1986–1987. See *Effective Sanctions on South Africa: The Cutting Edge of Economic Intervention*, George W. Shepherd Jr., ed., Praeger Publishing, 1991, pg. iii.

8. See UN General Assembly, *Declaration on the Granting of Independence to Colonial Countries and Peoples*, New York, Dec. 14, 1960; *Draft Declaration on the Rights of Indigenous Peoples*, 1994.

9. This struggle has become further complicated since the 11 September 2001 attacks on the World Trade Center towers in New York and on Washington, D.C. See www.saag.org/papers9/paper902.html.

10. See Naomi Schor, "French Feminism Is a Universalism," *Differences* 7, no. 1, (1995): 15.

11. To be sure, various theorists have struggled to reconcile these tensions. Will Kymlicka is but one such theorist. The point here is that no proposed reconciliation has gained the support of anything like a general consensus.

12. Slavoj Zizek, "Critical Responses: A Symptom—of What?" *Critical Inquiry* 29, no. 3 (2003): 499.

13. See Seyla Benhabib, "Sexual Difference and Collective Identities: The New Global Constellation," *Signs* 24, no. 2 (1999): 335.

14. Stacy, *supra*.

15. See Helen Stacy, *Postmodernism and Law: Jurisprudence in a Fragmenting World*, Ashgate Publishing, 2001, pgs. 1–19.

16. California State Prohibition of Female Genital Mutilation Act (CA) AB 2125, 1995; *State of Michigan HB 6095*; Federal Prohibition of Female Genital Mutilation Act of 1995, U.S. Senate, S. 1030, 1995; UN Beijing Declaration and Platform for Action of 1995.

17. Tom Campbell, *The Legal Theory of Ethical Positivism*, Dartmouth Publishing, 1996.

18. *Ibid.*, 129.

19. *Id*, 126.

20. *Id*, 10.

21. See Hans Georg Gadamer, *Truth and Method*, Crossroad Publishing, 1989; and G. W. F. Hegel, *Phenomenology of Spirit*, trans. by A. V. Miller, Clarendon Press, 1977.

22. See Charles Taylor, *Sources of the Self*, Harvard University Press, 1989, pg. 36.

23. Taylor, *ibid.*, pg. 27.

24. See Slavoj Zizek, "Critical Responses: A Symptom—of What?" *Critical Inquiry* 29, no. 3, 2003, pg. 486.

25. Taylor, *supra*, pg. 36.

26. I am indebted to the comments of Diana Tietjens Meyers for pointing this out and suggesting to me the thoughts in the remainder of this paragraph and in the next.

27. Jurgen Habermas, *Between Facts and Norms: Toward a Discourse Theory of Law and Democracy*, MIT Press, 1996, pg. 460.

7

Rights against Institutions: What Governments Should and Can Do

William Nelson

Human rights surely include specific rights, such as rights against force and violence, that hold as much against individuals as against institutions or governments. My focus here, however, is on the more general and vague rights to democratic government and to (some level of) economic and material well-being. And my question concerns what such rights might require governments and other institutions to do. This is a broad question, so I can develop only partial answers here. I argue, first, that obligations to promote democracy are somewhat limited, at least in the short run, partly by the difficulty of devising effective strategies but also because there is no unconditional right to democratic institutions. I argue, second, that even if everyone has a right to some level of material well-being (a claim I do not question), specifying a fair and effective assignment of the obligations corresponding to this right is no mean feat. Relying on some recent books on international trade and financial institutions, I undertake to begin this task by outlining what seem to me to be fair and reasonable (if minimal) requirements to which governments can be held in virtue of these rights.

I devote the second section to some general remarks about rights and their justification. In the third section, I address democratic rights, and in the fourth section, I address economic and material rights.

RIGHTS AND THEIR JUSTIFICATION

The rights on which I focus are human rights, and so are held, at least conditionally, by all humans. In this chapter, I focus on those human rights held against governments or other institutions. Such rights play a role in the assessment of governmental and nongovernmental institutions and in the assessment of institutional officials. How large a role they play, relative to other considerations, I am unable to say.[1] Nevertheless, it seems safe to say that we would not consider a government fully legitimate if it violated the human rights of its subjects and that we would also think it defective if it violated the human rights of others. Hence, the question of what human rights require of governments and other institutions and how they might meet their obligations is an important one.

In focusing on rights held against governments or institutions, I do not mean to restrict my discussion only to rights held by subjects against their own governments. There are often good reasons to hold that governments have the primary responsibility for the rights of their own subjects, but there are certainly exceptions to this generalization. Indeed, the economic rights I discuss toward the end of this chapter are clearly held both against other governments and against various international institutions. When we talk of such rights and their corresponding obligations, it is important that we be prepared to say something about how, in practice, such obligations might be discharged by the various institutional bodies subject to them.

Since rights impose requirements on others, and thus limit their freedom, rights require justification. The justification of any right must take into consideration the restrictions it imposes on others, since it is these restrictions that underwrite the need to justify rights. (It would be a mistake to convince ourselves that there is a certain right and only then to look at what it might require.) Rights are justified only if the obligations they imply are fair and reasonable.[2] Of course, whether the obligations imposed by a right are fair and reasonable will itself depend in part on other aspects of the justification of the right in question. Rights justified as being necessary and sufficient to secure the most fundamental of human interests might fairly and reasonably demand quite a lot of others.[3]

Some human rights—and especially those I focus on here, such as democratic rights and rights to a certain level of economic and material well-being—seem to present at this point two significant problems. First, notwithstanding their appeal, they may on reflection come to seem little more than vague aspirations—what Joel Feinberg once called rights in a "manifesto sense."[4] They sound good, but when we think of what they might really require, their requirements seem so demanding or open-ended as to be unreasonable. Second, differences from one country to another in culture and in political and social institutions are bound to affect what it would be reasonable to require of other governments. At the extreme, local cultural patterns or institutional arrangements may leave other governments with no effective way to discharge any putative obligation to persons in that society, in which case the obligations would represent an unreasonable demand.

Now, someone might conclude that to the extent that these problems arise for the human rights under discussion here—democratic rights and rights to a certain level of economic or material well-being—these rights are never genuine human rights, since the obligations they impose on others are sometimes unreasonable and thus not genuine obligations. But we need not draw this conclusion. On any plausible moral view, specific moral requirements will depend on circumstances. We can continue to say that there are universal human rights but still insist that we have to look at both the arguments in support of any given right and the specific circumstances of different countries before we can draw any conclusions about what those rights require of any particular institutional agent. In some cases, it may be best to think of rights as being universal but only conditional. Indeed, that is what I suggest later regarding democratic rights.

It is sometimes said that not only must the obligations implied by rights be reasonable and fairly distributed but also that rights must always serve the interests of right holders.[5] Of this I am not convinced, though I do not offer here a general account of rights.[6] I do want to insist, though, that rights can perform various functions. One is to secure goods or benefits to right holders, and rights performing this function are also most likely justified by only the interests persons have in these goods. But another function is to secure to a certain person some degree of control over various decisions. There may be many reasons for using rights to secure such control. We might grant a person a right of this type, for example, because her having it is in the interest of a third party.[7] Or we might do so because we endorse various indirect consequentialist arguments for distributing control over certain decisions in some particular way. In any case, whether a person has a right of this sort will turn not on any direct benefit to the right holder but rather on how that person can be expected to exercise the right if it is granted and on a comparative judgment as to how others might exercise it were it granted to them instead.

Recognizing that different rights may call for different patterns of justification is crucial if we are to carry out a fully adequate analysis of any particular right. Consider, for example, the human right to democratic institutions. This is essentially a right to play some role in deciding questions of law and policy within the body politic to which one belongs; it is a right conferring some measure of control over decisions of a certain sort. And, as such, it may be justified, indeed may best be justified, not by any benefit to the rightholder but rather by the more indirect sorts of considerations just described. But the force of these considerations will depend on circumstances, including especially cultural circumstances, that vary among countries. Thus, the strength of the justification for democratic rights may vary with the cultural context within which the right is asserted or claimed and, thus, may vary our sense of whether any particular obligation or distribution of obligations in light of such rights is fair or reasonable.

DEMOCRATIC RIGHTS AS HUMAN RIGHTS

The rights I discuss can be somewhat arbitrarily, but not unconventionally, divided into two groups: civil or political rights and economic or social rights. (I say "somewhat arbitrarily" because there are arguments that "civil or political" rights of free expression and democratic control may also be among the more effective protections of economic security and well-being.)[8] I start with civil or political rights and, in particular, with the right or rights to a democratic form of government (along with associated rights of free expression and association).

Some form of a right to democracy is among the most commonly mentioned human rights, and it is quite clearly a right against institutions. To be sure, the Universal Declaration of Human Rights of 1948 does not speak of democracy per se. It speaks, instead, of a right "to take part in the government of [one's] country"; it also says that "the will of the people shall be the basis of the authority of government" and that "this will shall be expressed in periodic and genuine elections" with "universal suffrage" (art. 21).[9]

Let us assume that there is a human right to democracy. If subjects have such a right, then this right would seem to impose obligations not only on their own government but also on the governments of other countries and on various international institutions, at least to the extent that the behaviors and attitudes of either may facilitate or frustrate subjects in their enjoyment of this right. If there is a human right to democracy, many countries may have to reconsider how they deal with undemocratic regimes. And international financial institutions may be duty bound to create incentives for democratic reform and disincentives for those wanting to overthrow democratic governments.[10]

However, the question on which I focus here is, what is the best justification for accepting these rights as human rights? There are many arguments for democratic government. The universal declaration suggests an argument when—echoing literature from the founding era of the United States—it speaks of the "will of the people" as the basis of governmental authority. The suggested argument is that we ought to have democratic government on the ground that only then is the government's authority based on the will of the people. The trouble with this argument is that we must either simply identify the will of the people with the outcome of free elections, in which case the argument gives no independent support for such elections, or offer an independent and morally relevant definition of "the will of the people," an undertaking with which philosophers and political theorists continue to wrestle. Further, there is, I think, some danger in talk of the will of the people in this context. If we insist that there is such a thing, independent of an electoral process, then we risk affirming a key claim typically invoked by undemocratic rulers or groups who claim to represent the will of the people and to possess legitimate political authority on this basis.

Another argument for a right to democratic government appeals to the moral proposition that individuals ought to govern themselves or be governed only by persons and laws to which they consent. Again, claims of this sort are not uncommon within the political literature of the founding period in the United States. However, the idea that a person becomes genuinely self-governing or genuinely consents to his or her rulers or laws by virtue of having and casting one vote out of millions seems extravagant.

There are, of course, more sophisticated arguments for democracy. There are, for example, various arguments connecting democracy with various values or virtues closely associated with public deliberation. But these are arguments, not so much for institutions such as elections, but for certain attitudes toward political argument and certain ways of carrying it out. Typically, these arguments begin with an ideal of substantively desirable legislation defined as that which results from a kind of ideal deliberative process. They then endorse democratic procedures, if carried out in appropriate ways, on the grounds that they best enable us to approach the relevant ideal of substantively desirable legislation. This is an argument for a democratic system, provided we have reason to expect that politics will be carried out in the appropriate way. But the argument is pretty weak if it is meant to establish that every society ought to be run democratically, for surely there is no reason to think democratic procedures likely to yield laws approaching the ideal of substantively desirable legislation unless we have reason to believe that all the essential elements of a democratic culture are present.[11]

A stronger argument for a human right to democracy affirms it as being a necessary institutional protection against abuses of autocratic power. According to this argument, it is simply less dangerous to put power in the hands of voters than to put it in the hands of, say, hereditary elites, revolutionary vanguards, or self-selecting religious clerics. Indeed, one could even argue that democratic government benefits the citizens of other countries if it reduces the kind of political volatility that can spill over borders. These arguments, of course, defend democracy as a means to an end, not as something intrinsically valuable, and they rest essentially on comparative judgments. Is it really true that democracy better protects citizens against abuse than all competing forms of government? Are democratic governments really less volatile and less likely to cause problems for other states than are nondemocratic governments? These are difficult questions to which there are no easy or obvious answers.

Yet another argument for a human right to democratic government appeals to political legitimacy. Here the idea is that, where citizens disagree over substantive values and ideals and thus public policies, they must each and all enjoy at least a fair chance to have their convictions reflected in law and policy. This argument is consistent with the argument for democracy from the value of self-government, but it is distinct insofar as political legitimacy or the legitimacy of coercive political authority is the grounding value. It is also consistent with, but distinct from, the arguments in favor of deliberative democracy, distinct in that it is a commitment to legitimacy in the face of disagreement, not a substantive ideal of just legislation, that underwrites the demand for democratic institutions.

Both this (argument from legitimacy) and the argument for democracy as a bulwark against abuses of power respond to the general question of who should control what decisions. Democracy requires undemocratic rulers and ruling parties to give up exclusive control over a certain range of political decisions. Of course, whether for good reasons or bad, rulers rarely look forward to giving up power. This is understandable. We should be surprised neither by the difficulty with which many European Union states have given up areas of sovereign control for the sake of European integration nor by the current U.S. administration's repeated refusal to sign on to international accords that involve ceding political control in one or another area to other bodies. It is risky to put decision-making authority in the hands of someone else. Of course, that is just what rights often require of us. And thus refusing to give up decision-making authority can sometimes be both understandable and morally deplorable.

In the end, whether there is a human right to democratic institutions or, better, whether that right is being violated in any particular case depends on a comparative assessment of the available alternatives paying close attention to the good of both those citizens for whom the right to democracy is being asserted as well as others outside the relevant state or states. There is, I think, nothing anomalous about this result. There are many considerations relevant to the distribution in any body politic of decision-making authority over matters of public or common interest. It is not irrelevant that voters often do not make good decisions, nor is it irrelevant when there are in a country many and serious potential demagogues ready to exploit democracy for their own ends. Even the best arguments for democratic rights end up being probabilistic in character. Of course, they might still be, in the end, sufficient. Indeed, I think they often are.

Still, any human right to democratic self-government is going to be conditional on several things, including the existence of, or potential for, the development of a democratic culture. What might be required of others, then, by the right to democratic government may be limited in various ways and will certainly vary with the circumstances.

ECONOMIC RIGHTS AS HUMAN RIGHTS

I now turn to economic rights, rights to at least a minimum level of economic opportunity and well-being. These are widely regarded as being more controversial than political rights and liberties. One reason is that they appear to impose "positive" rather than merely "negative" duties. I will not, however, dwell on this issue (though I do argue that one requirement of economic rights is that wealthy countries merely refrain from some of what they now do). Neither will I attempt a precise specification of the aim of these rights—the exact level of economic well-being required. Rather, I simply assume that persons in poor countries have rights to significantly better economic prospects than they now face. Drawing on recent books by George Soros and Joseph Stiglitz, I describe some ways in which current institutions either fail to improve the situation or even make it worse. I also describe a promising proposal from Soros for a program of direct aid.[12]

It is, I think, not unreasonable to expect well-off nations to change harmful and unfair practices and to adopt policies of the kind Soros proposes. These are feasible concrete reforms. Of course, one could consistently accept economic rights and recommend different policies, but one cannot accept them and recommend no reforms. In any case, establishing that there is at least one set of fair and feasible policy initiatives for implementing economic rights is an important part of the argument in support of regarding such rights as human rights.

A variety of factors influence the level of economic well-being of persons in the poorest countries:

1. the organization of domestic politics, the domestic infrastructure, and the form of domestic economic institutions;
2. the nature of international institutions governing trade and capital movements; and
3. the level and form of direct aid from wealthy to poor nations.

I focus my discussion here on the second and third factors. So let us turn to institutional issues.

In standard economic theory, there are strong arguments supporting free international trade. In particular, there is good reason to believe that free trade yields significant net benefits in the aggregate. I accept these arguments. Nevertheless, we should not ignore the indirect costs of trade and the distribution of these costs among nations. Moreover, we should not confuse support for free trade with support for the present system of rules governing international trade and being enforced by the World Trade Organization (WTO).

Consider first the built-in costs of trade. One such cost is the risk of a certain kind of response to competition. When every nation competes with every other nation, both for export markets and for capital investment, it is possible for all to get trapped in the kind of downward spiral characteristic of a multiperson prisoners' dilemma. To attract foreign capital, countries have to forego some of the taxes that could have funded investment in public goods, including the goods that can make such countries more competitive and productive—education, roads, communications, and so forth.[13] Similarly, to keep down the price of exports, countries cannot afford to enforce the protections for workers that would drive up costs.[14] While the market offers many benefits, it also carries important costs, including increased obstacles to the securing of public goods (or to the fair distribution of "negative externalities"). Managing these costs requires more direct intervention.

These problems affect every country, but they fall especially hard on poorer countries that do not already have a large capital stock, domestic sources of investment, an educated workforce, and so on. "Market discipline" makes it very difficult to catch up. Surely, a commitment to economic rights requires that we address these systemic problems. The difficulty is that the problems are inherent in the system of international market competition.

The second set of problems is not inherent in the idea of free trade but stems, instead, from the fact that trade under WTO rules is in fact neither free nor fair. Powerful players such as the United States have simply rigged the rules. For example, the obvious point of WTO rules is to reduce tariff barriers to international trade. But, under these rules, tariffs on advanced industrial goods are phased out much more quickly than tariffs on the agricultural products that poor nations seek to export. Moreover, the United States has retained the right to invoke antidumping provisions to protect itself against low-cost imports.[15]

All this is politics, of course. International organizations such as the WTO depend on near-unanimous agreement among countries, and this organization is one of the few to which the United States has been willing to agree. We should not be surprised that powerful countries will rig the rules in their favor nor that, in a period in which corporations have more political clout than labor, the rules should favor corporations. While the United States accepts WTO rules, it has ratified only 13 out of 182 of the conventions of the International Labor Organization.[16] Of course, that this is the way things are does not mean that they should not be otherwise.

Here there can be little doubt as to what the human right to economic well-being requires. It requires, in this instance, no actions being undertaken in the spirit of honoring "positive duties" of aid but concrete actions being undertaken in the spirit of honoring "negative duties" not to impose unfair rules. What so-called First World nations must do is act to eliminate unfair trade rules and replace them with fair trade rules.[17]

Consider now the question of direct aid to poor countries. Let us assume that to the extent poor countries can be helped simply by changing rules of trade that unfairly disadvantage them, these rules ought to be changed. As I have just argued, this seems to me a minimal implication of economic human rights. But not all disadvantages or deprivations result from unfair trade rules. Some are simply natural side effects of competition, such as the loss of control over taxation that makes it difficult for poor countries to invest adequately in public goods. Here I think the solution, again, is not to abandon free trade but rather to develop supplementary institutional arrangements. I conclude by briefly describing one proposal, from George Soros, for how institutions for foreign aid might be redesigned or reformed to serve this end. But first we need a clear view of the problems with existing foreign aid practices.

Genuinely humanitarian aid is not politically popular, at least in the United States. The United States contributes a smaller percentage of its gross domestic product than does any other developed country.[18] This is partly a matter of selfishness, of course. But it is also partly a political response to the fact that traditional approaches to foreign aid are often genuinely problematic.

One problem, or class of problems, has to do with the politics of foreign aid in donor countries. Asking for sacrifice is not easy for politicians. This leads them, first, not to ask at all and, second, if they do ask, to try to give aid in forms that benefit powerful constituencies in their own country or in forms that at least indirectly serve national self-interest. But all this means that donor countries will try to keep a lot of control over how the aid is used and that the aid may not be all that helpful to those who need it.

A second problem has to do with the governments and political institutions in poor countries. In short, they are often a significant cause of the poverty to which foreign aid is a response. And they are often ill-disposed to put foreign aid to its proper uses. Even when developed countries do give genuinely selfless aid to these governments, much is lost to corruption or inefficiency. Yet the governments in poor countries have a powerful interest in keeping control over expenditures of aid. And some international institutions, such as the World Bank and the

International Monetary Fund, are constrained by the rules under which they operate to work only through governments.

A third problem is that too much foreign aid is reactive rather than proactive. Sending food in a time of famine may be sometimes necessary. But famines are rarely the result of food shortages, and they are best avoided through the proactive development of markets, transparent political institutions, a free press, the rule of law, and much else. It is toward these proactive developments that most foreign aid ought to be directed.

Genuinely beneficent foreign aid would be more politically palatable, I suspect, if it were part of an organized, international program to which the developed countries all contributed proportional to their means. Voters at least would not feel that other countries were taking advantage of "our generosity." It would also be more politically acceptable, as well as morally better, if we could avoid corruption and inefficiency in the use of aid dollars. Soros has a proposal designed to meet these objectives.[19]

The International Monetary Fund has the power to create special drawing rights (SDRs), which function (roughly) as grants underwritten by proportional contributions from all member nations and which may be put to use for various development purposes. A proposal for an issue of SDRs is currently on the table and awaits only the approval of the U.S. Congress. Soros proposes that we approve this issue of SDRs, to be distributed to all member nations, with the added proviso that all the wealthy nations will be required to donate their SDRs to projects in poorer nations.

This proposal institutionalizes an arguably fair distribution of the burden of direct aid, and, in the initial distribution of SDRs, it also promises some immediate, though small, benefit for poor countries. The rest of the proposal is designed to respond to the inefficiencies in the way aid is used. Rather than simply ask wealthy countries to give their SDRs to poor governments, various organizations in poor countries, both governmental and nongovernmental, would be invited, in effect, to submit "grant proposals." These would be subject to an international approval process, and then donor countries would choose which of the approved proposals to fund. This gives some control to donor countries—they can choose plans they think likely to be effective—but it does not allow them to tailor their donations entirely to their own interests. Neither does it put them in the position of dictating to others what they need. At the same time, if recipients of aid misuse it, they cannot expect to be funded in the future. Thus, several features of the proposal conspire to make it more likely that foreign aid distributed in this way will actually be effective in bringing about the universal realization of basic economic rights as human rights.

CONCLUSION

In this chapter, I focus my attention on rights held by all persons and held against institutions—governments and various international institutions. I begin by discussing in a general way what kinds of argument are appropriate for rights, and I also discuss the need to specify what those rights imply in the way of obligations. If talk of human rights is more than empty rhetoric, then we have to be prepared to say what these rights concretely imply, and we have to be prepared to defend these requirements as being both reasonable and fair. In the remainder of this chapter, I offer notes toward this end. I argue that careful attention to the justifications for a human right to democratic institutions forces the conclusion that this right is in an important sense conditional and that, accordingly, the duties it imposes on others will vary from case to case if the circumstances are sufficiently different (e.g., the presence of a background culture favorable to justifiable democracy). And I argue that there is no reason to reject economic rights as being human rights on the grounds that they impose unfair or unreasonable duties or that there is no fair and reasonable way to distribute their corresponding duties. Indeed, I claim that there are some obvious and reasonable steps that wealthy states can take now to improve significantly the chances that the economic right to subsistence is universally secured, notwithstanding the great diversity of circumstances characterizing those nations where basic economic rights are not secure.

NOTES

1. This is partly so because I do not know how many human rights there are and how many considerations might be brought under their umbrella. If we assume that human rights are rights possessed by all human beings, that would give us a test for whether something is a human right, but it is not an easy test to apply, since a person who does not have a claim under an alleged human right in given circumstances might still be held to have the right conditionally.
2. Here I follow Alistair Macleod. See chapter 2 in this volume.
3. Here we might add the corollary that rights that demand a great deal of us must, if those demands are fair and reasonable, be strongly supported or justified as being necessary to secure very fundamental interests.
4. Joel Feinberg, *Social Philosophy* (Englewood Cliffs, N.J.: Prentice Hall, 1973), 95.
5. See McLeod's and Martin's contributions to this volume (chapters 2 and 3) for articulations of this view.
6. I have learned from several essays by and conversations with George Rainbolt on these matters.
7. H. L. A. Hart distinguishes right holders and "third-party beneficiaries" in "Are There Any Natural Rights?" *Philosophical Review*, 64 (1955): 180.

8. Henry Shue examines this idea in *Basic Rights*, 2nd ed. (Princeton, N.J., Princeton University Press, 1996), 74–87.

9. www.hrweb.org/legal/undocs.html.

10. Thomas Pogge, "The International Significance of Human rights," *Journal of Ethics*, 4 (2000): 57f.

11. Tony Judt, in a review of Fareed Zakaria, *The Future of Freedom: Illiberal Democracy at Home and Abroad*, observes that constitutionalism and the rule of law may be far more important and valuable aspects of what we think of as democracy than the mere institution of voting. *New York Review of Books* 50 (April 10, 2003), 30–31.

12. George Soros, *On Globalization* (New York, Public Affairs, 2002). Joseph Stiglitz, *Globalization and Its Discontents* (New York, Norton, 2002).

13. Nicolaus Tideman pointed out to me in conversation that, other things equal, while lower tax rates will reduce the revenues available to the host government, foreign investment can increase the value of the tax base and so may raise tax revenues even if tax rates are reduced. As a consequence, the problem in the text may not be as serious as it otherwise seems.

14. Soros, 3, 39–42, 49.

15. Soros, 33f., Stiglitz, 60–61, 172–73, 244–45.

16. Soros, 39f.

17. I focus here on WTO rules governing trade. Stiglitz also argues that the IMF imposes unfair rules on developing countries and that these often seem designed more to protect financial interests in developed countries than to address the needs of poor countries. The issues here are complex, and Soros is more circumspect in his discussion of the IMF.

18. Soros, 21.

19. Soros, 73–96.

III

ENFORCING UNIVERSAL HUMAN RIGHTS

8

Human Rights and Humanitarian Intervention

Steven P. Lee

In the late summer of 2000, the Canadian government established the International Commission on Intervention and State Sovereignty to study the growing divide between human rights and "national rights." Canadian foreign minister Lloyd Axworthy said, "Our take has been that since the end of the cold war, we have to focus on individuals, on the people. That is as much in the [United Nations] charter as sovereignty."[1] Axworthy and his Canadian colleagues have indeed identified an important problem, perhaps the central problem in international relations since the end of the Cold War. Do national rights against outside intervention—that is, national sovereignty—always trump a concern about the violation of human rights within states, or must sovereignty sometimes give way and, if so, when? Posing the problem in terms of rights, human and national, makes it clear that philosophers, political theorists, and international lawyers have an important role to play in addressing the necessary balance.

THE PROBLEM

Humanitarian intervention is the use of military violence in the territory of another state to provide humanitarian assistance to some of the citizens of that state. Often, the need for humanitarian assistance is due to the fact that the citizens are having some of their basic human rights violated. Humanitarian intervention is a method of enforcing human rights and is normally justified on such grounds. The universality of human rights provides the basis of this justification.

The justification of intervention through appeals to universal human rights presents some problems. The standard theoretical foundation for justifying the international use of military force is just war theory, and just war theory is based on respect for national sovereignty. Yet, humanitarian intervention often violates national sovereignty. It is true that the part of just war theory concerning how force may be used, *jus in bello,* is sensitive to human rights, as reflected, for example, in the principle of discrimination. But the just war doctrines of *jus ad bellum,* which concern the use of military force across borders, generally regard national defense as a necessary condition for such justification. Force can justifiably be used only in response to aggression by another state. In contrast, the rights violations that justify humanitarian intervention occur within a state. The state commits aggression against its own citizens but not against another state.[2]

This tension between national sovereignty and humanitarian intervention highlights a basic difficulty with just war theory that has long been apparent. The theory, as its name suggests, should be about the achievement of justice and, if it is not, will have little reason to be followed. Justice requires respect for human rights. Traditional doctrines of *jus ad bellum,* which emphasize respect for national sovereignty, seem to stand in the way of achieving justice in the case of rights violations that occur within states.

This objection is often expressed by claiming that *jus ad bellum* has an unacceptable statist orientation. *Jus ad bellum* treats states as the relevant moral patients and agents. It is the rights of states that are violated when aggression occurs, and, according to traditional just war theory, only this sort of violation can justify the cross-border use of force. Such a perspective is problematic for the liberal, for whom individual human rights are of the highest importance. Liberals will find the old rules of *jus ad bellum* excessively deferential to the importance of national sovereignty.

This criticism is not completely fair to just war theory. In most accounts of *jus ad bellum,* humanitarian intervention is a recognized category of justification. When a state commits massive human rights violations against its citizens, violations that "shock the moral conscience of mankind," most accounts of just war theory recognize that military intervention may be justified.[3] The humanitarian intervention justification within *jus ad bellum* doctrine may be referred to as the "humanitarian intervention exception."

But if *jus ad bellum* permits the humanitarian intervention exception, the problem for the theory then shifts. How is the exception to be understood as one consistent with the general theory? The task of this chapter is to address the theoretical problem of how to understand the humanitarian intervention exception within the general structure of just war theory. How can the humanitarian intervention exception be made consistent with the general impermissibility of the nondefensive cross-border use of force that characterizes *jus ad bellum*? This specific problem represents the more general problem referred to earlier. How can *jus ad bellum* be reconciled with the fundamental importance of human rights in the liberal worldview? Perhaps efforts to show consistency between the humanitarian intervention exception and the general noninterventionist stance of *jus ad bellum* can also show that *jus ad bellum* is consistent with liberal morality. In addition, an answer to these questions may help to solve the more practical problem that was Axworthy's main concern: What are the proper boundaries of humanitarian intervention?

MICHAEL WALZER'S RIGHTS-BASED APPROACH

One way to resolve the apparent tension within the *jus ad bellum* doctrine between the respect for national sovereignty and the humanitarian intervention exception would be to offer an account of national sovereignty in terms of individual human rights. Can national rights be derived from individual rights? If so, both aspects of *jus ad bellum* would be grounded in human rights. Both justificatory parts of the theory would be in the same moral coin.

Some have thought that such a resolution may be achieved by presenting an account of respect for sovereignty in terms of the domestic analogy, a comparison between the autonomy of the individual and the sovereignty of the state. The argument from this analogy is this. Because an individual is allowed to use force against another only in self-defense, so too a state should be allowed to use force against another state only in self-defense. As a matter of right, I cannot be legitimately aggressed against unless I first aggress against others. Likewise, as a matter of right, a state cannot be legitimately aggressed against unless it first aggresses against another. National sovereignty is on the same moral footing as individual autonomy. Indeed, the national right against aggression is simply the collection of the individual rights of its citizens against aggression. In this way, the moral force of sovereignty is derived from individual rights.

The inadequacy of this reasoning is notorious and readily apparent. The argument commits the fallacy of composition. A property of individuals, their autonomy, and the moral consequences that flow from it cannot necessarily be attributed to a collection of individuals, such as the state. Because individuals who are not aggressing against other individuals cannot be interfered with, it does not follow that groups of individuals not aggressing against other groups cannot be interfered with. The state does not collect the rights of its individual citizens in this way.

The state is not a superindividual. I can abuse a part of myself (my lungs, say, by smoking) without losing the right I have against aggression on the part of those who may wish to interfere with me to get me to stop such abuse. A part of me has no rights against me, but an individual has rights against his or her state, and those rights may stand against respect for national sovereignty.

Michael Walzer presents his well-known account of *jus ad bellum* in terms of the domestic analogy: "Our primary perceptions and judgments of aggression are the products of analogical reasoning." The rights of sovereignty "belong to states, but they derive ultimately from the rights of individuals, and from them they take their force." How does this happen? "States' rights are simply the collective form [of individual rights]."[4] Is Walzer in fact basing his argument for respect for national sovereignty on the discredited argument from analogy? Perhaps not. He seems to use the analogy primarily heuristically rather than as the basis of his argument.

What is his argument? Speaking of how states' rights can be derived from individual rights, he says that "the process of collectivization is a complex one."[5] The individual right on which national sovereignty is based is a right of citizens "to live as members of a historic community and to express their inherited culture through political forms worked out among themselves." Individuals have a right to "participation in the 'development' that goes on and can only go on within the enclosure [of the state]." This is an individual right that amounts to a right of the state against aggression: "Against foreigners, individuals have a right to a state of their own."[6] Aggression against a state disrupts and perhaps destroys the community created by the citizens of that state. This right is, Walzer says, an individual right with a collective reference. We may call this right the "right of political participation." Aggression against the state, in usurping the established indigenous political forms, is a violation of the right of political participation.

Thus, it seems, Walzer does not rely on the domestic analogy for his argument. The domestic analogy attributes to the state a right that individuals have—namely, a right against aggression. However, Walzer also argues that a different right that individuals have, a right to participation in the development of their political life, implies that the state has a right against aggression. This argument avoids the fallacy of composition because the individual right in question is different from the state right on which it is based and the nature of the individual right shows how it yields that state right.

But there are two problems with Walzer's argument, either of which may be sufficient to reject his position. First, the nature of the right of political participation is unclear, and its status as an individual right is questionable. Second, the scope that Walzer gives to the right is controversial.

With respect to the first problem, it is unclear whether the right of political participation, as Walzer understands it, is an individual right at all. It seems rather to be a communal or collective right, a right that belongs primarily to the group rather than to the individual. Walzer presents it as an individual right from which a group right can be derived, but it might be more accurate to see it the other way around. The property the right protects is fundamentally collective rather than individual. Of course, there may be nothing wrong with collective properties and the claims that have moral implications. But if Walzer's account does depend on a collective right, it would not by itself show how to reconcile *jus ad bellum* with concern for individual rights, as represented in the humanitarian intervention exception.

To explore this issue a bit further, consider the moral force of the comment "It's none of your business," used to rebuff interference with a group of people in a relationship.[7] Can it ever be someone's moral business to interfere with what is going on among individuals in a long-standing relationship so long as their activity does no serious harm to anyone outside the group? The moral right to interfere in a conflict between individuals would seem to be more constrained when they are in a long-standing relationship than when they are strangers. This is a problem at the normative center of family law. If I come upon two adults fighting or an adult acting aggressively toward a child, and if I am trying to decide whether it is permissible for me to intervene, it seems that my judgment would and should be influenced (though not necessarily determined) by information about whether the former adults are a couple or whether the latter adult is the parent of the child. The apparent relevance of such information is the basic moral intuition on which Walzer's argument for the right of political participation hangs. One could generalize the moral point in these terms: Individuals have a right to live their lives in relationships that have been shaped through their own choices. From such a right may be derived a right of a relationship group against outside interference in the relationship. (Of course, any such right does not imply that intervention is always wrong, but more on this later.) Walzer's right of political participation would be a specification of this general right in cases where the relationship group is a state.

But should this kind of special moral consideration given to relationship groups, in contrast with stranger groups, be understood as being based on an individual right of participation in relationships as Walzer would have it? I think not. Another way to understand the greater moral constraints on intervening in relationship groups (in comparison with stranger groups) is to observe that relationship groups create a special presumption against intervention. This presumption is based, in part, on the increased likelihood that individuals in relationship groups are consenting to apparently aggressive behavior toward themselves by others in the group. There is an individual right against unconsented-to aggression, and this is the justification for intervening in the case of apparently aggressive behavior within groups. But in the case of relationship groups, it is simply more likely than in the case of stranger groups that the aggressive behavior is something that those in the group have consented to. The aggressive behavior is likely to be an expression of the nature of the relationship that has developed among the members of the group and that has been shaped by them over time. Some families are dysfunctional, but the members of the family have accepted that their relationships will be structured in it that way. This may be part of what supports the special moral consideration against intervention given to individuals in relationship groups.[8]

The second problem is related to the first. Walzer gives wide scope to the right of political participation, and it is not clear, even if there is such a right, that it would have such a broad application. A number of Walzer's critics have focused on this point. What kind of regimes does the right of political participation protect from outside interference? What counts as participation in the development of, or consent to, the set of political and social relationships within a state? The practical issue here is whether authoritarian, undemocratic regimes are protected from intervention when they violate the human rights of some of their citizens. Walzer gives the right of political participation wide scope so that it does protect most such regimes. Walzer joins John Rawls in embracing a wide range of acceptable forms of government. The right of political participation is, collectively, a right of self-determination, and "self-determination and political freedom are not equivalent terms."[9] Authoritarian regimes often "fit" the political culture and society of the people they govern.[10] The people usually identify with the regime and hence can be said to have consented to it or helped to make it what it is through their political participation—that is, understanding consent and political participation in a broad sense.

On the other hand, critics of Walzer would narrow the scope of what counts as being political participation such that some respect for basic civil rights and some kind of democratic mechanism are necessary for there to be political participation in the morally relevant sense. In other words, the critics would connect the alleged right of political participation much more closely with respect for more traditional individual rights. But in that case, it may be best to say that the right of political participation is otiose. It is simply a different name for an array of traditional civil and political rights, the recognition of which are the hallmarks of a regime that a liberal would regard as being morally legitimate. This reinforces the previous point in that it supports the view that the right of political participation, if it exists, plays little or no role in explaining our inclination to intervene (or not) in the case of aggressive behavior in relationship groups.

This inclination requires an explanation that the alleged right of political participation cannot supply.[11]

A RECONSTRUCTED JUST WAR THEORY?

Walzer's attempt to show how the deference to national sovereignty characteristic of traditional accounts of *jus ad bellum* could be shown to be consistent with the importance of individual human rights is problematic at best. Perhaps his attempt to reconcile *jus ad bellum* to individual rights demonstrates the necessity of reconstructing just war theory in the image of individual rights. Why not simply restate the theory directly in terms of individual rights, abandoning its long-standing commitment to respect for national sovereignty?

This is what one of Walzer's critics, David Luban, proposes: "Wars are not fought by states, but by men and women."[12] As a result, *jus ad bellum* must explain "how a crime against a state is also a crime against its citizens, that is, by relating men and women to their states in a morally cogent way." This is what Walzer tries to do with his right of political participation. But Luban rejects Walzer's account, partly for some of the reasons discussed earlier. Instead, Luban suggests, "We should be able to define *jus ad bellum* directly in terms of human rights, without the needless detour of talk about states."[13] Luban suggests that "a just war is a war in defense of socially basic human rights (subject to proportionality)."[14] Gone is the pretext that respect for national sovereignty can be a stand-in for the individual rights that war may be fought to defend, as Walzer would have it. There is no morally acceptable defense for the traditional *jus ad bellum* focus on national sovereignty, so reconstruction of the theory is necessary if it is to deserve any role in contemporary public policy.

One reaction to Luban's proposal might be that it is too permissive, that it permits humanitarian intervention in too broad a range of cases. Indeed, under his proposal, it seems that humanitarian intervention ceases to be the exception and becomes the norm, the only factor that justifies the international use of force (or resistance to such force). But, of course, not every domestic human rights violation would justify the use of force against the state, and Luban recognizes this by inclusion of the caveat that the use of force is "subject to proportionality." Intervention is justified only when the harm done by the intervention would be no more than proportional to the benefit achieved by preventing the human rights violations that justify the intervention. This seems to be a sensible limitation on the permissibility of intervention, and it is consistent with the fact that proportionality is one of the traditional criteria of *jus ad bellum* (as well as *jus in bello*). In the traditional view, proportionality is another condition, along with the defensive nature of the military action, necessary to justify use of force.[15]

But the limitation provided by the proportionality requirement, though extensive, does not seem sufficient. Even with its inclusion, the use of force would be too often justified. Luban, in a later essay, recognizes this kind of problem with his reconstruction of *jus ad bellum*.[16] Further limitations are needed on the use of force in response to human rights violations beyond those implicit in the notion of proportionality. Luban's response in the later essay is, in part, to argue that another necessary condition on the use of force is that it have political legitimacy in the state using the force. Such legitimacy is likely to exist only when the citizens are truly horrified by the rights violations in question, to the point of regarding the violations as an instance of barbarism. But then we seem to be back to something close to the traditional formula of the humanitarian intervention exception, where the intervention is justified in response only to a state's domestic rights violations that "shock the moral conscience of mankind."

This may remove the objection that Luban's reconstruction of *jus ad bellum* is too permissive, but it raises other problems. Tying the permissibility of use of force to the political legitimacy of the decision to use that force seems both an empirical and a conceptual mistake. Empirically, many of the acts of humanitarian intervention cited as acceptable examples were undertaken by states where the nature of the regime precluded the decision to use force having political legitimacy in the liberal sense—for example, Vietnam's intervention in Cambodia and Tanzania's intervention in Uganda. Conceptually, when a liberal regime is considering humanitarian intervention, the permissibility of the intervention is one of the factors that is cited to build the case for a decision to intervene. Hence, the question of the permissibility of the intervention is logically made before the decision to intervene. One further difficulty with Luban's reconstruction lies in his claim that the political legitimacy of the decision depends on democratic support and that such support is likely only when the rights violations at issue are regarded as being barbaric. The problem is that this introduces the issue of moral motivation, a notion more at home in discussions of obligation than of permissibility.

Perhaps the traditional formula involving respect for national sovereignty can be revived and restated in a way that resolves the apparent inconsistency between sovereignty and the humanitarian intervention exception.

RESPECT FOR NATIONAL SOVEREIGNTY AS A RULE OF THUMB

One solution to the apparent inconsistency in traditional accounts of *jus ad bellum* would be to regard the rule of respect for national sovereignty as a rule of thumb, which may be ignored in those kinds of cases where the humanitarian intervention exception traditionally applies. Walzer is mistaken to look for an individual right underlying respect for national sovereignty, and Luban is mistaken in abandoning the national sovereignty standard in favor of one that appeals directly to individual rights. Walzer is mistaken because there is no individual right that can do the job, and Luban is mistaken because the moral decision whether to go to war on humanitarian grounds is more complicated than what can be encompassed in the notion of proportionality and because it logically cannot involve reference to the political legitimacy of the decision itself.

The factors that a state should take into account in deciding whether it is morally permissible to respond with military force to domestic rights violations in another state include the following:

1. *Epistemological considerations*. Knowledge of the nature and extent of the rights violations that might justify a military response is inevitably limited by distance from the scene of the violations, both in space and in understanding of the context in which they arise. This is a point raised earlier regarding outsiders' perceptions of the behavior of people in relationship groups. Rights violations are generally closely tied to the question of whether the victim of an aggressive action has consented to the aggression. If there is consent, there may be no violation. But the presence or absence of consent to aggressive behavior in relationship groups is at least in part a function of the history of the relationship and the way it has been formed by the participants through their choices over time. Hence, we should exercise some caution in judging that rights violations are occurring in a relationship group other than our own. Walzer makes this kind of argument, though it is logically separate from his main line of argument concerning a right of political participation.[17] But, as Luban points out in response to Walzer, it is wrong to treat our ignorance as something that is necessary and inevitable. It is possible to acquire sufficient knowledge of other relationship groups in order to make accurate judgments about rights violations.[18] The epistemological argument can establish, at most, a presumption against reliable judgment, as discussed earlier in the general case of relationship groups. But there are other factors, too.
2. *The expectation of resistance*. Any military intervention is bound to be met with military resistance, and a judgment of the moral acceptability of an intervention must take this into account. This is a large part of what would come under the category of proportionality in *jus ad bellum*. It is what makes military action a very expensive undertaking in terms of all that humans value. But Walzer, though he

would not deny the roll of resistance in calculations of proportionality, understands the expectation of resistance in another way. He sees resistance to intervention as being an expression of the right of political participation. If the citizens of a state regard their state as being legitimate, however outsiders may view it, they will justly resist intervention. But as an argument for the right of a state against intervention, this proves too much because citizens would feel that their state is legitimate and they would defend it even if intervention were justified under the humanitarian intervention exception.[19]

3. *The risks of humanitarian intervention becoming a false rationale for intervention.* Any humanitarian intervention exception will make it possible for states to intervene under a humanitarian intervention rationale when humanitarian intervention is not justified and the rationale is meant to mask other motives. The concern here is not cases where a humanitarian intervention rationale is justified but cases where states intervene with other motives. Motives are always mixed, and no state is likely to intervene with a purely humanitarian motive. So long as there is a genuine humanitarian intervention rationale and states do no more than what is needed to correct the rights violations, the presence of other motives is irrelevant to whether states' interventions are justified on humanitarian grounds.[20] But the availability of a humanitarian intervention rationale for states to use as a justification when the rationale is inapplicable is a real danger. As many authors have pointed out, a humanitarian intervention exception can tend to increase the degree of intervention by strong states in the affairs of weak states. A respect for national sovereignty protects weak states, and this is one reason for a rule requiring such respect. Indeed, this can be seen as a human rights issue. As Henry Shue has noted, the United States' policy on human rights in the 1970s had an anti-interventionalist motivation.[21] The point in part was to get the United States to stop intervening on the behalf of regimes that systematically violated human rights. In addition, intervention on ideological or religious grounds can be given a false humanitarian rationale. The religious wars of the sixteenth and seventeenth centuries were one of the reasons for the adoption of the *jus ad bellum* condition that all wars must be defensive.[22]
4. *The danger of precedents.* The more often states intervene in the affairs of other states, the easier it is for interventions to occur in the future, whatever their purpose. For example, some have speculated that the United States' intervention in Iraq (whether or not it is considered a case of humanitarian intervention) may serve other states that have their own interventions to pursue, interventions that might be easier

to get away with were the Iraq intervention available as precedent. The Iraq intervention may be useful to rationalize, for instance, Russia's intervention in Georgia or India's intervention in Pakistan.

Those states contemplating humanitarian intervention must make sure that the cure is not worse than the disease.[23] The four areas just outlined can all lead to problems. It is important that the dangers they pose be recognized, but the dangers are easy to overlook. Some may be captured by the condition of proportionality, but not all of them. It would help to have a general condition that would serve to encompass the whole set. Establishing a rule of thumb that mandates respect for national sovereignty would cover all four of these possible limitations on humanitarian intervention and help to ensure that humanitarian intervention will be undertaken only when the disease is so severe that the cure is not likely to be worse. When the disease of human rights violations becomes so severe that it "shocks the moral conscience of mankind," then the rule of thumb would be superseded by the humanitarian intervention exception to the ordinary *jus ad bellum*.

The first of the four factors that constrain humanitarian intervention, the epistemological consideration, is the one that creates a presumption against intervening in the case of relationship groups (including states). But the other three factors can also be included under such a presumption, strengthening it. Take the case of a family. First there are the epistemological considerations of our not knowing whether apparently aggressive behavior within the family is genuinely consented to. Second, there is the expectation of resistance to intervention, even when it is otherwise justified, that may make the intervention counterproductive, the cure worse than the disease. Police officers dealing with domestic disputes know well that couples in a physical fight may turn on someone seeking to intervene to stop the aggression.[24] Third, the state or other parties may seek to use any rule allowing intervention in families as a false rationale to justify intervention sought for some other reason, a feature common in totalitarian states. Fourth, in families, as in states, the more often intervention occurs, the easier it is to justify it in the future.

How is this rule-of-thumb analysis of the respect for national sovereignty a solution to the apparent inconsistency between respect for sovereignty and the humanitarian intervention exception? The rule-of-thumb analysis archives consistency by adopting a moral pluralism, recognizing a combination of deontological and teleological factors that bear on situations when intervention is being considered and that must be weighed in particular situations to determine the morally preferable action. Respect for national sovereignty, understood as a rule of thumb, can express several such important factors, while sometimes allowing the respect that states owe their subjects' individual rights to trump the general presumption against intervention. Humanitarian intervention should be permitted to protect individual human rights only when extensive rights violations outweigh the other moral factors covered by the moral rule of thumb mandating respect for sovereignty.

This account can explain the changes that take place over time in the scope of the humanitarian intervention exception. At this moment in international relations, the scope of morally permissible humanitarian intervention seems to be growing. This is understandable because some of the factors comprehended by the rule of thumb of respect for national sovereignty are subject to change with changing circumstances. For example, the epistemological considerations may grow less important as information about other parts of the world becomes more plentiful and more widely shared. The expectation of resistance may grow weaker as citizens of various nations come increasingly to appreciate that some humanitarian interventions are actually intended to provide humanitarian rescue and are not aggression in the traditional sense. In addition, the likelihood of interventions on false humanitarian rationales and the danger of interventions as precedents may grow less likely in cases where humanitarian intervention is authorized through a world body such as the United Nations.

Analogous things could be said about legal interventions in families. The scope of morally permissible interventions seems to have grown in recent decades, and a similar explanation could be given. We have more information, if not about particular families, at least about the nature of family dynamics, patterns of coercive behavior, and the effects of dysfunction on children. As members of the family, especially women, have come to appreciate that the state often intervenes on their behalf, they are less likely to resist such interventions. In addition, as our legal response to family dysfunction grows more discriminating and professional, the danger posed by the prospect of false rationales for intervention and intervention as precedents is likely to diminish. The upshot is that the presumption against intervention in the case of families, like respect for national sovereignty in the case of states, has grown weaker.

Note finally that *jus ad bellum* concerns only the permissibility of the use of military force and not its obligatoriness. *Jus ad bellum* establishes when force may be used, not when it must be used. Consistent with this, the humanitarian intervention exception shows that humanitarian intervention is in some cases permitted, not required. Some would see this as being an inadequacy in the theory's account of humanitarian intervention. Human rights, being what they are, may obligate us not only to not violate rights of others but also to defend others whose rights are being violated by third parties. Just war theory cannot require us to use force in defense of human rights, but our conception of human rights may require this.[25] Some have argued that if there is a duty of humanitarian intervention, it is an imperfect duty, like the duty of charity, and thus does not fall on any state in particular. Others have argued that, on analogy with the conditions of "good Samaritan duties," a duty to rescue cannot require great sacrifice on the part of the rescuer. As a result, there can be no duty of humanitarian military intervention because any military intervention requires a sacrifice of life.[26] Further investigation will be needed to determine in what circumstances humanitarian intervention might become a duty, but intervention is at least permitted so long as the costs of intervention outweigh considerations that support the usual rule-of-thumb presumption in favor of sovereignty.

NOTES

1. Barbara Crossette, "Canada Tries to Define Line between Human and National Rights," *New York Times*, September 14, 2000, p. A11.
2. Situations justifying humanitarian intervention do not always concern a state's aggressing against its citizens. Sometimes, for example, in the case of so-called failed states, the violations of rights may be perpetrated by substate groups, groups that the state is either unable or unwilling to control. While I generally speak in what follows of the state as being the perpetrator of the rights violations, what I say applies to this other possibility as well.
3. The quoted phrase is used by Michael Walzer in his account of just war theory, in *Just and Unjust Wars* (New York, Basic Books, 1977), p. 107. Walzer's account is one of those that recognizes the justifiability of humanitarian intervention.
4. Walzer, *Just and Unjust Wars*, pp. 58, 53, 54.
5. Walzer, *Just and Unjust Wars*, p. 54.
6. Michael Walzer, "The Moral Standing of States: A Response to Four Critics," in Charles Beitz et al. (eds.), *International Ethics* (Princeton, NJ: Princeton University Press, 1985), pp. 219, 236.
7. The remark is, of course, also used to rebuff interference with a single individual.
8. There are other factors as well, as discussed later.
9. Walzer, *Just and Unjust Wars*, p. 87.
10. Walzer, "The Moral Standing of States," pp. 232–33.
11. There is another possible problem with Walzer's account, which is how the humanitarian intervention exception is to be explained in the context of a right of political participation. Walzer would like to see the humanitarian intervention exception not as an exception, strictly speaking, to the right but as a negative demonstration of the right (*Just and Unjust Wars*, p. 90). He claims, for example, that in the case of humanitarian outrages, there is no longer a community in the state in which a right of political participation can be exercised. But there is still a political life in such states, so his argument may not be persuasive.

12. David Luban, "Just War and Human Rights," in Beitz, *International Ethics*, pp. 195–216.

13. Luban, "Just War and Human Rights," p. 201.

14. Luban, "Just War and Human Rights," p. 210.

15. There are other conditions as well, such as the decision to use force being taken by proper authority.

16. David Luban, "Intervention and Civilization: Some Unhappy Lessons of the Kosovo War," in Pablo De Greiff and Ciaran Cronin (eds.), *Global Justice and Transnational Politics* (Cambridge: MIT Press, 2002), pp. 79–115.

17. Walzer, "The Moral Standing of States," p. 220.

18. Luban, "The Romance of the Nation-State," in Beitz, *International Ethics*, pp. 240–41.

19. The United States intervention in Somalia may fall into this category.

20. Walzer, *Just and Unjust Wars*, pp. 101–08.

21. Henry Shue, *Basic Rights: Subsistence, Affluence, and U.S. Foreign Policy*, 2nd ed. (Princeton, NJ: Princeton University Press, 1996), p. 175.

22. Nigel Biggar, "Christianity and Weapons of Mass Destruction," in Sohail Hashmi and Steven Lee (eds.), *Ethics and Weapons of Mass Destruction* (New York): Cambridge University Press, 2004), pp. 169–170.

23. Shue, *Basic Rights*, p. 175.

24. "My partner may be a son of a bitch, but at least he (or she) is my son of a bitch."

25. Some, such as Robert Nozick, see rights as corresponding only to negative duties of nonviolation, while others see there being corresponding positive duties as well. For example, Henry Shue speaks of default duties, which are positive duties to take action to restrain others when they are violating their negative duties of nonviolation. See *Basic Rights*.

26. Luban, "Intervention and Civilization," pp. 93–94.

9

Genocide and Political Responsibility

Larry May

> It is quite conceivable that certain political responsibilities among nations might some day be adjudicated in an international court; what is inconceivable is that such a court would be a criminal tribunal which pronounces on the guilt or innocence of individuals.
>
> —Hannah Arendt[1]

Human rights abuses are increasingly subject to international prosecution. One would think that mass human rights abuses, such as genocide, would be particularly worthy of international criminal prosecution, for genocide seems to be the worst form of human rights abuse; but in recent debates about genocide, a conceptual problem has arisen. Criminal trials seek to hold individuals accountable, yet genocide is perpetrated by organized groups and institutions. William Schabas notes, "At the drafting convention in 1948 for the Genocide Convention, the United Kingdom refused to participate because it felt that the convention approached genocide from the wrong angle, responsibility of individuals, whereas it was really governments that had to be the focus."[2] This chapter assesses this criticism of genocide prosecutions, as well as the similar criticisms voiced by Hannah Arendt.

Political responsibility concerns group responsibility, either collective or shared, for political crimes. Political crimes are crimes that are large scale and involve many people, most of whom do not cause harm directly. When large-scale consequences occur, "collaboration can be assumed."[3] Individuals are normally not capable of producing large-scale consequences on their own; individuals must usually act as members of groups to produce such consequences. One of the chief difficulties in determining individual guilt for political crimes such as genocide is the sheer number of people who participated in the crime. As Arendt has said, "where all are guilty, nobody . . . can be judged."[4] This situation does not seem to comport well with criminal law that seeks objective determinations of guilt, separating the guilty from the nonguilty. For example, in the Rwandan genocide, the perpetrators constituted more than a tenth of the population, and most of the rest were in some sense accomplices. Despite such facts, I argue that prosecutions of individuals for genocide are conceptually and normatively plausible.

Genocide is a crime that seems to fit the conception of something for which political responsibility, but not moral or criminal responsibility, should be assigned. Genocide is committed by a state or statelike entity against a people, often a group of its own people.[5] In a sense it does not matter so much what each person has done, since so many are complicit. Genocide has as its defining characteristics the specific intent to destroy a group, and it is this intent for which individuals are held responsible. The skepticism about prosecutions of individuals for political crimes in general can easily be applied to international trials for individuals accused of genocide. These trials seem to hold individuals improperly accountable for what others have done, since it is a social group that commits the criminal act. Yet, there are criminal trials against individuals currently proceeding for genocides allegedly committed in the former Yugoslavia and Rwanda. Other trials are planned to punish genocides in Cambodia, East Timor, and elsewhere. Arendt's very important challenge to these sorts of criminal tribunals requires a response.[6] Such tribunals are justified by the fact that a person's intentions, along with what he or she indirectly causes, can be a basis for individual criminal liability.

Political responsibility is the responsibility of the *polis*—either that of the *polis* itself or that of the citizens who compose the polis. So, political responsibility is a form of either collective or shared responsibility. It is a form of collective responsibility if the subject of the responsibility is something that only the state as an actor could accomplish and that is largely indivisible. It is a form of shared responsibility if the subject of the responsibility can indeed be divided into parts where any given part is accomplished by subparts of the state—in this case, by individuals. Political crimes are crimes that are committed by a state or by a statelike entity. The chief conceptual question is how much responsibility individual citizens share for what the state or other group has done. How much does it matter whether the individual personally committed deeds that constitute genocide, such as killing? The emerging genocide jurisprudence seems to accept that a weak act element is enough. All that is needed is that the act in some sense caused the harm in question. Yet political responsibility tracks what groups of people do together, and in the case of genocide what matters more is what one's intentions were rather than what one's actions were. Political responsibility is not primarily about blame for what one has directly caused but rather about one's role in a larger group activity that necessarily involves wide-scale complicity.[7]

This chapter focuses on the responsibility of individuals for genocide. Genocide involves two parts: some act that promotes the destruction of a group and "the intent to destroy, in whole or in part, a national, ethnical, racial, or religious group, as such." It is unlikely that a single individual would be able to destroy a whole group. But an individual could destroy a part of that group. One individual might kill another. What makes this individual's act a political act of the sort condemned by the genocide convention seems to be its collective dimension, some kind of intentional connection to the action of a state or other group. Understanding the collective dimension of individual responsibility for political crimes is crucial if individuals are to be justifiably prosecuted for genocide.

THE ACT ELEMENT IN THE CRIME OF GENOCIDE

Arendt worries that if individuals are prosecuted for political crimes, they will be held accountable for what others have done. In a sense, this is surely right. One individual's act alone does not normally amount to genocide. The combined acts of many are required to make these individual acts into actual genocide. So when individuals are prosecuted for genocide, they are, in this sense, almost always being held accountable in part for what others have done. This would be especially worrisome if an individual were to be held solely responsible for what these other people did or if the individual had no other connection to the acts of the others than that they happened to have a single set of consequences. But neither of these worries will apply if the act that the individual is held responsible for is his or her own act, as part of a plan that included the acts of others. The individual is prosecuted for what the group does but is only held accountable for his or her share. The most morally troubling aspect of prosecuting individuals for political crimes can thus be averted.

The act element in the genocide convention's construal of the crime of genocide should not be seen as being an independent element but rather as being linked with the aim, or intention, to follow a plan. It is this link to a plan that transforms the individual's act into a part of a collective act, and that makes the individual complicit in what others are doing. So, individual responsibility for political crimes does not have to be like holding the child responsible for what the parent has done, to use Arendt's own metaphor. Rather, the better image is that of holding one responsible for one's contribution to a common undertaking. This makes individual responsibility for political crimes into a subspecies of shared responsibility. One is held responsible for the aim of one's acts in a larger plan.

The 1948 genocide convention defines *genocide* as being a "normal" crime, which is to say a crime that requires *mens rea* (guilty mind) as well as *actus reus* (guilty act). Yet, the act element is best understood as being subordinate to one particular type of intent. Even though the genocide convention calls for both an intent and an act element, the act element need not be the serious acts of directly destroying a group or even directly killing its members. The acts that satisfy the act requirement of the crime of genocide include the following:

1. Killing members of the group
2. Causing serious bodily or mental harm to members of the group
3. Deliberately inflicting on the group conditions of life calculated to bring about its physical destruction in whole or in part
4. Imposing measures intended to prevent births within the group
5. Forcibly transferring children of the group to another group[8]

The International Criminal Tribunal for Rwanda (ICTR) has said, in the *Rutaganda* case, that the third point is to be construed "as methods of destruction by which the perpetrator does not necessarily intend to immediately kill the members of the group, but which are ultimately aimed at their destruction."[9] Of course, this brings a kind of intention element into the act element, since discerning the aim of the act means looking at the intent behind the act, making this crime very different from "normal" crimes.

The act of killing another person, or even several other persons, is not ordinarily an act of genocide or, indeed, an international crime at all. What makes the act of killing an instance of genocide is the intent behind it, what the ICTR calls the aim of destruction of the group. This aim in the crime of genocide does not refer to a person's understanding that what he or she is doing is an instance of killing or even that killing is what is directly aimed at. Such an aim is the way to characterize the intent behind the crime of killing. But for the crime of genocide, there is an additional special element of intent: the intent to destroy the group. This element is already a part of the act element in the aim mentioned in the genocide convention's description of the relevant acts. This aim transforms a normal act of killing, along with similar acts by others, and makes it into an act of genocide due to the additional aim of the destruction of a group. The intent element in genocide is what makes the crime into an international crime at all.

The act element does not appear to be able to stand on its own conceptually as a separate element of the crime of genocide. The third and fourth acts listed refer to intention outright in the description of these act elements. The fifth act also needs some reference to intention, since it is not clear what would be meant by the notion of transferring children from one group to another without the intention to remove them permanently. The first and second acts appear to be more straightforward act categories. Killing and causing bodily or emotional harm to individuals are relatively discrete acts. But the category is not merely killing individuals but killing or harming members of a group. Here there is an aim element that must be added to the more straightforward act element. One must aim by killing an individual to kill a member of a specific group. It is for these reasons that the act element is not conceptually isolatable from the intention element.

Two recent international court cases, one from the International Criminal Tribunal for Yugoslavia (ICTY) in The Hague and the other from the ICTR in Arusha, Africa, illustrate what it might mean that an individual has acted in a way that makes him or her responsible for a political crime such as genocide. In the Yugoslav case, a particularly vicious individual stole into concentration camps to kill. In the Rwanda case, a town leader who seemingly could have stopped mass killing did not act to do so. In both cases, while there were many things the defendants could have been prosecuted for, a decision was made to prosecute these individuals for genocide. Examining these cases sheds light on how these individuals' acts contributed to the crime of genocide as opposed to the crime of murder or the putative crime of neglect (perhaps even reckless neglect) of one's duty to preserve human life. The key consideration in ultimately determining their guilt or innocence was not how they acted but what their aims were in so acting and, specifically, whether either of these defendants was acting in a way that was designed to harm individuals as members of a group, as a way of destroying that group.

In the Yugoslav case, a Serb civilian, Goran Jelisic, snuck into Bosnian concentration camps and killed at least a dozen Muslims, claiming to be the "Serbian Adolph." The trial chamber of the ICTY claimed that it was "theoretically possible" that a single perpetrator could commit an act of genocide.[10] In this case, Jelisic displayed a discriminatory motive in that he attacked these people because he hated Muslims. Nonetheless, these were seemingly random murders. Jelisic killed people who were Muslims, and he had hatred against Muslims. But in order to be convicted of genocide, the accused had to act in a way that had as its aim to kill members of the Muslim group and thus destroy the group.

Here following a plan aimed at destroying a group would indeed link the individual accused to the larger political harm and make him individually guilty of the political harm, of genocide.[11] Was Jelisic following a plan or not? This is not merely a matter of looking at his acts but of also considering what others were doing. If his acts were random in that, while based on hatred of Muslims, they were not part of a larger plan, then he could not be found guilty of genocide. If he were not following such a plan, then his acts would still meet the elements of persecution, as a crime against humanity, but not as the separate elements of genocide. The Jelisic trial court ruled that the defendant was not guilty of genocide since his assaults on Muslims were more likely random than planned. The conceptual question is this: How does one tell when an act is random as opposed to being part of a plan? The answer is that we must look to the defendant's intent. Hence, the act element appears to be subordinate to the intent element.

In the Rwandan case, a Rwandan civilian political leader, Jean-Paul Akayesu, apparently knew that Hutu townspeople were killing Tutsi civilians in large numbers. He was present at many of the killings and participated in several of these killings. The ICTR trial chamber claimed that genocidal intent can be inferred "from the general context of the perpetration of other culpable acts directed at the same group, whether these acts were committed by the same offender or others." Other factors include whether one group was targeted for attack and another group was excluded from these attacks.[12] Here, command responsibility was crucial, inasmuch as Akayesu knew what was occurring and could have, but did not, stop it from occurring. His participation in some of the killings, his knowledge that a group was being targeted in the larger plan, plus his intentional failure to stop the killings made him responsible for what occurred and, ultimately, for genocide. The conceptual question is, why should his failure to act be viewed as part of a plan? Should the plans of others change what might otherwise have been random acts of violence into acts aimed at members of a group? This is a variation of Arendt's worry expressed at the beginning of this chapter. What matters is the defendant's aim to allow a genocidal plan to succeed.

Two possible bases exist for linking an individual's acts to the crime of genocide. One avenue is for an individual to follow the plan of a group that has as its aim the destruction of another group. A second avenue is for an individual to be aware of the ongoing plan of a group to destroy another group, to be able to stop such a plan, and to choose not to. In both cases, it is the intention of the defendant that makes a defendant's acts complicit in the larger political harm. The acts alone are not enough to link the individual to a political crime. The positive or negative role that the accused intends to play is what makes him or her responsible for the political harm of genocide.

THE INTENT ELEMENT IN THE CRIME OF GENOCIDE

The key to justifying the prosecution of an individual for a political crime such as genocide is to show that an individual was aiming to do a certain thing as one significant step toward destroying a group. Normally, this means that the individual intended his or her act to advance a plan that had harmful large-scale consequences. Intentional participation in such a plan makes the individual complicit in the harms that result from carrying out that plan. Various problems arise in construing this element of intent. How large a proportion of the group must the individual actually intend to destroy, and, if only a small part, how is genocide to be distinguished from other group-based crimes, such as persecution or discrimination? There may also be some question whether it makes sense to hold individuals accountable for this supposedly most serious of all international crimes merely on the basis of genocidal intentions in those cases in which their actual acts were fairly inconsequential.

Arendt and others have also raised the related objection that many of those who participate in mass atrocities do so intending to obey orders or perhaps to advance what are perceived as legitimate plans of the state rather than specifically to do harm. This seems improbable. Participation in a plan of genocide usually involves some knowledge of the likely consequences of one's actions. Those participating in a plan of genocide may intentionally deceive themselves, but those who truly participate in the destruction of a people or social group usually intend to do so, and understand that what they are doing is wrong, even if they also intend to follow orders or advance some other collective project.

Consider the case of Slobodan Milosevic. He has not denied that intentional participation in the extermination of Muslims is wrong. Rather, his defense has been either the claim that this was not at all the plan he participated in or the related claim that this plan was only to remove people who had demonstrated their own genocidal intent so that genocidal ethnic cleansing was a kind of self-defense on the part of the Serbs. Milosevic was of course a leader, not merely a follower. So we could consider Milosevic to be someone like Jelisic. Jelisic claimed that he acted out of hatred for Muslims rather than out of an intention to exterminate Muslims. If this is accurate, then Jelisic cannot plausibly be convicted of genocide. It is interesting to note, however, that Jelisic, like Milosevic, did not argue that he did not know that it would have been wrong to intend to destroy the group Muslims. Indeed, the presentation of his defense suggests that he certainly did know that such genocidal acts were wrong. Those who engage in a plan of genocide will find it very hard to argue that they were not aware that genocide is wrong.

Genocide is currently an international crime that is prosecuted against individual persons. The defining intent element is that acts (enumerated earlier) have been "committed with the intent to destroy, in whole or in part, a national, ethnical, racial or religious group, as such."[13] It is rare that an individual person intends to destroy an entire population or group. For this reason, the 1948 genocide convention adds the words "in whole or in part" to the definition of *genocide*. The ICTR specifically said that "genocide does not imply the actual extermination of a group in its entirety."[14] Yet the International Law Commission wrote, in 1966, that the intention element in genocide "must be [the intent] to destroy the group 'as such' meaning as a separate and distinct entity, and not merely some individuals because of their membership in a particular group."[15]

There is another international crime, persecution (one of the crimes against humanity), that is meant to cover murders or tortures directed at individuals because of their group membership. According to the ICTR's *Akayesu* judgment, the point of prosecutions for these crimes is to "protect civilian populations from persecution." On the other hand, the point of prosecutions for genocide is to "protect certain groups from extermination or attempted extermination."[16] The difference between persecution and genocide is not the specific acts committed, which may be the same, but rather the defendant's intent. More is required than that an individual person acted in a way that contributed to a genocidal plan and that the person knew that the plan could destroy a group. The individual must also have intended to destroy the group, and this is the essential element in the crime of genocide.[17]

The United States attached an interpretive declaration to Article II of the Genocide Convention: "the phrase 'intent to destroy in whole or in part, a national, ethnical, racial, or religious group as such' appearing in Article II means the specific intent to destroy, in whole or *substantial* part."[18] So, from all of these sources, the idea seems clear enough that the individual person must intend to destroy a substantial part of a group and not merely an individual person who happens to be a member of the group, even if the point of killing that member was because of that person's group membership. To be guilty of genocide, one must participate in such a plan and intend to do so, but one need not have directly committed the harm, such as the killing of members of a group.

Individuals can hate whole groups and can even intend to discriminate against all of the members of a group, but generally individuals do not intend to destroy whole groups. Individuals may wish that whole groups would be destroyed. Yet, even this is not the same as intending their destruction. With regard to intending to destroy a group, it must be plausible to think that one could do so. It does not make sense to say that one intends to do that which one knows one could not do, only perhaps that one intended to do that which turns out to be impossible to do. It is generally implausible for one person to be able to destroy an entire group, and hence it is also implausible for that person to intend to do so. It is plausible for a person to destroy a group in part, depending on the size of the part. Hence, it is plausible to knowingly intend to destroy a group in part.[19]

It is plausible for an individual to intend to destroy a part of a group, since at the limit an individual is part of a group and one individual can destroy another individual. It is nonetheless generally implausible to intend to destroy a group by planning to kill just one member of that group. But if one intends to destroy a part of a group and the part that one intends to destroy is itself a "substantial" part of the group, then it can plausibly be said that the intent was to destroy the group, and this is something that individuals can both intend and accomplish, but only with the help of many others. This is why the United States made the qualification to the genocide convention that the "in part" aspect of the intent element must refer to a "substantial part."

The emerging jurisprudence on the crime of genocide distinguishes between "the collective genocidal intent underlying the plan" and the "genocidal intent of the individual."[20] The *Jelisic* court looked for "an affirmed resolve to destroy in whole or in part a group as such."[21] This was the link thought to be necessary between the collective and the individual genocidal intent. This standard can be difficult to meet, and the ICTY Trial Chamber said that it was not met in the *Jelisic* case since Jelisic appeared to use a random-selection mechanism in his killing. Indeed, the ICTY said that "it will be very difficult in practice to provide proof of the genocidal intent of an individual if the crimes committed were not widespread and if the crime charged is not backed by an organization or a system."[22] Hence, the emerging jurisprudence requires that there be more than a plan. There must also be a group, normally an organized group, of which the defendant is a part, that has attempted to carry out this plan. While it may be possible for an individual, on his or her own, to hatch a plan to destroy a group and carry out that plan, in practice it will be very difficult to prove genocide in such cases.

There is a fairly large conceptual gap between intending to destroy a part of a group and intending to destroy the group as a whole. The larger the group that one intends to destroy, the greater the likelihood that the group as a whole is the real target.[23] But what of the parts of groups that are geographically confined and isolated? If the relevant part of the group is confined geographically, can it really be true that the intent to destroy this part of the group should count as the intent to destroy the group as a whole? Should intent make any difference?

The crime of genocide requires the intent to destroy a group "as such." The intent to destroy only a part of a group must be in furtherance of the destruction of the group as such. This complicates the required element of individual genocidal intent. To be guilty of genocide, either the defendant must have an intent to destroy a whole group as such, or the defendant must have the intent to destroy a part of a group and must have the further aim of ultimately destroying the group as such. Thus, even the "in part" aspect of genocidal intent must be accompanied by the further intent ultimately to destroy the group. It is not enough to intend ultimately to destroy only this particular geographically isolated part of the group, even though it is enough to intend at the moment only to destroy that part of the group. The "as such" requirement means that one must also intend at the moment only to destroy that part of the group, thereby ultimately to destroy the group as a whole.[24] Recall the International Law Commission's statement that "the intention must be to destroy the group 'as such' meaning as a separate and distinct entity" and that the way to accomplish this is to commit an act against an individual because of his or her membership in a group "as an incremental step in the overall objective of destroying the group."[25]

The acts and intentions of individuals can thus contribute to the political crime of genocide. International criminal jurisprudence has specified the requisite act and intent necessary to make an individual guilty of genocide. The individual's act must in some sense be connected to the larger act of group destruction to the extent that, with the acts of others, it could plausibly achieve its goal. The individual's intent must be not only destruction of a part of a group but also, ultimately, destruction of the larger group as a whole.

POLITICAL CRIMES

A political crime is a crime that is committed by many people, many of whom have done nothing directly harmful themselves. To call something a political crime is to say that it is a crime committed by a collectivity, typically by a state or an organized group of people in some way acting systematically. Typically, the group that commits a political crime has a structure that endures through time such that it makes sense to say of the group that it is responsible for what has occurred, even though no current members played a role in the harm for which the group is held responsible.[26] Arendt's position, discussed earlier, is that it is not plausible to hold individuals accountable for what organizations do, especially since organizations have lives of their own that do not correspond to the life of the individual and since current members would then be held responsible for what earlier members have done.

Karl Jaspers provides useful insights into the distinction between political crimes and legal or moral crimes, in his discussion of political and moral guilt.[27] Jasper describes political guilt as guilt such that citizens must bear the consequences of the deeds of the state whose power governs them and under whose laws they live. Everybody is co-responsible for the way he or she is governed. Jurisdiction rests with the power and the will of the victor in both domestic and foreign politics.[28]

Political guilt is to be contrasted both with legal guilt, which Jaspers says involves crimes that are "capable of objective proof and violate unequivocal laws," and with moral guilt, which involves one's own judgment of another's personal deeds. In legal guilt, jurisdiction lies with the courts; in moral guilt, jurisdiction lies with the conscience. But in the case of political guilt, "success decides," and "natural and international law serves to mitigate arbitrary power."

Jaspers's reference to international law is noteworthy, since in Jaspers's day (the 1940s) international law had only begun to include international criminal tribunals. Indeed, international criminal law would have been a kind of oxymoron. But today there has to be a blending of categories whereby political crimes such as genocide are indeed judged not by victors' success but by judges acting according to international law and assigning legal guilt. Nonetheless, Jaspers's main point is still relevant that in political crimes, political guilt belongs to many people and that many in political society will be co-responsible. But how that political co-responsibility translates into legal guilt remains a deeply divisive matter, even if not the purely subjective matter Jaspers thought it was.

In political crimes, a lot of people, even if not all people in a political community, are co-responsible, and hence many more people than those who directly acted to cause harm are also guilty of the harms that have transpired. It is for this reason that the emphasis on intent is so crucial for justifying the prosecutions of individuals for genocide. Genocide is itself a crime that is an attack against individual persons, on groups of persons, and against humanity. But it is very different from more ordinary crimes, such as persecution and discrimination. Persecution and discrimination are directed at a group and might also be quite widespread, but there is a clearly harmful act for each individual actor. Genocide is much more like a conspiracy than an individual crime.

In normative terms, there is shared criminal responsibility for those individual members of organizations who commit political crimes. The main point to be noticed here, in keeping with the views of Jaspers and Arendt, is that crimes of states and other organizations involve acts of many individuals, many of whom are merely blindly following orders, but some of whom are giving those orders, and others of whom are following orders but share the goals of those who are giving the orders. For this reason, it is plausible, especially concerning people in the second and third categories mentioned earlier, that individuals be held criminally liable for their roles in these so-called political crimes. There is normative implausibility only when an individual is held criminally liable for all that a state has done. When one speaks of shared rather than sole responsibility or liability, the evident normative implausibility does not arise.

Shared responsibility involves responsibility not merely of those who directly cause harm but also of those who cause harm indirectly and in other ways are complicit in a crime. A person is complicit in a crime if he or she intentionally participates in a collective endeavor that brings about the crime. All those people who are complicit in a crime can plausibly be said to share in responsibility for the crime. Once one plays a role or generally participates in an event and does so intentionally, one becomes a normatively proper subject of responsibility.[29] Not only those who directly cause harm but also those who do so indirectly can be plausibly said to be responsible for that harm.

Indirect causation of harm that is nonetheless intentional is a plausible basis for ascriptions of responsibility, even of ascriptions of criminal liability, if it is intentional. Direct causation of harm is necessary to create sole responsibility for a harm. But even in that case, it is somewhat doubtful that one person should be forced to shoulder all of the responsibility when there were others whose indirect help made them complicit in the harm. If normative plausibility of responsibility ascriptions is connected to what one did, then not only direct causation but also indirect causation should give rise to responsibility. Forming an intention can give rise to responsibility in the same way. In this sense, shared responsibility is much more plausible than sole responsibility when more than one person participates in a harm. Hence, it is normatively plausible that individuals who are complicit but not the direct causes of harm be held liable for their share in these harms.

Jaspers and Arendt would challenge the possibility of objective proof in the case of political crimes. For while it may be conceptually and normatively plausible to assign guilt or blame for each person's role in a political crime such as genocide, there may appear to be, as in conspiracy cases, overwhelming practical difficulties with doing so, and because of this it may be nearly inconceivable that trials could ever take place. There are difficult practical problems with legally proving intent and in establishing the kind of intent that seems necessary for genocide to occur. But these practical difficulties can be overcome.

Recall that in the *Jelisic* case, what mattered was whether his acts were random or designed to be part of a larger, genocidal plan. If his aim was to be part of a genocidal plan already shown to exist, then he is complicit in it and thus plausibly responsible for it. In the *Akayesu* case, what mattered was whether his omissions were designed to allow the genocide to continue or not. Given that Akayesu was a high-ranking political leader, his intentional failure to act definitely allowed a plan to be carried out that he otherwise could have stopped. He was thus responsible for the role he played in the ensuing mass harms. In the *Jelisic* case, the evidence turned out to be inconclusive, and Jelisic was exonerated of genocide charges. In the *Akayesu* case, the evidence was conclusive, and Akayesu was convicted of genocide. In both cases, it was plausible that these individual defendants could be judged to be criminally guilty of genocide.

Leaders such as Akayesu will be easier to convict than minor players, since their leadership roles in the society mean that they are more influential in the setting and maintaining of mass plans. The relatively small fish such as Jelisic should be harder to convict than the leaders and, when convicted, should be given lesser punishments than those given the leaders, since the small fish's role in the setting and maintaining of the plan is much less influential.[30] But even the small fish can sometimes plausibly be held responsible for the part he or she played in a political crime such as genocide.

SHARING RESPONSIBILITY FOR GENOCIDE

There are positive advantages of prosecuting and punishing individuals for political crimes that become clear when one views individual political responsibility as a form of shared responsibility. Shared responsibility is that form of responsibility according to which the individual is responsible for the contribution that the individual has made to a larger plan of crime or the contribution that an individual makes to a continued pattern of behavior that makes certain crimes more likely than not to occur. So there are both active and passive contributions that can be counted as being contributions to a larger plan of crime. The leaders of a group are particularly subject to accountability for collective crimes based on their passive, as well as their active, contributions. Shared responsibility generally makes the most sense for concerted efforts undertaken by a number of people, each intentionally participating in what should be viewed as a collective action.[31]

The major normative advantage of employing individual criminal punishment for political crimes such as genocide is that this makes clear that in the end it is individuals who are the perpetrators of these collective crimes. Punishment is normally a fitting response when individuals are responsible for having done, or contributed, to harm. When individuals share in responsibility for harm, they should also share in punishment for harm. To do less than this in response to harm is to succumb to the temptation to let people off the hook merely because large numbers are complicit. Even if all members of society share at least some of the blame for harm, there is nothing in principle wrong with having each member of a society experience some punishment, although jail time is almost surely excluded (in such cases) in any reasonably large society.

Contrary to what Jaspers and Arendt claim, an international criminal tribunal that metes out punishment need not be a form of victor's justice where success in battle is the determiner of who gets to judge whom. Generally, the states from which the judges of the new International Criminal Court will be drawn have not themselves been engaged in any form of war, nor has the United Nations that sponsors the court. But this does not mean that bias will be easily eliminated on the part of those who are judging.[32] All that needs to be established at this point is that it is plausible that an international criminal tribunal could truly represent the world's interests rather than merely the interests of the victorious parties in a particular war. Hence, it will not necessarily be true that success or strength must be the basis for judging in international criminal tribunals.

Nonetheless, politics, in another sense of the term from its use in "political" crime, may still intrude into the judicial process. Especially when political crimes are alleged, with their hard-to-pin-down emphasis on the intentions and attitudes of individuals, considerations of ideology will often surface. While politics do not always take the form of so-called victor's justice, a strong Western bias is readily apparent in the International Criminal Court, where Western-style cross-examination and the adversarial method generally will be the order of the day. Defense lawyers trained in non-Western legal systems find it difficult to operate in international criminal courts. This problem is unlikely to go away, since courts must follow some model, whether Western or non-Western, and hence someone will be disadvantaged.

One of the reasons why convictions are so hard to obtain in such courts is that genocide, the destruction of a group or a people, is ultimately a collective crime rather than an individual crime. Courts are generally not well set up for such crimes. Perhaps more important, many people's moral intuitions are offended by the thought of collective responsibility or punishment. Even if it is clear that a state is responsible for perpetrating a harm against a group, it is unsettling to think that the members of a state would be held responsible for the harm that has clearly been done by their state. It is troubling to contemplate the possibility of collective responsibility for the harms of one's group. But, such a strong view is not necessary to defend the position that criminal tribunals can appropriately judge individual guilt for political crimes such as genocide.

Consider the bombing of the World Trade Center towers.[33] If United States prosecutors are correct, the nineteen people who boarded planes were only the tip of the iceberg of that conspiracy. Zacarias Moussaoui, the so-called twentieth hijacker, did not contribute anything directly harmful to the September 11 deaths, and yet federal prosecutors are seeking the death penalty in his case. Moussaoui's alleged criminal acts include attending a training camp in Afghanistan operated by al Qaida, taking flying lessons, buying flight-training videos, researching crop dusting, buying knives, joining a gym, buying fighting gloves and shin guards, and receiving money from an alleged terrorist in Hamburg, Germany.[34] It was also alleged that he funneled money that he received from Germany to the other hijackers. Nonetheless, at the time of the bombing of the World Trade Center towers, Moussaoui was in jail and had been in jail for several months. Yet, he is said to be a part of the conspiracy to blow up the World Trade Center towers and as guilty as those who actually flew the planes into the towers. For this reason, the federal prosecutors seek the death penalty in his case.

This seems an odd result. Moussaoui is not just as guilty as those who directly caused the harm. But, assuming that the allegations are correct, Moussaoui may be guilty to a more limited degree because of what he intended to do. If Moussaoui had been the ringleader and had orchestrated the event, he might be just as guilty as those who actually flew the planes into the World Trade Center towers. But this was not the case. Moussaoui was at most a minor player who perhaps did play some role for which he should be held guilty and punished, assuming that the facts are indeed as they have been alleged to be. Prosecutors assert that he intended to be on one of the planes or that he intended to be one of the backups for one of those who boarded the planes. In the end, though, Moussaoui did not cause harm directly. He is not as guilty as those who did.

If Moussaoui was a fellow conspirator, he should be found guilty of participating in the crime and should be convicted and punished for his own role (and only for his own role) in the attack. It may be true that Moussaoui shared some of the guilt for the bombing of the World Trade Center towers, even though he was not there and hence did not play a direct causal role in the harms. One of the questions asked in conspiracy law is whether someone knew about the plan and understood that pursuing the plan risked loss of life. In the genocide case, the question is whether the accused intended to destroy a group. Similar things are true of genocide that are true of conspiracies. In genocide, it is quite appropriate to say that many people share in the responsibility for the collective harm. While it is sometimes difficult to determine precisely the extent of each person's share in the guilt for such harms, these determinations can be made, as prosecutors have made similar determinations on almost a daily basis in conspiracy cases.

People such as Moussaoui, if they have demonstrated the intention to cause harm in a conspiracy-like arrangement but do not themselves directly cause the main harm in question, should still legitimately be tried and punished for what they have done. This does not mean that it would be justifiable to punish all of the participants in the same way. Lesser participants deserve lesser punishments. Not only must the punishment fit the crime, but, especially in complex cases, it must also fit the degree of guilt. Minor players generally do not have as much guilt in political crimes as do major players, and punishment schemes should reflect this fact.

International prosecutions for genocide should focus primarily on political leaders, and should pay much more attention to *mens rea* than to *actus reus,* as is actually reflected in a proper reading of the elements of the crime of genocide in the 1948 Genocide Convention and in the way that the new International Criminal Court has interpreted the criminal elements of genocide. Through a focus on the criminal intention, it is possible to overcome the justificatory hurdle of prosecuting an individual for what is largely a political crime. Responsibility for such crimes is best seen as a form of shared responsibility where the leaders of the group or institution should be singled out for their intentional acts of planning the mass human rights abuse. While it is difficult for criminal tribunals to deal with political crimes, it is not, as Arendt claims, conceptually or normatively "inconceivable" or implausible.

Mass human rights abuses such as genocide involve the participation, at many levels, of large segments of a population and not normally the single, isolated acts of an individual perpetrator. But it does not follow from this that it is implausible to establish individual legal guilt for political crimes. The difficulty is that individuals seem to be held liable for what others have done. But where many participate in harm, it is at least conceivable to assign criminal guilt and punishment for precisely what each one did and for what each intended to do. While practical difficulties abound, it is plausible to apportion guilt to contribution in the collective enterprise. Hence, in some cases, the international community should prosecute and punish individuals for political crimes such as genocide.

NOTES

1. Hannah Arendt, *Eichmann in Jerusalem,* NY: Viking Books, Postscript, p. 298, 1964.

2. William A. Schabas, *Genocide in International Law,* Cambridge: Cambridge University Press, 2000, p. 79, citing UN Doc. A/C.6/SR.132 (Fitzmaurice, United Kingdom).

3. Berel Lang, "The Concept of Genocide," *The Philosophical Forum,* vol. XVI, nos. 1–2, Fall 1984–85, p. 7.

4. Hannah Arendt, "Organized Guilt and Universal Responsibility," *Jewish Frontier,* 1948, reprinted in *Collective Responsibility,* eds. Larry May and Stacey Hoffman, Savage, MD: Rowman & Littlefield, 1992, p. 278.

5. See Mark Osiel's wonderful book *Mass Atrocity, Ordinary Evil, and Hannah Arendt,* New Haven, CT: Yale University Press, 2001.

6. Arendt actually makes several significant objections to criminal prosecution of midlevel figures such as Adolph Eichmann. Perhaps the most famous of her criticisms is that these individuals were not intending to do wrong but only to do

what they had been ordered to do. I only touch on this point in the second section of this chapter. Rather, I focus on a much less-well-known criticism concerning the sheer number of people involved and the inability to distinguish those who are guilty from those who are not. For an excellent discussion of the more famous of her charges, see Osiel, *Mass Atrocity*, chapter 2.

7. For a discussion of the difference between various models of responsibility, see Larry May, *Sharing Responsibility*, Chicago: University of Chicago Press, 1992.

8. Convention on the Prevention and Punishment of the Crime of Genocide, adopted Dec. 9, 1948, entered into force Jan. 12, 1951, 78 U.N.T.SW. 277, Art. II.

9. The Prosecutor of the Tribunal against Georges Anderson Nderubumwe Rutaganda, International Criminal Tribunal for Rwanda, Case No. ICTR-96-3, Judgment and Sentence, 6 December 1999, para. 52.

10. *Prosecutor v. Goran Jelisic*, Case No. IT-95-10, Trial Chamber Judgment, December 14, 1999, para. 100.

11. *Prosecutor v. Goran Jelisic*, Case No. IT-95-10, Appeals Chamber Judgment, July 5, 2001, para. 4.

12. *Prosecutor v. Jean-Paul Akayesu*, Case No. ICTR-96-4-T, Trial Chamber Judgment, Sept. 2, 1998, para. 523.

13. Genocide Convention, Art. II.

14. Akayesu Trial Chamber Judgment, para. 497.

15. Report of the International Law Commission on the Work of its 48th Session, UN GAOR, 51st Sess., Supp. No. 10, at 87, UN Doc. A/51/10 (1996) at 88.

16. Akayesu Trial Chamber Judgment, para. 469.

17. See Alexander K. A. Greenawalt, "Rethinking Genocidal Intent: The Case for a Knowledge-Based Interpretation," *Columbia Law Review*, vol. 99, no. 8, December 1999, pp. 2259–2294.

18. My italics, quoted in Guglielmo Verdirame, "The Genocide Definition in the Jurisprudence of the Ad Hoc Tribunals," *International and Comparative Law Quarterly*, vol. 49, no. 3, July 2000, p. 580.

19. Intending is like promising; it has a performative aspect. Normally, one cannot promise to do something and yet not have any plan to do so, and similarly one cannot intend to do something and yet not have a plan to do so. Of course, one could have a plan that was doomed from the start. But normally one cannot have an intention to do something that one knows one has a doomed plan to accomplish. It simply would not be intending. And just as one cannot make a promise that one intends not to keep, one cannot intend to do something that one knows one cannot accomplish. Intending is different from attempting. In the case of attempting, there is some sense to the concept of attempting to do the impossible. If I know in advance that I will not be able to influence my dean, I may attempt to do so anyway, and my colleagues would not be talking nonsense when they said that I had made a valiant attempt. But it would be nearly inconceivable that I would be said to have intended to do the impossible. This is one of the reasons why the "in part" is added to the intent element of the crime of genocide.

20. See Verdirame, p. 588.

21. Jelisic Trial Chamber Judgment, para. 107.

22. *Ibid.*, para. 101.

23. See William A. Schabas, "Was Genocide Committed in Bosnia and Herzegovina? First Judgments of the International Criminal Tribunal for the Former Yugoslava," *Fordham International Law Journal*, vol. 25, no. 1, November 2001, p. 40.

24. Perhaps it could be argued that the destruction of a whole group is different from the destruction of a group as such. Intending to destroy a whole group might mean doing what is necessary to bring about the group's end all at once by somehow assaulting the entire group. Intending to destroy a part of a group would be less than this—that is, intending to do what is necessary to bring about part of a group's demise by assaulting part of the group. Both forms would involve the ultimate aim of destroying the group as such, not merely ending the lives of the individual members of the group. Even if we take this route, it remains unclear what it would mean to destroy a group in whole as such.

25. Cited in Greenawalt, p. 2265.

26. A surprising result of all of this is that some groups, such as the mafia, can commit political crimes. This is one reason why I later explore the analogy between conspiracy law and the international law concerning genocide.

27. While Hannah Arendt and Karl Jaspers held somewhat different views of these matters, I ignore these differences here and treat them as having roughly the same view, as the authors themselves have maintained.

28. Karl Jaspers, *The Question of German Guilt*, NY: Capricorn Books, 1947, p. 31.

29. See Kutz, *Complicity*, NY: Cambridge University Press, 2000.

30. I defend this view in chapter 6 of my book *Crimes against Humanity*, Cambridge U.P., 2004.

31. For an analysis of collective action see chapter 2 of my book *The Morality of Groups*, Notre Dame, IN: University of Notre Dame Press, 1987. For more on the nature of shared responsibility and how it is related to collective action, see my book *Sharing Responsibility*, Chicago: University of Chicago Press, 1992.

32. The major disadvantage of trials for political crimes is that it is very difficult to find unbiased witnesses and impartial judges when nearly everyone in a society is one of the perpetrators of the crime. When all are guilty, there is little possibility of having the nonguilty as judges and, hence, little possibility in that society's having impartial trials. In addition, when all are guilty, the testimony of one's neighbors or coworkers will not be believable since it is so likely to be biased by self-interested considerations. Of course one way to get around the first of these problems is to have the judging party be selected from outside the society in question, which is what international criminal tribunals have been primarily constructed to do. Unfortunately, these tribunals have yet to figure out an answer to the latter problem, since even when a trial is held far away from the society where the crime occurred, one will still need witnesses from that society, and bringing them hundreds or thousands of miles from home does not necessarily make their testimony any more trustworthy.

33. This is an example that may not be technically classified as genocide but that concerns large-scale harm committed by a political group. I employ this example to illustrate the conspiracy model of understanding why even some minor players should be prosecuted for political crimes.

34. John Gibeaut, "Prosecuting Moussaoui," *ABA Journal*, July 2002, p. 41.

10

Human Rights and the Rule of Law: Sovereignty and the International Criminal Court

Kenneth Henley

The creation of the International Criminal Court (ICC) raises questions about the nature of state sovereignty in relation to the rule of law. The ICC is part of the international protection of human rights through an enforcement regime that already includes other tribunals, customary international law, and various conventions or treaties, some of which create universal jurisdiction in municipal courts for specific violations of core human rights. The long-term goal of the entire project is to bring the effective rule of law to the fundamental core of human rights. Some human rights norms cannot appropriately become part of such an enforcement regime within a state or through international institutions. Strong Hobbesian or Rousseauian theories of state sovereignty imply that no human rights of any kind should prevail against the state, but most states now recognize some fundamental civil rights in their internal institutions. The same thing should be true at the international level. Just as the rule of law requires that there be no single unlimited site of sovereignty within the state, so too the international community will benefit by dispersing sovereignty and protecting universal human rights through judges and the rule of law. The perception of opposition between state sovereignty and complementary international judicial implementation of the most fundamental human rights results from an untenable conception of sovereignty and the state.

Perhaps the most puzzling aspect of human rights discourse has been what may be called the "puzzle of vindication": the sense that talk of human rights is often mere hortatory rhetoric. It is not simply that there is no clear, assigned correlative duty to seek, however imperfectly, to implement and vindicate the asserted rights. To be disturbed by the puzzle, one need not accept the analysis of rights that denies the logical possibility of a right without a correlative duty. The puzzle is that there seems to be no practical reality to supposed human rights, not even an indirect connection to human institutions or practices (even without assigned correlative duties). Nor does there seem to be any consensus about which rights should be universal and who possesses them. If one supposes, for example, that women share in universal human rights,[1] then some response is needed for nations such as Saudi Arabia, which abstained from the Universal Declaration of Human Rights because of objections to equality for women (and objections to the right to change one's religion).[2] Similarly, the assertion that any person detained by a government has a right to impartial adjudication seems to be weakened as a universal right when sovereign states disdain to implement this right, even when it is nominally protected by law.[3] This puzzle of vindication was ironically emphasized by the adoption of the universal declaration, which was dependent upon rejection of its bindingness upon sovereign states.[4] Now the puzzle of vindication may disappear for a crucial subset of fundamental human rights: the International Criminal Court seeks "an end to impunity" for those who commit genocide, war crimes, and crimes against humanity.[5]

The Rome Statute of the ICC has great rule-of-law virtues, in contrast to ad hoc tribunals, such as the one established at Nuremberg, the International Tribunal for the Former Yugoslavia, or the International Tribunal for Rwanda. It is arguable whether these ad hoc tribunals have relied on ex post facto law, but certainly the jurisdiction, authority, and procedure of these tribunals were not established beforehand by any kind of law, treaty, or convention. The Rome Statute of the ICC respects the fundamental maxim *nullum crimen sine lege* (no crime without law),[6] strengthened by an explicit restriction against extension by analogy in the definition of a crime and the commitment that all ambiguities of definition be resolved in favor of the accused.[7] The ICC also delimits territorial considerations relevant to its jurisdiction in a way that is not arbitrary or ad hoc. Except when there is a direct referral by the Security Council (comparable to the mode of origin of the ad hoc Yugoslav and Rwandan tribunals), the court's jurisdiction extends only to conduct within a state party or within a state that has accepted the jurisdiction of the court or the conduct of a national of a state party.[8] This is in accordance with the rule of law to a much greater extent than the territorial restrictions of the ad hoc tribunals, which exercised jurisdiction with no basis in prior agreement or law as to the territory included. The same arbitrariness infects the starting dates of the Yugoslav and Rwandan tribunals—not only is there procedural retroactivity, but there are also dates attached to the retroactivity. The ICC scrupulously promulgates the temporal limits of its jurisdiction, including the time needed to end jurisdiction by withdrawing from the statute.[9]

Powerful states, which engage in armed international interventions, understandably fear that politically motivated prosecutions might occur in the ICC. But unjustified political prosecutions are sufficiently guarded against in the Rome Statute. The statute establishes only backup, complementary jurisdiction for the ICC regarding the crimes of genocide, crimes against humanity, war crimes, and perhaps eventually (if there is ever a definition) the crime of aggression. The statute places the primary responsibility to prosecute upon the state parties themselves, within their own legal systems, if the accused are within their jurisdiction. The ICC's jurisdiction is "complementary to national criminal jurisdictions."[10] A state party or the Security Council of the United Nations may refer a case to the prosecutor. The prosecutor may also act on his or her own motion, but this requires judicial authorization from the Pretrial Chamber.[11] A case is inadmissible if it is being "investigated or prosecuted by a State which has jurisdiction over it, unless the State is unwilling or unable genuinely to carry out the investigation or prosecution." It is also inadmissible if it has been investigated by the state and if the state has decided not to prosecute, "unless the decision resulted from the unwillingness or inability of the State genuinely to prosecute"; and it is inadmissible if there has already been a trial for the conduct, unless that trial is deemed by the court to have been for the purpose of shielding the person from the court or not to have been independently conducted.[12] It is for the court, not the prosecutor, to determine whether there is a lack of willingness or whether there has been a sham trial. States may appeal decisions of the Pretrial Chamber to the Appeals Chamber regarding any matter concerning the admissibility of a case.[13]

If these judicial safeguards are not sufficient to prevent politically motivated, unjustified prosecutions, there is a final line of protection. The Security Council has the authority to halt prosecutions for a year, and it may then by new resolutions each year halt prosecution for another year.[14] Such a deferral is possible only in the absence of a veto by a permanent member and thus is likely only when a strong case can be made that proceeding with the case would endanger the stability and peace of the international order. Of course, this provision could be used for other purposes than that of halting unjustified prosecutions—for instance, to halt justified prosecutions. But that seems an acceptable arrangement, given the rule-of-law virtues of the ICC when compared to such ad hoc, procedurally (at least) retroactive tribunals as Nuremberg, the International Tribunal for the Former Yugoslavia, and the International Tribunal for Rwanda. Some have argued that with all of the protections of states, especially members of the Security Council, the ICC is of little value.[15] But the final safeguard through the Security Council's authority to halt proceedings is arguably analogous to the political questions doctrine in U.S.

constitutional law. Under this doctrine, the courts may refuse to adjudicate a matter that is seen as being more properly left to other branches of government because of its distinctively political character or because of danger to the integrity of the whole governmental system through judicial encroachment. The difference, of course, is that the Security Council is not a judicial body deciding not to exercise its jurisdiction but a political body deciding to block a judicial body's jurisdiction. But it can be argued that when the Supreme Court decides to invoke the political questions doctrine, the judicial role is all but abandoned. As suggested in the following, there are both practical and normative limits to international criminal tribunals, for there neither is, nor ought there be, a strict world hierarchy of courts (at least in respect to criminal jurisdiction). And so it is appropriate that whether a matter should be removed from the ICC's jurisdiction finally rests, in extraordinary cases, with a very special political, nonjudicial body charged with keeping world peace. The ICC depends upon the United Nations, so the stability of the United Nations is necessary to the ICC's jurisdiction, just as the political integrity of a state is necessary to the jurisdiction of its courts.

Given the safeguards of the statute, a state's refusal to allow the court's jurisdiction, even when its nationals act within the territory of a state party, must rely on an assertion of unlimited sovereignty. And this assertion of impunity, even within other states, seems inconsistent with the obligation under Article 55 of the United Nations Charter to promote observance of human rights.

Some may view this commitment to promote the observance of human rights as being empty because of the abstractness of the concept. And they may find the Universal Declaration of Human Rights unhelpful because it includes so much that cannot be fundamental—for instance, the right to "periodic holidays with pay," in Article 24. This response is unjustified. The commitment to promote observance of human rights must include an obligation to participate in specifying and delimiting fundamental human rights sufficiently to make the obligation practical. The concept of human rights must be made applicable through less-abstract conceptions, and the fundamental must be distinguished from the peripheral or optional. This is a historical process that has been proceeding and needs to continue. There is a necessary distinction to be made between abstract normative concepts and the less-abstract (and more controversial) conceptions that instantiate them. The bare concept of human rights is the abstract idea of potentially enforceable norms specifying justifiable individualized claims belonging to all human beings, simply in virtue of their humanity. Of course, it is possible to be a human rights skeptic, denying that the concept has any instances, regardless of how it is made less abstract through one or another conception. But those who affirm the existence of human rights need to develop a less-abstract conception, bringing the concept down toward application. There are many competing conceptions of human rights, distinguished from each other on various dimensions.

The first dimension differentiating conceptions is the structure of human rights discourse. As described by Rex Martin,[16] rights include a claims-to element and a claims-against element. The claims-to element has a content that is universal within a particular state for civil rights, and the claims-against element is specified by the governmental bodies and institutions of that particular state. For human rights, the claims-to element includes all human beings, and the claims-against element includes all governmental bodies and institutions. But rights, including human rights, are more than claims. "A human right is defective, not as a claim but as a right, in the absence of appropriate practices of recognition and maintenance. The absolute difference between morally valid claims and human rights, then, is that rights do, and claims do not, include such practices within their concept."[17] As used here, this is not equivalent to the thesis of the analytical correlativity of rights and duties. Rather, it has the pragmatic point that to be committed to human rights includes commitment to fostering practices that respect those rights. Practices need not yet be in place for the assertion of the human right to be warranted, but that lack is seen as a defect. Nor need one assert that any particular, detailed rights-supporting practice or institution is necessary—a wide variety of practices, with differing strengths and weaknesses, might be developed. Early-stage practices include beliefs that are connected to developing practices, including institution-reforming and institution-building activities.

Human rights can be viewed as universal civil rights. They are the rights that belong to citizens of the world community, which encompasses not only international institutions but also the shared core of respect for individual dignity within the domestic institutions of states and, above all, within the institutions of constitutional democracies. The idea of world citizenship in the intended sense is not connected to a world government or a worldwide state. There should be many sites of vindication, each bolstering and checking the others. The need to vindicate human rights through the civil rights within states leads naturally to the need to vindicate the most fundamental human rights concurrently through "practices of recognition and maintenance" in international organizations and tribunals such as the International Criminal Court. It is not desirable that there be any hierarchical ordering of the various sites of vindication at the national and various international levels, for doing so would leave the summit of the hierarchy both too powerful and too detached from local circumstances. A world sovereign would be both impracticable and undesirable. Even the world sovereignty of law would be undesirable if it were understood to require a single legal hierarchy of jurisdiction. But neither the ICC nor other practices such as the universal jurisdiction of municipal courts for specified core rights depend on any universal sovereign. The worldwide sovereignty of law will be a desirable and practicable goal only if it consists of diverse legal practices, and the most important will be situated within individual states or unions such as the European Union. The international criminal tribunals occupy a separate and nondominant role. The Rome Statute of the ICC provides one reasonable model of nondominant, complementary jurisdiction.

There is no danger that the principle of complementarity will be circumvented, for the delivery of defendants to the ICC requires the cooperation of individual sovereign states. There is no enforcement arm of the ICC within the sovereign states (whether or not they are state parties) nor any jurisdiction within the states, except that through treaty and by operation of municipal courts and governments in extradition proceedings (as is already the case regarding the jurisdiction of the ad hoc international criminal tribunals).

The jurisdiction of the International Criminal Court will not undermine the existing sovereignty of states. A contrast with the radical change in sovereignty between the U.S. Articles of Confederation and the constitution of 1787 is illuminating. Alexander Hamilton argued that a crucial defect of the articles was that the national government was denied "the power of extending its operations to individuals."[18] Under the articles, each individual state retained full, complete sovereignty. Under the new constitution, "the majesty of the national authority must be manifested through the medium of the Courts of Justice."[19] The ICC does not threaten to bring about any comparable decrease in the sovereign independence of states. Like the ad hoc international criminal tribunals, and the various states' enforcement of universal jurisdiction for certain crimes against humanity, implementation of the ICC will depend upon the municipal courts and governments of the states themselves to either prosecute defendants or hand them over to the international tribunals (or other municipal tribunals exercising universal jurisdiction). There is no enforcement arm or judicial organ of the ICC within the territory of the sovereign states. The ICC will not function as the arm of an international sovereign, reaching out directly into the territories of states.

Different conceptions of human rights may differ according to the epistemological or ontological basis that they give to universality. Both theological and secular conceptions are possible, as are conceptions that are difficult to categorize in such terms. The drafting of the Universal Declaration of Human Rights inspired philosophically fascinating debate about whether to conceptualize human rights as being based on humanity's relation to God. The need to be inclusive, drawing as many as possible into the declaration, led to a neutral, nontheological statement.[20] This result strengthens John Rawls's observation that comprehensive doctrines of the good cannot be the basis for either liberal nation-states or an international order.[21] There needs to be a conception of human rights that avoids competing ontological conceptions by refusing to commit itself to any particular ontology of rights. Working out the content of human rights will achieve the best results through the processes of dialogue, interaction, and institution building found in individual states committed to human rights and through the treaties and conventions that they adopt. Federations such as the European Union and its tribunals can also contribute to this dialogue, as can nongovernmental organizations and the United Nations, including the Commission on Human Rights of the Economic and Social Council, the special tribunal for the former Yugoslavia and that for Rwanda, the International Criminal Court, and future structures.

The concept of human rights presented here has strong similarities to John Rawls's view of public reason's working to develop an overlapping consensus and with Jürgen Habermas's communicative rationality (despite their assertions of disagreement).[22] Immanuel Kant is not normally thought of as being a pragmatist, but his conception of a peaceful international order also relies on a form of public reasoning that even the unethical must recognize because it serves the interests of all. Kant believed that "the problem of setting up a state can be solved even by a nation of devils (so long as they possess understanding)."[23] A pragmatic and dialogic conception of human rights fits the analytical model derived from Rex Martin, requiring the development of functioning institutions and practices that give effect to universal claims and, in giving effect, also further clarify and specify, separating that which is fundamental and capable of universal vindication from that which must remain less than universal and confined to particular kinds of states. The pragmatist proponent of human rights sees the human rights skeptic as being yet another disappointed absolutist. Human rights exist as they evolve within human political life, both within states and internationally. The human rights skeptic is like someone who denies that there are civil rights because there is no Hegelian metaphysical state to undergird their reality.

Attempts to state or specify the content of universal human rights seem to fail in two ways: either they are so abstract that they allow for radically divergent interpretations, or they are so specific that they cannot be expected ever to be implemented, even imperfectly, throughout the international community. Similar conceptual difficulties have arisen with basic civil rights within nation-states, especially federal ones. For instance, the equal protection clause of the Fourteenth Amendment of the U.S. Constitution could not be more abstract, and divergent interpretations abound. On the other hand, the Fifth Amendment right to be indicted by a grand jury seems excessively detailed and historically conditioned. Courts of the United States have developed distinctions and midlevel interpretations of abstract fundamental rights that allow for judicial enforcement.[24] The discarding of the inessential and the further specifying of the fundamental depend upon developing midlevel interpretations within judicial institutions at the international level, just as has been done within municipal law. The process of interpretation requires that there be authoritative interpretive sources. Judicial tribunals are not the only source of authoritative interpretation, but they are the most reliable in developing shared practices. This process cannot proceed at the international level without the participation of the most powerful states.

Thus the practices that make human rights a practical reality are found within that municipal law that recognizes fundamental human rights as civil rights; in municipal courts exercising universal jurisdiction under conventions and treaties concerning fundamental protections (such as the Torture Convention); and (increasingly) in international institutions, including international tribunals.

Rights-protecting practices of this kind should not be understood as being a violation of sovereignty. A distinction must be made between internal and external applications of the concept of sovereignty.[25] Internally, sovereignty belongs to the final political authority of the state, at the apex of the state's system. The internal structure is in some sense pyramidal, though this need not be a simple pyramid, as Hobbes thought: the apex may itself have structure and internal complexity, as long as finality is achievable concerning the exercise of the state's coercive powers. But among states, sovereignty expresses the absence of an apex—each state is independent and formally equal. The international structure is a horizontal grouping of sovereign states, with multiple lines of interaction through international institutions, alliances, treaties, and shared conceptions of international law. Sovereign independence requires the exclusion of other powers from the sovereign state's territory and other jurisdictions. There is no expectation in the international arena of complete finality, or any assumption that all issues can be resolved through the plurality of municipal and international jurisdictions. Some issues may simply remain unresolved or be resolved through war.

Historically, the rule of law within states has emerged concurrently with the final sovereignty of the people, constitutionally limiting themselves through structures that protect individual rights. And so, in terms of governmental functioning, despite the final sovereignty of the people (*imperium populi*), they constitutionally limit themselves through structures that protect individual rights. In a sense, this makes the law itself the ultimate sovereign power (*imperium legum*). Rule-of-law states are committed to core universal human rights within their municipal law and should find little difficulty accepting an international regime that implements core human rights with a complementary jurisdiction, as long as there is no diminution of sovereign independence through intrusion into the state without its consent. States that are not ruled by law internally cannot expect to participate in an international human rights regime without either changing their own systems of government or encountering repeated conflicts with the international community.

A state follows the rule of law within its own legal system to the extent that government proceeds through established, general, prospective laws that are applied impartially by an independent judiciary.[26] Rule-of-law nations do not recognize any sovereign one or many as being above the law. There is no Hobbesian sovereign within such a state. The law itself is sovereign—a conceptual impossibility according to imperativists such as Hobbes.[27] In its corporate capacity, a rule-of-law state may choose to maintain a form of sovereign immunity (as that against private suits), but the natural persons who wield power do so only under the law and can have qualified immunity only within these bounds. The corporate capacity of the state itself is at play in the international arena. In its dealings with other nation-states, rule-of-law states are sovereign in the sense that they are independent—one state does not have rule over another state. The fundamental principle is *par in parem non habet imperium*—"an equal cannot have sovereignty over its equal."

Many politicians and commentators (some with disapproval, some with approval) see the international protection of human rights as limiting state sovereignty both externally and internally.[28] This tendency of opposing camps to see international protection of human rights as eroding sovereignty results from a failure to make distinctions among conceptions of sovereignty and to discard those conceptions that are no longer tenable. The external sovereignty of a state is simply its participation as formally an equal in the various structures of the international community. Some early authors had an almost mystical sense that sovereignty should not be divided. Rousseau vested sovereignty in the General Will, viewed as infallible, indivisible, and inalienable.[29] Hegel imagined an internally unified state, acting as an autonomous individual against the outside world.[30]

Hobbes's conception of sovereignty has had the greatest influence in subordinating all law to sovereignty and denying the possibility of international law without a world sovereign to regulate it. But the absence of a world sovereign need not mean the absence of international law. Each state government enforces the law within its own jurisdiction, through its own judiciary. States coordinate their enforcement of international law through treaties and customs. For rule-of-law states with independent judiciaries, there is no tension between fundamental human rights and their sovereign independence, because it is their own institutions that apply international law. Even Rousseau's absolute sovereign makes general laws that must be interpreted by judges. The application of human rights norms by national or international courts fully respects the sovereignty of the separate states. The complementary jurisdiction of the ICC is no more a threat to state sovereignty than the acceptance of the jurisdiction of a state's own municipal courts.

If a rule-of-law state becomes a state party to the Rome Statute of the ICC, there is no danger of eroding the legal supremacy of its fundamental law. The primary responsibility for prosecution under the statute is placed upon the state party having the accused within its jurisdiction, with all of the legal procedures and protections of its municipal law. If the ICC's Pretrial Chamber unjustifiably deemed nonprosecution unacceptable or a trial a sham, there are safeguards to halt any further proceedings in the ICC, through intercession of the Security Council. Even if the Security Council did not end the matter, municipal judges under their own municipal law would still decide the application of treaty obligations in regard to extradition as long as the accused remained within their jurisdiction.[31] Of course, citizens of one state who find themselves within the jurisdiction of another rule-of-law state will be dealt with under its laws, including questions of extradition either to other states or to international tribunals. Authoritarian or dictatorial states, on the other hand, will not find their internal sovereignty compromised by the recognition of human rights through practices such as the ICC, because their internal sovereign is not law in any case but some powerful one or many whose power is a matter of fact, incapable of erosion except through actual intervention. Such intervention is not at issue in international tribunals but rather a separate matter for either individual states, unions of states, or the Security Council of the United Nations. Wars undertaken to vindicate human rights do indeed directly violate the sovereign independence of the state attacked, but this is a very special case, not to be conflated with the peaceful creation of institutions such as the ICC and the European Court of Human Rights and the recognition of human rights within the municipal law of rule-of-law states.

Citizens of one sovereign state can fall under the jurisdiction of another sovereign state, as when accused of crimes in another state's jurisdiction. There are no conceptual differences if the second jurisdiction is an international tribunal, unless the alleged crime occurs in the citizen's own state. But as long as a state remains a nonparty to the Rome Statute, internal matters cannot come under the ICC's jurisdiction, except by direct referral of the Security Council, on which the permanent members have a veto. This mode of jurisdiction through the Security Council already exists in the form of ad hoc tribunals, so the ICC raises no additional concerns about sovereignty in such cases. For state parties, the jurisdiction of the ICC would extend only to cases in which there was an unjustifiable decision not to prosecute within the state or (implausibly, in the case of rule-of-law states) the ICC found that the prosecution was a sham. There might indeed be no prosecution of government officials or military leaders in matters of genuine controversy, raising the specter of political prosecution. But as explained earlier, the Rome Statute has nearly insurmountable barriers to the ICC's pursuit of such problematic cases, especially if the case concerns a permanent member of the Security Council.

Questions concerning state sovereignty seem minor under the ICC when compared to those arising from the universal jurisdiction of municipal courts either under stand-alone statutes or through integrating international conventions into domestic law. There are many such treaties conferring universal jurisdiction on municipal courts, and the United States is a state party to several, including the Torture Convention.[32] Universal jurisdiction under these treaties includes jurisdiction over nationals of nonparty states.[33] Universal jurisdiction under the Torture Convention was at issue in the United Kingdom case concerning the extradition of Augusto Pinochet, the former dictator of Chile. Although on humanitarian grounds, due to his age and health, the decision was eventually reached not to extradite him to Spain for trial under the Torture Convention, the UK law lords found as a matter of UK law that he could be extradited.[34] Any issue of sovereignty seems more pointed when the tribunal is a municipal one exercising universal jurisdiction rather than an international tribunal. The principle *par in parem non habet imperium* is arguably violated or at least undermined when there is prosecution invoking universal jurisdiction in municipal courts.

Consider the prosecution of a foreign citizen by a municipal tribunal (exercising universal jurisdiction) for a crime against humanity that occurs outside its territory. This seems to be one equal state asserting authority over the judicial affairs of another equal state. This undermining of sovereignty may be acceptable, since most states would get no benefit from protecting their government's sovereign prerogative (for example) to torture citizens with impunity. But the ICC itself does not undermine sovereignty in this way. The jurisdiction of the ICC is only supplementary to the jurisdiction of the state parties themselves. The jurisdiction over foreign citizens of nonparties acting within the territory of a state party (or acting against its nationals from a distance) operates only through the state party and its judicial system when the accused is under its jurisdiction. This requires no violation of the principle of equals not ruling over equals any more than it does in cases involving the violation of municipal law by a foreign national.

Perhaps the real worry of the powerful is a different question of sovereignty. The Rome Statute allows for no immunity based on official capacity.

Even current heads of state or government and others acting in their official capacities are under the law of the statute.[35] Thus, the statute rejects the well-established doctrine of official immunity for heads of state and other high officials, whether *ratione personae* or *ratione materiae*. This is indeed a major departure.

The statute of the ICC expressly rejects immunity for those acting in their official capacity, *rationae materiae* or *ratione persona*. This rejection of criminal immunity respects a basic principle of the rule of law: that all are subject to the law and accountable for their actions. Of course, the other jurisdiction provisions of the Rome Statute would have to be satisfied for a head of state or other high official to be prosecuted in the ICC, and all of the safeguards would make such prosecutions unlikely, except in extreme cases similar to the current prosecution of Slobodan Milosevic in the tribunal for the former Yugoslavia. The officials of powerful nations have much more to fear from the universal jurisdiction of municipal courts under conventions such as the Torture Convention than from the ICC.

Whatever happens to any future attempts to create freestanding universal jurisdiction that rejects immunity for current high officials, there will continue to be universal jurisdiction under international conventions and customary international law, where such immunity is not at issue. If apprehended in a foreign state, former officials of powerful nations may be liable to prosecution in municipal courts if there is a credible case under the Torture Convention. Those who have reason to fear such prosecution may need to restrict their travel.

The international judicial implementation of some of the most fundamental human rights furthers the rule of law both through universal jurisdiction and international tribunals such as the ad hoc tribunals and the ICC. The ICC, however, has greater rule-of-law virtues than either universal jurisdiction or ad hoc tribunals. But the rule of law cannot be pursued even gradually and imperfectly if the most powerful nations are outside its domain. The perception of opposition between sovereignty and an international judicial implementation of human rights results from an untenable conception of sovereignty. This Hobbesian conception of absolutely powerful sovereign rulers is particularly untenable for states that seek justice through limited government and respect for the rule of law.

NOTES

1. Universal Declaration of Human Rights, Articles 2, 6, 7, 16.2.
2. Johannes Morsink, *The Universal Declaration of Human Rights: Origins, Drafting, and Intent* (Philadelphia: University of Pennsylvania Press, 1999), 24–25.

3. Universal Declaration of Human Rights, Articles 7–11.

4. H. Lauterpacht, *International Law and Human Rights* (London: Stevens & Son, 1950), 397–408, and Morsink, *The Universal Declaration of Human Rights: Origins, Drafting, and Intent*, 320–24, 331.

5. Rome Statute of the International Criminal Court, UN Doc. A/CONF.183/9 (1998), Preamble.

6. Rome Statute, Article 24.

7. Rome Statute, Article 22.

8. Rome Statute, Article 12.

9. Rome Statute, Article 11, Article 127.

10. Rome Statute, Article 1.

11. Rome Statute, Article 15.

12. Rome Statute, Article 17, Article 20.

13. Rome Statute, Article 18.

14. Rome Statute, Article 16.

15. David Rieff, "Court of Dreams," *New Republic*, Sept. 7, 1998, 16–17.

16. Rex Martin, "Human Rights and Civil Rights," *Philosophical Studies* 37 (1980): 391–403.

17. Martin, "Human Rights and Civil Rights," 395.

18. Alexander Hamilton, *The Federalist Papers*, Number 16.

19. Alexander Hamilton, *The Federalist Papers*, Number 16.

20. Morsink, *The Universal Declaration of Human Rights: Origins, Drafting, and Intent*, 284 ff.

21. John Rawls, *The Law of Peoples* (Cambridge, Mass.: Harvard University Press, 1999), 122–23.

22. John Rawls, *Political Liberalism (with the "Reply to Habermas")* (New York: Columbia University Press, 1996), 385ff.

23. Immanuel Kant, "Perpetual Peace: A Philosophical Sketch," first published 1796, trans. H. B. Nisbet, in *Kant's Political Writings*, ed. Hans Reiss (Cambridge: Cambridge University Press, 1970), 112.

24. For the idea of midlevel principles, see Michael D. Bayles, "Mid-level Principles and Justification," in *Justification: Nomos 28*, ed. J. Roland Pennock and John W. Chapman (New York: New York University Press, 1986), 49–67; and Kenneth Henley, "Abstract Principles, Mid-level Principles, and the Rule of Law," *Law and Philosophy* 12 (1993): 121–32.

25. Cornelius F. Murphy Jr., *Theories of World Governance: A Study in the History of Ideas* (Washington: Catholic University of America Press, 1999), 145.

26. For a more extensive account, see Kenneth Henley, "The Impersonal Rule of Law," *Canadian Journal of Law and Jurisprudence* 5 (1992): 299–308.

27. For an analysis and rebuttal of this claim of Hobbes, see Jean Hampton, "Democracy and the Rule of Law," in *The Rule of Law: Nomos 36*, ed. Ian Shapiro (New York: New York University Press, 1994), 13–44.

28. For disapproval of the limits, see Gary T. Dempsey, "Reasonable Doubt: The Case against the Proposed International Criminal Court," *Cato Institute Policy Analysis* 311 (July 16, 1998); and Jeremy Rabkin, *Why Sovereignty Matters* (Washington, D.C.: AEI Press, 1998). For approval see Rawls, *The Law of Peoples*, 26–27, 42; and Lauterpacht, *International Law and Human Rights*, 304–8.

29. Jean Jacques Rousseau, *The Social Contract and Discourses,* trans. G. D. H. Cole (New York: E. P. Dutton, 1950), 23–27.

30. G. W. F. Hegel, *Hegel's Philosophy of Right*, trans T. M. Knox (Oxford: Oxford University Press, 1952), 179–81, 208–10.

31. For a thorough discussion of the issue of possible constitutional concerns were the U.S. to become a state party, see Ruth Wedgwood, "The Constitution and the ICC," in *The United States and the International Criminal Court*, ed. Sarah B. Sewall and Carl Kaysen (Lanham, Md: Rowman & Littlefield Publishers, 2000), 119–36. For an analysis of a broad range of issues concerning the opposition of the United States to the ICC, see Diane Marie Amann and M. N. S. Sellers, "The United States of America and the International Criminal Court," *American Journal of Comparative Law* 50 (2002): 381–404.

32. Convention against Torture and Other Cruel, Inhuman, or Degrading Treatment or Punishment (1984), UN Doc. A/39/51, Articles 4, 5, 7, 8 with special attention to 4 and 8.4.

33. For an account of U.S. participation in treaty-based universal jurisdiction, see Michael P. Scharf, "The ICC's Jurisdiction over the Nationals of Non-party States," in *The United States and the International Criminal Court*, ed. Sarah B. Sewall and Carl Kaysen (Lanham, Md: Rowman & Littlefield Publishers, 2000), 220–21.

34. *Regina v. Bartle and the Commissioner of Police for the Metropolis and Others, Ex Parte Pinochet*. House of Lords, decided 24 March 1999.

35. Rome Statute, Article 27.

IV

RIGHTS IN EXTREMIS

11

Is Terrorism Ever Morally Permissible? An Inquiry into the Right to Life

Stephen Nathanson

Is terrorism ever morally permissible? Even asking this question can seem like an insult, both to the victims of terrorist actions and to moral common sense. The victims have suffered injury and death for actions and policies for which they were not responsible, and moral common sense resoundingly condemns terrorist acts as paradigms of immorality. One wants to say, if the murder of innocent people by terrorists is not clearly wrong, what is?

While it is easy to condemn terrorist killings, these condemnations begin to look problematic when we broaden our focus and examine a wider range of moral judgments made by people who denounce terrorism. For people who condemn all killing, condemning terrorism is not problematic. But very few of us condemn all killing. In fact, most of us think that war—which is simply organized killing, injuring, and destroying—is sometimes morally permissible, even though we know that in warfare, many people are killed and injured, innocent civilians as well as soldiers.

Terrorism is generally thought to violate the rights of its victims. When terrorists kill people, we generally see this as a violation of the victims' right to life. The question "Is terrorism ever morally permissible?" could be framed in terms of whether there are circumstances in which terrorists may justifiably violate the rights of victims, even the right to life.

In this chapter, I critically examine various responses to the question of whether terrorism is ever morally permissible. Although my discussion is not expressed in the language of human rights, most of what I say here can easily be translated into a rights, or human rights, vocabulary, and I try to link my points to a rights perspective at the end of the chapter. The connections should be clear throughout, however. Indeed, asking whether terrorism is ever morally permissible amounts to asking whether the right of innocent people not to be attacked can be overridden by the right of people to use violent means to defend themselves and their way of life.

If people believe that wars in which civilians are killed are sometimes morally permissible, can those people consistently condemn terrorism? Or are such condemnations hypocritical and self-serving? Judgments condemning terrorism often seem hypocritical. Sometimes this is so because the person making the judgment relies on a self-serving definition of terrorism that makes it analytically true that no act of killing of innocents by his or her own country or group could be an instance of terrorism. Sometimes it is so because the person making the judgment applies relevant moral principles in a biased and uneven way so as to reach different judgments, depending on whether the conduct being judged is that of a friend or foe.

To avoid this sort of hypocrisy, we need three things. The first is a definition of terrorism that does not restrict the terrorist label to conduct undertaken only by one's enemies. The second is a set of relevant moral principles that apply to a broad range of actions that includes, but is not restricted to, acts of terrorism. The third is a willingness to apply both the definition and the moral principles in an evenhanded way.

I begin with a definition of terrorism that I have developed and defended elsewhere.[1] Here I simply offer it to launch my discussion of the moral issues. Terrorist acts have the following features:

1. They are acts of serious deliberate violence or destruction.
2. They are generally committed by groups as part of a campaign to promote a political or social agenda.
3. They generally target limited numbers of people but aim to influence a larger group and/or the leaders who make decisions for that group.
4. They either kill or injure innocent people or pose a serious threat of such harms to innocent people.

The crux of the moral question about terrorism concerns the fourth point. Anyone who thinks that war is sometimes morally permissible accepts that actions that meet the first three conditions are sometimes morally right because war involves acts of serious violence that are committed by groups for political purposes and that target some people in order to influence others. So, if terrorism is always immoral, it must be so because terrorist acts kill and injure innocent people. But all wars involve the killing or injuring of innocent people. Thus, to sustain the view that all terrorist actions are wrong but that warfare is sometimes permissible, one must identify some morally relevant difference between the killing of innocents by terrorists and the killing of innocents in morally permissible acts of war. If this difference cannot be found, then anyone who wants to condemn all terrorism will be forced to revise their views. Either they will have to conclude that fighting a war is never morally permissible, or they will have to concede that terrorist acts may be morally justifiable.

I now examine this set of problems by considering several important discussions of the ethics of war and violence to see if a morally consistent position on these issues can be developed.

PRIMORATZ ON THE MORALITY OF TERRORISM

In his valuable article "The Morality of Terrorism," Igor Primoratz argues that while war is sometimes morally permissible, terrorism is never morally permissible because (1) by definition, terrorism always involves the intentional killing of innocent people; and (2) the intentional killing of innocent people is always wrong.[2] He also defends the thesis that moral consequentialism is false because in principle it could permit terrorism. For consequentialists, the rightness of actions depends only on their results: actions are right if the results of performing them are better than the results of not performing them. As Primoratz notes, consequentialism has the following implication regarding the morality of terrorism: "When its consequences are good enough, terrorism, just like everything else, is given moral consecration."[3] In his view, any moral theory that could "consecrate" terrorism must be false.

Primoratz offers a number of nonconsequentialist arguments against the morality of terrorism. The first two derive from the nature of persons as moral agents that are due a high level of respect. He writes, "Every human being is an individual, a person separate from other persons, with a unique, irreproducible thread of life and a value that is not commensurable with anything else."[4] Given the incommensurable value of individual persons, it is wrong to try to determine the moral permissibility of alternative courses of conduct aimed at some desired goal by calculating the number of lives preserved and lost under each alternative. This kind of moral and political arithmetic violates the ideal of giving individual lives our utmost respect and concern. Terrorists violate this central moral ideal. They treat innocent people as political pawns, giving no consideration to their individual worth and instead seeing their lives as useful only insofar as their deaths serve the terrorists' political cause. In this way, they violate the ideal expressed by Kant's injunction that we are to treat people as ends in themselves and not as means only.[5]

In addition, Primoratz argues, terrorists ignore the moral relevance of guilt and innocence in their treatment of individuals. They do not attack only those who are responsible for the alleged evils done to their own group or cause. They attack people with no causal or moral responsibility for these alleged evils and thus violate the principle that people, as moral agents, should be treated in accord with what they deserve.

Terrorists, Primoratz tells us, also forsake ideals of moral dialogue and moral equality. Not only do they decide who will live and who will die, but they also feel no burden to justify their actions in ways that the victims might understand and accept. Here Primoratz invokes a moral ideal of open discussion and debate. Morally justifiable conduct, he claims, must be justifiable to others, including those adversely affected by it. Terrorist killings, then, should in principle be justifiable to their victims.[6]

Though he does not fully develop his discussion of these moral values, Primoratz is surely correct to identify them as being among the important moral values relevant to any moral inquiry into the permissibility of terrorist killing. Because he sees these values as being widely accepted, he concludes that terrorism is incompatible with "some of the most basic moral beliefs many of us hold."[7]

After reaching this conclusion, Primoratz turns to Leon Trotsky's defense of terrorism as a tactic of revolution. Trotsky argues that there is no morally significant difference between the violence of traditional war and revolutionary violence. If wars that kill innocent people can be justified, then so can revolutions that kill innocent people.

Primoratz's criticism of Trotsky's view is important because Primoratz wants to denounce all terrorism but not condemn all war, even though innocent people are killed in both. To sustain this view, he must meet Trotsky's challenge by showing that war and terrorism are morally different. He writes, "The suffering of civilians . . . is surely inevitable not only in modern, but in almost all wars. . . . But we must attend not only to the suffering inflicted, but also to the way it is inflicted."[8]

To illustrate his point, he contrasts two imagined artillery attacks on a village. In one such attack, the intention is to kill the civilian inhabitants of the village. Morally, this attack is the equivalent of terrorism since both intentionally target innocent people. In a second case, the civilian deaths are foreseen but not intended. The artillery gunners' intention is not to kill civilians but to attack enemy soldiers stationed in the village. "Had it been possible to attack the enemy unit without endangering the civilians in any way, they would certainly have done so. This was not possible, so they attacked although they knew that the attack would cause civilian casualties too; but they did their best to reduce those inevitable, but undesired consequences as much as possible."[9] This is a case, then, of civilian deaths and injuries being morally permissible collateral damage. Primoratz contrasts it with the first case to show that justified war fighting differs from terrorism. While terrorists intentionally kill the innocent, those engaged in justified war fighting only do so unintentionally.

Primoratz appeals here to something like the principle of double effect. According to this principle, certain actions are permissible if their negative consequences are not intended, while actions that bring about the same consequences intentionally would be wrong.[10] Primoratz uses this idea to show that Trotsky and other defenders of terrorism are mistaken in their view that there is a moral equivalence between war and terrorism. No doubt, the intentional killing of civilians may occur in war, but when it does, Primoratz will condemn it for the same reason he condemns terrorism. But, contrary to Trotsky, the foreseeable death of innocents as an indirect effect of acts of war is not the same as the intentional killing of innocents. As long as those who fight wars do not intentionally kill innocent civilians, tactics that kill innocent civilians may be morally permissible. The key issue, for Primoratz, is one of intention. As long as soldiers and revolutionaries avoid the intentional killing of innocent people, they will not be guilty of terrorist acts. They become terrorists when they fail to do this.

PROBLEMS WITH PRIMORATZ'S VIEW

Primoratz's view has a number of attractive features. His condemnation of terrorism appears to be principled and firm, unlike the consequentialist arguments that can go either way depending on the circumstances. In addition, his view fits in with the widespread desire to permit justified wars but to rule out terrorism as always being morally beyond the pale. Nonetheless, it has serious weaknesses.

First, by stressing the role of intentions and drawing at least implicitly on the doctrine of double effect, Primoratz sides with those who claim that we should evaluate actions in terms of the intentions that produce them and not the consequences they produce. This principle is sometimes plausible. When people build highways, they intend to make it possible for people to travel with ease, but they know that another effect of their work will be auto accidents in which innocent people die. Since they do not intend the accidents or the associated deaths, we generally do not think that it is wrong to build highways.

While the doctrine of double effect is undeniably plausible in this and other cases, it is nevertheless seriously defective. To see this, suppose that the September 11 attackers had only intended to destroy the physical structures of the Pentagon and the World Trade Center and had no intention to kill anyone. Even if this were true, we would not take this as a reason for thinking that the attacks were either justifiable or excusable. As an argument for the moral permissibility of their actions, it would be insufficient, to say the least, for the terrorists to say that they had only intended to destroy buildings and that, although they foresaw the deaths of innocent persons, they did not intend these deaths. But this is just what Primoratz's emphasis on the intentions of those who kill innocent civilians would lead us to accept as a sufficient defense of their actions.

There are additional problems with Primoratz's attempt to differentiate the killing of innocents in war from the killing of innocents through acts of terrorism. In his own example, the artillery gunners attack the village even though they expect to cause civilian deaths. And while it does seem morally relevant that the artillery gunners would rather not cause the death of innocents and would even regret having done so, it is still the case that the artillery gunners know that they will kill innocent people, perhaps even in large numbers. In spite of this, they launch their attack.

A key problem for Primoratz is that his approval of these collateral damage attacks does not square with central values cited in his discussion. Primoratz insists on the incalculable value of individual lives and the moral demand that we respect individuals as ends and not means. And he denounces those who evaluate acts of killing through a consequentialist cost-benefit analysis. It is hard to see how his defense of collateral damage killings in war can be made consistent with these moral ideals and the principles he so strongly affirms. Surely the killing of innocent people is not justified by the fact that the people who are responsible for these deaths would rather not kill their victims.

One reason that Primoratz's view may seem plausible is that it echoes some common misconceptions about the law of homicide. It is widely believed that intentionally killing a person counts as first- or second-degree murder, while unintentionally killing someone is the lesser crime of manslaughter, and the conclusion drawn is that the law treats intentional killings as being more grievous crimes than unintentional ones. But this is not correct. Some unintentional killings are legally as bad as intentional killings. While intentional killings are the paradigms for first-degree murder, there are unintended deaths that count as murder rather than manslaughter. In what are sometimes called "depraved heart" murders, "the accused does not intend to kill, but . . . there is 'a wanton and wilful disregard of the likelihood that the natural tendency of [the] defendant's behavior is to cause death or great bodily harm.'" In such cases, the crime "manifests such a high degree of indifference to the value of human life that it may fairly be said that the actor 'as good as' intended to kill his victim."[11] Where such reckless indifference is evident, both law and morality condemn such unintended deaths very strongly, and they do so in a way that is incompatible with the principle of double effect. Many collateral damage killings satisfy the criteria of reckless indifference, and these actions should be criticized by anyone who condemns terrorism.[12]

Primoratz has one set of additional arguments in defense of collateral damage killings. In spite of his powerful denunciations of consequentialism, Primoratz relies on an appeal to the consequences of the act. Recall that in describing the artillery attack, he writes, "The military need . . . [was] so strong and urgent that it prevailed over the prohibition of killing or maiming a comparatively small number of civilians."[13] In claiming that the military need was "strong and urgent," he presumably means that the consequences of not destroying the military forces in the village would have been very bad. When he says that only a "comparatively small number of civilians" would be killed or injured, he presumably means that the losses are not that great. His claim implies that if the number of civilian deaths had been larger, the attack would have been wrong. Unfortunately, determining whether this requirement is satisfied requires exactly the kind of calculation that Primoratz denounces so fervently. Earlier in his essay, he writes, "It is precisely these calculations, in which human beings figure as units to be added and subtracted, that many find morally inappropriate and indeed offensive. Many will want to say, with Arthur Koestler's Rubashov, that 'twice two are not four when the mathematical units are human beings.'"[14] Primoratz's own argument fits this description precisely and thus qualifies as being "morally inappropriate and indeed offensive" by his own criteria.

Suppose we accept Primoratz's defense of collateral damage killings of innocents in wartime and set aside his earlier denunciations of all consequentialist calculations. We could then take seriously his claim that the killing of innocents in wartime is sometimes morally permissible. But the cost would be that his argument against terrorism would collapse, for if consequences are central to the justification for killing innocents in wartime, then terrorists can use Primoratz's analysis to show that their actions could also be justifiable. Terrorists might argue that they have a "just cause" and that a particular attack on innocent people arose from a need that was "so strong and urgent that it prevailed over the prohibition of killing or maiming a comparatively small number of civilians." If the terrorists did not intend to harm innocents and if the consequences were sufficiently good, then consistency would require Primoratz to agree that the act was morally permissible. The only way to avoid this result would be to reject the criteria he uses to justify collateral damage killings and to condemn collateral damage killings as being the moral equivalent of terrorism.

My conclusion is that Primoratz fails to show that terrorism is always immoral while collateral damage killing of innocents in wartime is sometimes morally permissible. This is a significant failure because many people hold just this view. Indeed, this appears to be the view of commonsense morality. So the difficulties I have described are not just problems for Primoratz. The view that he defends and many believe runs into problems because collateral damage killings can exhibit a profound indifference to the value of individual human beings even if these acts are not done for the purpose of killing innocent people.[15]

Having reached this conclusion, one way to proceed at this point would be to try to repair Primoratz's position by seeing if there is another way to articulate the difference between terrorism and collateral damage killings. I later pursue this strategy, but before considering this option, I want to examine more closely the idea that in some cases, the intentional killing of innocents in wartime is justified. I want to examine this because such killings are sometimes defended by those who want to condemn terrorism.

THE BOMBING OF CITIES IN WORLD WAR II: WALZER ON THE LIMITS OF CIVILIAN IMMUNITY

During World War II, Germany, Britain, and the United States all engaged in aerial bombardment of cities. I want to focus on the bombings by the Allies, since these are widely thought to have been justified. While some bombings by the Allies were directed at military or industrial targets, the main targets were cities themselves and the people who inhabited them. If these attacks can be morally justified, then the killing of innocent civilians is sometimes morally permissible, even when it is specifically intended. And if the killing of innocent people was justified in these cases, we will have to consider whether these cases can be differentiated from the killing of innocent people by terrorists. If not, then we may have to accept that some terrorist actions might be morally justifiable (if, for example, they are motivated by a just cause). I examine these issues through a discussion of two works that defend some instances of city bombing while condemning terrorism. These are Michael Walzer's well-known book *Just and Unjust Wars* and Gerry Wallace's challenging essay "Terrorism and the Argument from Analogy."[16]

One of Walzer's central aims in *Just and Unjust Wars* is the articulation and defense of what he calls the "war convention," a set of normative principles governing the conduct of war. These principles include what is sometimes called the "principle of discrimination" or the "principle of noncombatant immunity." It prohibits direct attacks on civilians. Walzer introduces his own version of this principle by asserting some fundamental moral claims regarding the ethics of killing in war. He writes, "A legitimate act of war is one that does not violate the rights of the people against whom it is directed. . . . No one can be threatened with war or warred against, unless through some act of his own he has surrendered or lost his rights. This fundamental principle underlies and shapes the judgments we make of wartime conduct."[17] In applying these fundamental norms, Walzer takes it as given that soldiers have surrendered their immunity to attack, while civilians have not. From this it follows that innocent civilians are not legitimate targets of attack.

In a later chapter, Walzer applies his principles to terrorism. Since he defines terrorism as being the "method of random murder of innocent people" for the purpose of destroying the morale of a nation or class, it is no surprise that he condemns all acts of terrorism.[18] If terrorism intentionally kills innocent people and the principle of discrimination prohibits this, then terrorism is wrong. In discussing an attack by Algerian terrorists on a milk bar frequented by teenagers, Walzer makes the following comment: "Certainly, there are historical moments when armed struggle is necessary for the sake of human freedom. But if dignity and self-respect are to be the outcomes of that struggle, it cannot consist of terrorist attacks against children."[19] Here and elsewhere, his denunciations of terrorism are categorical and deeply felt.

Nonetheless, when Walzer discusses the large-scale aerial attacks on civilians by the British early in World War II, he claims that these attacks were justified, and he develops the concept of a "supreme emergency" to show why. He introduces this concept to describe a situation that possesses two special features. The first is an extreme and extraordinary threat. Nazism, he says, was no ordinary enemy; it was an "ultimate threat to everything decent in our lives."[20] The second feature of a supreme emergency is that this extreme threat is imminent. In his view, the threat to Britain in 1940 was imminent. German armies dominated Europe and threatened to control the seas. Britain feared an invasion by a country that threatened both Britain itself and the basic values of civilization. Finally, at that point, Britain's air force was the only military means it possessed for inflicting damage on Germany.

According to Walzer, the enormity and the imminence of the threat transformed Britain's wartime situation into a supreme emergency. In such a situation the war convention's prohibition on intentionally killing innocent people is no longer binding. Because the British were in a situation of supreme emergency, their attacks against German cities and their civilian residents were morally permissible. To be clear here, Walzer does not approve of all of the city bombings by Allied Forces in World War II. He approves only of those that occurred while the supreme emergency lasted. This condition ceased to exist by late 1942. The threat of an invasion had diminished; the United States had entered the war; the Russians had weakened the Germans on the Eastern front. In short, the threat was no longer imminent, and the constraints of the war convention should have been honored once again. But they were not. Most of the city bombings of World War II occurred after 1942. They continued and even intensified throughout the war, climaxing in the bombing of Dresden, Germany; the fire bombings of Japanese cities by the United States; and the atomic bombings of Hiroshima and Nagasaki. None of these bombings were justified, Walzer insists, by the supreme emergency rule.[21]

While Walzer develops his account of the supreme emergency exception to the war convention in light of the Nazi threat to all civilized values, he extends the exception to other threats. Addressing the crucial question of the scope of the supreme emergency exception, Walzer asks, "Can a supreme emergency be constituted by . . . a threat of enslavement or extermination directed against a single nation? Can soldiers and statesmen override the rights of innocent people for the sake of their own political community?"[22] He answers, "I am inclined to answer this question affirmatively, though not without hesitation and worry."

To justify extending the supreme emergency extension to more limited but nevertheless grave threats, Walzer appeals to the role-based duties of a country's soldiers and statesmen. Even if they are willing to sacrifice themselves in the name of morality or fidelity to the war convention, they "cannot sacrifice their countrymen," who, Walzer assumes, are counting on them to defend their interests as a people or nation. If forced to choose between defending the fundamental interests of their own people or honoring the war convention's restrictions on the use of force, soldiers and statesmen are morally free, if not morally obligated, to defend their nation.

The trouble with this answer, from the perspective of Walzer's own defense of civilian immunity, is that what had appeared to be a unique circumstance when discussed with respect to Nazism now appears to be a more common occurrence—nations finding themselves threatened with serious losses of life and liberty. The extended "supreme emergency" exception appears in fact to be quite elastic and thus very permissive. Even somewhat uncertain threats to life and liberty are likely to appear urgent to military and national leaders (as we have seen recently with the alleged threat from Iraqi weapons of mass destruction).[23] Nor are military and national leaders likely to wait until defeat is imminent before attacking innocent civilians. And, as the experience of World War II shows, once nations have set aside the constraints of the war convention, they are not likely to reinstate them until hostilities end, and the precedent of setting aside these limits may remain in force when a new conflict arises.[24]

According to Walzer, then, military and national leaders may target innocent civilians when a supreme emergency exists. But if the intentional killing of innocents in wartime is morally permissible in these circumstances, might not the terrorist killing of innocents also be morally permissible in similar circumstances? Walzer's own denunciation of terrorism notwithstanding, the logic of his discussion suggests that the answer is yes. Indeed, while his official view must be that the justified city bombings were not acts of terrorism, he sometimes uses the expressions "terror bombing" and "terrorism" to describe them.[25] Unfortunately, Walzer never directly connects his discussion of the supreme emergency exception with his condemnation of terrorism. And so his position remains unclear. Terrorism is unconditionally condemned, and yet what appears to be its moral equivalent is sometimes said to be morally permissible.

THE BOMBINGS OF CITIES IN WORLD WAR II REVISITED: WALLACE'S DEFENSE

In "Terrorism and the Argument from Analogy," Gerry Wallace directly faces the question of whether the moral permissibility of bombing civilians in World War II provides grounds for thinking that some terrorist attacks on innocents might also be morally permissible. Like Walzer, Wallace believes that some civilian bombing in World War II was morally justified. According to Wallace, what justified the World War II bombings was the conjunction of four factors:

1. the bombing was a measure of last resort;
2. it was an act of collective self-defense;
3. it was a reply in kind against a genocidal, racist aggressor; and
4. it had some chance of success.[26]

After describing the four conditions that justified city bombing, Wallace asks whether terrorism "can mirror these features" so that acts of terrorism might be justified in a similar way. Describing the position he wants to examine, he writes, "The apologist [for terrorism] . . . is not holding that area bombing was terrorism but only that acts of . . . terrorism can be sufficiently like it . . . for the same conclusion to apply."[27]

Wallace constructs a powerful analogy that suggests that terrorism might sometimes be morally permissible. It comes as something of a surprise, then, when he argues that terrorism is always morally wrong. He defends this view by arguing that terrorist killings of innocents can never meet the four conditions that, taken together, justify the Allied bombing of civilian targets in World War II. More precisely, he claims that while terrorism might meet any one—or even several—of the conditions, it cannot simultaneously satisfy all four of them. To support this claim, Wallace imagines a community that satisfies both the second and third conditions: the community is combating a brutal regime that oppresses it, and its opposition is an act of collective self-defense against this regime.

So far this imagined community is relevantly similar to that of Britain in 1940. But, Wallace claims, if the conduct being contemplated is terrorist conduct, the first and fourth conditions will never be jointly satisfied. If a community is able to defend itself successfully through the use of terrorism, thus satisfying the fourth condition, it is unlikely that terrorism is a last resort; other means are likely to work as well. In this case, the community fails to meet the first condition. On the other hand, if a community truly turns to terrorism as a last resort, thus satisfying the first condition, it is unlikely to have a reasonable chance of success. In this case, the fourth condition is not met; if nothing else would work, it is unlikely that terrorism would have a reasonable chance of success of working either. Thus, it is impossible for terrorist acts both to be a genuine last resort and to have a reasonable chance of succeeding as a method of collective self-defense.[28]

This is the same comforting conclusion sought by Primoratz and Walzer: the British bombing of cities was morally permissible in at least some cases, but terrorist killings of innocents are always wrong. The trouble is that Wallace's imagined apologist for terrorism creates a powerful analogy between the Allied bombings of civilian targets in World War II and at least some terrorist killings. Either may be an instance of intentionally killing innocent human beings to promote an important political goal, and either may be an act of collective self-defense against a brutal regime. Wallace insists, however, that, unlike the World War II bombing of cities, the intentional killing of innocents by terrorists can never be justified. This is so because it is impossible that terrorist killings be both a last resort and an act likely to succeed. But there is no basis for claiming this circumstance to be impossible. Wallace himself argues that just this combination of circumstances occurred during World War II. There is no way to know that it could not occur again.

The conclusion Wallace should have reached is that just as the military targeting of civilians and cities is morally permissible in some circumstances, so too is the terrorist killing of innocents sometimes morally permissible. But this is a conclusion that neither he nor Walzer is prepared to reach, even though their own premises push them in this direction.

THREE POSSIBLE VIEWS ON THE KILLING OF INNOCENTS IN WAR OR THROUGH TERRORISM

If my analysis is correct, then Walzer and Wallace are both logically committed to acknowledging the possibility of morally justified terrorism.

The view that I believe they are forced to hold is represented in the following table:

	Sometimes Justifiable	*Never Justifiable*
Intentional attacks on civilians	X	
Foreseen but unintended civilian deaths and injuries	X	
War	X	
Terrorism	X	

People who condemn all wartime attacks against innocent civilians—whether intentional or not—are in a strong position to condemn terrorism across the board. But they would be required to condemn all wars, since war almost inevitably involves civilian deaths as collateral damage. This pacifist view is represented as follows:

	Sometimes Justifiable	*Never Justifiable*
Intentional attacks on civilians		X
Foreseen but unintended civilian deaths and injuries		X
War		X
Terrorism		X

Anyone who has reverence for human life and abhors the killing of the innocent would sometimes find pacifism to be an appealing option. Nonetheless, it is generally rejected, even by morally conscientious people.[29]

A third possibility is the one that Primoratz appears to defend. It may be represented as follows:

	Sometimes Justifiable	*Never Justifiable*
Intentional attacks on civilians		X
Foreseen but unintended civilian deaths and injuries	X	
War	X	
Terrorism		X

As we saw, however, Primoratz has trouble squaring the principles that he uses to condemn terrorism with his own approval of attacks that produce civilian deaths and injuries as collateral damage.

TOWARD A COHERENT VIEW OF TERRORISM AND COLLATERAL DAMAGE KILLINGS

In spite of the difficulties I have described with Primoratz's views, the conclusion he seeks to defend is plausible and attractive. The challenge is to find a better way to articulate and defend the idea that while terrorist attacks on civilians are always wrong, wartime attacks that cause civilian deaths and injuries are sometimes morally permissible. I want now to offer my own version of this view. I try both to articulate a principle that can serve as the basis of these plausible opinions and to provide an argument in favor of this principle.

In sketching out a better view, I begin with some of the problems I have raised concerning the principle of double effect. Neither the principle of double effect nor any other principle that relies on the distinction between intentional and unintentional killing can explain or justify the claim that terrorism and collateral damage killing are sometimes morally different. Intention-based criteria are simply too slippery to apply and are too permissive in their implications. As I noted, such principles would allow the September 11 attackers to defend themselves against murder charges by arguing that while they did foresee civilian casualties, they did not intend them and instead intended only to damage the World Trade Center and the Pentagon buildings.

Walzer criticizes the principle of double effect for related reasons. "Simply not to intend the death of civilians is too easy," he writes. "What we look for in such cases is some sign of a positive commitment to save civilian lives."[30] In other words, double effect requires too little. More than not intending must be demanded to justify an act that results in civilian deaths and injuries. Walzer proposes what he sees as an amendment to the principle of double effect. He calls his revision the principle of "double intention." It requires that military planners and soldiers take steps to avoid or minimize harm to innocent civilians, even if these precautions increase the danger to military forces.

This is definitely a step in the right direction, though Walzer's point would be clearer and more forceful if he described it as a rejection of double effect rather than an amendment to it. Primoratz suggests a similar idea but neither develops it nor emphasizes its importance. When arguing for the moral permissibility of a military attack that will kill civilians as collateral damage, he characterizes those making the attack as having done "their best to reduce those inevitable but undesired consequences as much as possible."[31]

Building on these remarks, I suggest the following set of requirements for just, discriminate fighting. People involved in acts of war must:

1. target attacks as narrowly as possible on military resources;
2. avoid targets where civilian deaths are extremely likely;
3. avoid the use of inherently indiscriminate weapons (such as land mines and cluster bombs) and inherently indiscriminate strategies (such as high-altitude bombing of areas containing both civilian enclaves and military targets); and
4. accept that when there are choices between damage to civilian lives and damage to military personnel, priority should be given to saving civilian lives.

I do not claim that these requirements are definitive or complete. Rather, they are meant to illustrate the kinds of things people would do if they were making serious efforts to minimize civilian casualties. What is crucial is the idea that morality requires soldiers and military planners to bend over backward to avoid civilian deaths and injuries. For this reason, I refer to this type of constraint as the "bend-over-backward rule." The specifics required to carry this out will vary, but no case of collateral damage killings is morally permissible if great efforts are not made to avoid civilian deaths and injuries.

If a group has a just cause for being at war and acts in accord with principles like those illustrated here, then the group could be said to be acknowledging the humanity and value of those affected by its actions, even in those cases where its attacks expose innocent people to danger. By adhering to these principles, group members would show that they are not indifferent to the well-being of these innocent people. In this way, they would satisfy the demands of the principles and ideals cited by Primoratz in his critique of terrorism.

I believe that the bend-over-backward rule constitutes an essential moral constraint on the use of warfare. Something like this rule is already recognized within international practice and politics. The International Conference of the Red Cross, for example, has asserted principles that prohibit indiscriminate attacks (i.e., attacks that "strike military objectives and civilians or civilian objects without distinction"). In addition, the Red Cross rules require military forces to take "constant care" to avoid harm to civilians: "In the conduct of military operations, constant care shall be taken to spare the civilian population."[32] These principles have been endorsed by the United Nations General Assembly.

In addition to being intuitively plausible, the bend-over-backward rule is also capable of satisfying Primoratz's requirement that military actions that kill innocent civilians be justifiable to the victims themselves. How might this be achieved?

One way to interpret this ideal of justification is to use a social contract model and to imagine people choosing the rule or policy that will govern killing in wartime. A rule will be justified if it would be chosen by people as the one to govern these acts, and a particular act will be justified if it is in accord with the rule. With this idea of justification in mind, we can ask people to consider the following choice situation:

1. You are a member of group A or group B, but you do not know which one you belong to.
2. Group A is facing an attack by group B; if successful, group B's attack will result in the extermination or grave oppression of group A.
3. Group A can defend itself only by using means that will cause death and injury to innocent members of group B.
4. You must select some rule or policy to govern the killing of innocent people in cases of collective self-defense; it may be a rule absolutely prohibiting such killing, absolutely permitting it, or conditionally permitting it.

In such a choice situation, I believe that people would reject a rule that permits either intentional or indiscriminate attacks on civilians. Such a rule would be rejected because it opens up members of both group A and group B to unrestrained attack. Similarly, people would reject a rule that absolutely prohibits any act that kills innocent civilians. Such a rule could make it impossible for members of group A to defend itself. Yet the ability to defend themselves is something that they will want to retain.

What people would accept is a rule that combines the moral right to collective self-defense with a strong protection from military attacks against innocent civilians. The bend-over-backward rule does precisely this. It ensures that members of an attacked group have a realistic right of self-defense by permitting them to fight defensive wars, even though these wars may result in the deaths of innocent people. At the same time, the bend-over-backward rule ensures that if one is an innocent citizen in either the attacked or the attacking group, one can count on all combatants taking serious and even costly steps to avoid injury or death to you and other civilians. Such a rule could be accepted by all who face this choice situation. If this is so, then attacks that conform to the bend-over-backward rule but nonetheless result in injury or death to civilians would be justifiable to potential victims themselves since they would accept the rule that permits these attacks. Attacks that do not follow the bend-over-backward rule would not be justifiable in the same way.

What does the bend-over-backward rule imply about terrorism? Since paradigmatic cases of terrorism are always intentional and always aimed at innocent civilians, they are blatant violations of the bend-over-backward test. Someone who intentionally engages in this kind of killing is not bending over backward to avoid it.

I believe that the bend-over-backward rule achieves what nonpacifist critics of terrorism want to achieve. It provides a principled basis for condemning terrorist acts, no matter who carries them out, and a principled justification of acts of war that are constrained by this rule. Moreover, the moral perspective described here is unified in a desirable way. The very same principle that justifies the condemnation of terrorist killings also shows why some collateral damage killings are permissible and why others are not.

The view I have defended is also immune to charges of hypocrisy. Just as terrorist killings are condemned, so too are the killings of innocents by states in wartime when they fail to comply with the bend-over-backward rule and either attack civilians directly or fail to take due care to avoid civilian deaths and injuries. Hence, the supreme emergency killings that are defended by Walzer and Wallace fail to be justified according to this test. If condemnations of terrorism are to have any moral credibility, then these moral lapses by established governments need to be acknowledged and criticized. In some cases, public repentance and apologies might be necessary to show that we apply our own moral standards to our own acts and our own history.[33] The most powerful way to achieve moral credibility, of course, is to adhere to these restrictions in ways that make clear that one is doing so.

CONCLUSION

Can terrorism be morally justified? At the start of this chapter, I suggest that while it is easy to give a resounding no to this question, it is not so easy to make this resounding no compatible with other beliefs that most people hold about the killings of civilians during war. I suggest that to make credible moral judgments about terrorism, we need both a clearer sense of what terrorism is and a more general set of impartial principles for judging acts of violence. My hope is that this chapter gets us closer to achieving these goals.

I suggested at the start that my view can be stated in terms of human rights. I conclude with a brief restatement of my view in these terms. I begin with the assumption that there is a right to life. Since some killings are permissible, however, it follows either that the right to life can be overridden by other moral considerations or that the right to life is forfeited or canceled in some circumstances. Whichever of these views we take, to say that the killing of a person is morally permissible is to say that it is not prohibited by the right to life. So, for example, to say that killing in self-defense is morally permissible is to say that it is not prohibited by the right to life of the attacker. Likewise, to say that soldiers are permissible targets in wartime is to say that their right to life is forfeited or overridden by their status as soldiers and by the circumstance that they are in.

When soldiers kill one another, their right to life is not violated. By virtue of their status, soldiers acquire a conditional right to kill other soldiers during wartime, but they lose their own immunity to injury or death at the hands of other soldiers.

Civilians retain their right to life even in wartime. It is not permissible to kill them in the way that it is permissible to kill soldiers. This is the doctrine of noncombatant immunity. Terrorism is wrong because it violates this right in a direct way through the intentional targeting of civilians. Such terrorist killings are often contrasted with collateral damage killings, and the principle of double effect has been used to show that collateral damage killings may be justified because they are not intended. A rights version of double effect would say that the right to life protects people from being intentionally killed but not from being killed as an unintended side effect of a military attack. I have rejected the principle of double effect because it weakens the right to life too much.

In defending the bend-over-backward rule, I have defended an understanding of the right to life that requires military personnel to take strong precautionary measures to avoid causing the deaths of innocent people in the course of military activities. When soldiers kill civilians without taking these precautions, they violate the right to life of these civilians. If they take the necessary precautions and innocent people are still killed or injured, the protections afforded by the right to life have still been respected. The soldiers have done all they could do to avoid harm to innocent people in a context in which they are carrying out otherwise legitimate military activities. In such cases, we may want to say that the right to life has been overridden, or we may want to say that the scope of the right to life does not include protection from being killed when others have bent over backward to avoid doing so. Whichever formulation we choose, the killings in these cases are permissible. In those cases where the proper precautions are not taken, the killing of civilians is wrong, whether the killings are instances of terrorism or instances of collateral damage attacks. We need to be as critical of these collateral damage attacks as we are of terrorism. If we are not, we undermine both our own moral credibility and the credibility of moral criticism itself.

NOTES

1. For development and defense of this definition, see my "Prerequisites for Morally Credible Condemnations of Terrorism," in William Crotty, ed., *The Politics of Terror: The U.S. Response to 9/11* (Northeastern University Press, 2003); and "Can

Terrorism be Morally Justified," in James Sterba, ed., *Morality in Practice*, 7th ed. (Wadsworth, 2004).

2. Igor Primoratz, "The Morality of Terrorism," *Journal of Applied Philosophy*, Vol. 14 (1997), 221–33. In my discussion, I attribute to Primoratz view that terrorism is always wrong. In correspondence, he informs me that his own view is less absolutist than I say. His less-absolutist view is suggested in his essay "State Terrorism," in Tony Coady and Michael O'Keefe, eds., *Terrorism and Justice* (Melbourne: Melbourne University Press, 2002), 39–40. For Primoratz's discussion of the definition of terrorism, see his "What Is Terrorism?" *Journal of Applied Philosophy*, Vol. 7 (1990), 129–38. For other helpful discussions of this issue, see Haig Khatchadourian, "Terrorism and Morality," *Journal of Applied Philosophy*, Vol. 5 (1988), 131–45; and C. A. J. Coady, "The Morality of Terrorism," *Philosophy*, Vol. 60 (1985), 47–69.

3. Primoratz, 222.

4. Primoratz, 224.

5. I. Kant, *Grounding for the Metaphysics of Morals*, trans. James Ellington (Hackett, 1981), 36.

6. For a similar idea, see Thomas Nagel, *Equality and Partiality* (Oxford, 1991), 23. "We are looking for principles to deal with conflict that can at some level be endorsed by everyone."

7. Primoratz, 225.

8. Primoratz, 227.

9. Primoratz, 227.

10. P. A. Woodward, in his edited volume of essays *The Doctrine of Double Effect* (University of Notre Dame Press, 2001), briefly explains double effect as being the view that "an agent may not run afoul of, for example, the prohibition on killing civilians, if in acting the agent kills civilians unintentionally, even when those killings are foreseen" (p. 2). He goes on to note that other conditions may be added to this one for the act to be fully justified. A prominent additional condition in just war theory is proportionality.

11. Joshua Dressler, *Understanding Criminal Law*, 3rd ed. (Lexus Publishing, 2001), 513.

12. My thanks are due to Michael Davis for emphasizing the role of "reckless indifference" as a moral criterion and to both Ursula Bentele and Dan Givelber for clarifying the law of homicide for me.

13. Primoratz, 228.

14. See Primoratz, 224.

15. I discuss the morality of collateral killings in "Is the War on Terrorism a Defense of Civilization?" *Concerned Philosophers for Peace Newsletter*, v. 22 (Spring/Fall, 2002), 19–27, www.cpp-phil.org/newsltr.htm

16. Michael Walzer, *Just and Unjust Wars* (Basic Books, 1977); Gerry Wallace, "Terrorism and the Argument from Analogy," *Journal of Moral and Social Studies*, v. 6 (1991), 149–60.

17. Walzer, 135.

18. Walzer, 197.

19. Walzer, 205. Walzer's condemnation of terrorism is located in "Terrorism: A Critique of Excuses," in S. Luper-Foy, ed., *Problems of International Justice* (Westview, 1988), 237–47.

20. Walzer, 253.

21. For a valuable account of the bombing campaigns, see Stephen Garrett, *Ethics and Airpower in World War II: The British Bombing of German Cities* (St. Martin's Press, 1993). For contrasts between the British operational bombing policies and their public statements, see the appendix to chapter 1 of John Finnis, Joseph Boyle, and Germain Grisez, *Nuclear Deterrence, Morality, and Realism* (Oxford University Press, 1987), 38–44.

22. Walzer, 254.

23. For a reminder of how this threat was portrayed, see the "2003 State of the Union Address" by President George W. Bush, available at www.whitehouse .gov/news/releases/2003/01/20030128-19.html.

24. Kenneth Brown, "'Supreme Emergency': A Critique of Michael Walzer's Moral Justification for Allied Operational Bombing in World War II," *Manchester College Peace Studies Bulletin*, 1983. Walzer's use of the "supreme emergency" concept is also criticized by Tony Coady in "Terrorism, Just War and Supreme Emergency," in T. Coady and M. O'Keefe, *Terrorism and Justice* (Melbourne University Press, 2002), 15–20; and by Michael O'Keefe in "Responding to International Terrorism," in *Terrorism and Justice*, 108.

25. E.g., Walzer, 257. Walzer moves slightly away from absolutely condemning terrorism in his recent *Arguing about War* (Yale University Press, 2004), 54.

26. Wallace, 155.

27. Wallace, 155.

28. Wallace, 155–56.

29. For philosophical defenses and discussions of pacifism, see, e.g., Robert Holmes, *On War and Morality* (Princeton University Press, 1989); Richard Norman, *Ethics, Killing, and War* (Cambridge University Press, 1995); and John Yoder, *Nevertheless: Varieties of Religious Pacificism* (Herald Press, 1976). For an effective statement by a longtime proponent of nonviolence, see David McReynolds, *A Philosophy of Nonviolence* (A. J. Muste Memorial Institute, 1997).

30. Walzer, 155–56.

31. Primoratz, 227.

32. For these points regarding international rules for the conduct of war, see Fritz Kalshoven, *Constraints on the Waging of War*, 2nd ed. (International Committee of the Red Cross, 1991), 92–93.

33. On these issues, see Ian Buruma, *The Wages of Guilt* (Farrar, Strauss & Giroux, 1994); Donald Shriver, *Ethics for Enemies: Forgiveness and Atonement in Politics* (Oxford, 1995); and Robert Jay Lifton and Gregg Mitchell, *Hiroshima in America: Fifty Years of Denial* (Putnam, 1995).

12

Thwarting Suicide Terrorists: The Locus of Moral Constraints and the (Ir)Relevance of "Human Rights"

Jonathan Schonsheck

On September 11, 2001, the United States suffered a terrorist attack—and as regards property destroyed and lives disrupted or lost, it was the most devastating in our country's history. The U.S. response to this attack is generally referred to as the war on terrorism.[1] I believe that this name is a misnomer. Our concern is not about the abstract concept of terrorism and our endeavor—to invoke a neutral term—is not literally a war.

Four airliners were hijacked on September 11. Their flight crews were not killed by abstract nouns, and the planes were not piloted by terrorism. The hijacking, the killing, the crashing were done by small groups of identifiable individuals—suicide terrorists. And as we shall see, focusing on the fact that we are threatened by particular individuals is essential to meeting the threat they pose.

Typically, we use the term *war* and the *declaring of war* metaphorically—as a way of indicating that we are really upset about something and to convince others (and perhaps ourselves) that we are really going to do something about it. So we have declared metaphorical war on poverty, and we've declared metaphorical war on drugs.[2] In neither case is it clear just what should be done to prosecute the war—recall the late comedian Jackie Vernon, who claimed to be so enthused about Lyndon Johnson's "declaration of a war on poverty that he went out and threw a hand grenade at a beggar."[3] Using *war* metaphorically tends to befuddle rather than enlighten.

We need to rethink, to reconceptualize, our endeavor if that endeavor is to be both effective and morally upright.

David Luban has recently taken on this task.[4] What he has to say is interesting, insightful, important—and profoundly exasperating. I agree with many of the premises of Luban's arguments. But I believe that his central argument and a number of subsidiary arguments are instances of the fallacy of ignoratio elenchi. The premise sets of these arguments lead to conclusions different from—sometimes quite different from—the conclusions drawn by Luban.

Luban sketches out two competing models of the war on terrorism: the war model (within which terrorists are soldiers) and the criminal justice model (within which terrorists are criminals). However, Luban argues that the war on terrorism does not fit the war model: it has some elements of war but not others. I agree. He argues that the war on terrorism does not fit the criminal justice model: it has some elements of the criminal law model but not others. Again, I agree. Luban argues that the Bush administration seems to have constructed—perhaps by default—a hybrid model: some elements of the war model, some of the law model. And Luban argues that this hybrid model is morally problematic. The elements of the two models have been selected in a way that facilitates U.S. actions but in one that was not selected on the basis of any recognizable moral principles. Yet again, I agree.

But at this point, just when we (or at least I) expect Luban to construct a new model, sketch a new model, outline a new model, or at least to issue an urgent call for a new model, he does not. The crescendo of the article is, rather, a lament for the "death of human rights." So here, and at other crucial junctures, I supply the conclusions that should have been drawn, the conclusions that the various sets of premises that Luban gathers really support. And I hope to contribute to the reconceptualization that I say is necessary: the construction of a new model for our endeavor, a model that is cognizant of the new realities that we confront and that explains how we can go about preventing attacks by suicide terrorists while maintaining moral integrity.

My proposal is that we think about and talk about this endeavor as "thwarting suicide terrorists."

This proposed change is not a matter of mere semantics. While I do believe that thwarting suicide terrorists is indeed more accurate than fighting a war on terrorism, far more than clarity and precision are at stake. Much is revealed in arguing that this endeavor is not a war and that our adversary is not an abstraction. Most important, the moral justification for engaging in certain actions aimed at thwarting suicide terrorists is very different and significantly stronger.

TERRORISTS: SUI-CIDE IS SUI GENERIS

The U.S. response to September 11 is neither a war, despite the extensive engagement of the military, nor a police activity, despite the extensive engagement of police forces across the entire spectrum. The place to begin the reconceptualization, I submit, is not with the various models but with an investigation of the precise nature of the threat. Suicide terrorists are neither soldiers per se nor criminals per se. Suicide terrorists are sui generis. In consequence, the threat that is posed by suicide terrorists is sui generis—both like and unlike the threats posed by soldiers and criminals. Let us see how this is so.

Suicide terrorists are like soldiers in many respects: in operating across international borders and in weaponry—including the use of weapons of mass destruction—if they can obtain them. Furthermore, like soldiers, they are not motivated by personal gain but by some alleged "higher cause."

But suicide terrorists are unlike soldiers in crucial respects. They do not act on behalf of, nor under the control and direction of, the government of any nation-state. Nor do they wear any uniform or other fixed insignia of members of the military. Typically, nation-states go to war only after failing, in other ways, to secure some vital objective—for example, access to natural resources or for defensible borders. They consider these objectives as being essential to their prosperity or even to their very survival. This point is crucial—the goal of a nation-state is to survive the conflict and indeed to emerge from it in a superior condition. Of course, nation-states can miscalculate, and some are defeated. But nation-states are not suicidal.

Suicide terrorists are like criminals in many respects: they conspire; they plot actions that violate numerous criminal statutes. They are mass murderers.

But suicide terrorists are unlike criminals in other crucial respects. Typically, the goal of criminals is (in the words of *Star Trek*'s Commander Spock) to live long and prosper. Typically, criminals want, intend, to survive their criminal activities. They want to live, to enjoy their ill-gotten gains. When Willie Sutton was asked "Why do you rob banks?" he famously replied, "Because that's where the money is." Outlaws—from Butch Cassidy and the Sundance Kid to Willie Sutton to the corporate crooks in the news today—want to live lavishly. The necessary first step: live. Suicide terrorists, in sharp contrast, intend to die.[5]

Suicide terrorists are unlike soldiers and criminals in two additional respects, both of which are essential to understanding the threat that terrorists pose—and thus to understanding the measures necessary to thwarting that threat.

First, suicide terrorists quite intentionally target noncombatants. The deliberate killing of civilians—especially children, the elderly, and so on, who quite decidedly cannot defend themselves—enhances the terror and thus is tactically preferred. Soldiers do not intentionally target noncombatants—or if they do, their actions constitute war crimes. To be sure, various militaries are sometimes more and sometimes less scrupulous about preserving the safety of noncombatants—and the same must be said about criminals. But it is not the intention of either soldiers or criminals to injure bystanders.

The second respect in which suicide terrorists differ from soldiers and criminals follows from the fact that such terrorists intend to die. The fact that soldiers and criminals want, intend, to survive their respective activities—they want to live long and prosper—means that both are, in principle, deterrable. Individuals (both crooks and soldiers) and governments can at least in principle be dissuaded from taking a particular path by credible deterrent threats. An adversary can persuade the threatened persons or government that, unless they do differently, the outcome will be worse for them, not better. They will be defeated or even annihilated—not the outcomes they intend to bring about.

Focus now on the particular individuals who pose the danger of a suicide terrorist attack, and ask: What deterrent threat could we make, what could we threaten to do to them, that would dissuade them from their contemplated course of action? The answer is, of course: nothing. They are intending to die; they welcome death—and its promised or alleged rewards.[6] Unlike the deterrable criminal, who seeks to live lavishly, unlike the deterrable nation-state, which seeks to survive and prosper as a nation-state: suicide terrorists intend not to survive. The terrorist threat is posed not by some abstraction, terrorism, but by undeterrable individuals. They cannot be dissuaded by threats; nothing we could plausibly threaten to do to them could be worse than what they intend to do to themselves—and in the course of doing it to themselves, inflicting great evil on us.[7]

Let us now consider what Luban calls the hybrid model, which combines elements of both the war model and the law model. But be forewarned: even though he rejects the war model, Luban relies heavily upon it and uses its terminology. Note also: here is an instance of the ignoratio elenchi. Luban does not see the conclusion that these considerations (and their implications) most strongly support: that the threat posed by the suicide terrorist is indeed sui generis. He writes,

> Enemy soldiers in the War on Terrorism are, by definition, those who have embarked on a path of terrorism. They are neither morally nor politically innocent. Their sworn aim—"Death to America!"—is to create more 9/11s. In this respect, they are much more akin to criminal conspirators than to conscript soldiers. Terrorists will fight as soldiers when they must, and metamorphose into mass murderers when they can.
>
> Furthermore, suicide terrorists pose a special, unique danger. Ordinary criminals do not target innocent bystanders. They may be willing to kill them if necessary, but bystanders enjoy at least some measure of security because they are not primary targets. Not so with terrorists, who aim to kill as many innocent people as possible. Likewise, innocent bystanders are protected from ordinary criminals by whatever deterrent force the threat of punish-

> ment and the risk of getting killed in the act of committing a crime offer. For a suicide bomber, neither of these threats is a deterrent at all—after all, for the suicide bomber one of the hallmarks of a *successful* operation is that he winds up dead at day's end. . . . Add to this the danger that terrorists may come to possess weapons of mass destruction, including nuclear devices in suitcases. Under circumstances of such dire menace, it is appropriate to treat terrorists as though they embody the most dangerous aspects of both warriors and criminals. That is the basis of the hybrid war-law model.[8]

I have no quarrel with Luban's claim that this is the basis of the hybrid model. But it is vastly more than that. Among other things, it embodies some of the harsh new realities that must be accommodated by any new model of the United States's endeavor to counter suicide terrorists.

Luban exhibits a very strange reticence here: "to treat terrorists *as though* they embody the most dangerous aspects of both warriors and criminals." Surely they do; that's part of the reason that they are sui generis. The other part of the reason that they are sui generis: the ways in which they differ from both soldiers and criminals.

I want to consider now Luban's crescendo—but not uninterrupted. At this point, I interpose a running commentary based on what I have argued to this point. Luban writes,

> Here, the chief problem is that the War on Terrorism is not like any other kind of war.[9]

Quite so. Indeed, it's not a war at all; continuing to think of it as such leads to serious confusion. Luban continues,

> The enemy, Terrorism, is not a territorial state or a nation or a government.

Our concern is not, and cannot be, with the abstraction of terrorism. Our focus must be on terrorists and the unique threat posed by suicide terrorists. Luban continues further,

> There is no opposite number to negotiate with. There is no one on the other side to call a truce or declare a cease-fire, no one among the enemy authorized to surrender. In traditional wars among states, the war aim is, as Clausewitz argued, to impose one state's political will on another's. The *aim* of the war is not to kill the enemy—killing the enemy is the *means* used to achieve the real end, which is to force capitulation. In the War on Terrorism, no capitulation is possible. That means that the real aim of the war is, quite simply, to kill or capture all of the terrorists—to keep on killing and killing, capturing and capturing, until they are all gone.

Once again, it is not a war; Luban himself has identified many of the reasons for which it is not. But more important, what other real aim of the

U.S. response could there be? What—other than killing and capturing—could be the objective? Luban notes,

> Of course, no one expects that terrorism will ever disappear completely. . . . It follows, then, that the War on Terrorism will be a war that can only be abandoned, never concluded. The War has no natural resting point, no moment of victory or finality. It requires a mission of killing and capturing, in territories all over the globe, that will go on in perpetuity.[10]

Yes, it will. This is not, however, a choice made by the United States; it is one of the stark, harsh new realities of the post–September 11 world. The endeavor of thwarting suicide terrorists is indeed open-ended because it must be coextensive with the threat of those terrorists. And as it is not unreasonable to believe that the threat will indeed continue into the foreseeable future, so must the endeavor.[11]

> It follows as well that the suspension of human rights implicit in the hybrid war-law model is not temporary but permanent.[12]

Of course we need not subscribe to the hybrid war-law model. What Luban's critique really supports is the need to develop a new model for responding to suicide terrorists—one that acknowledges their sui generis threat—and to determine the place within that new model (if any) of human rights. But again—and it is difficult to overemphasize this point—the endeavor of thwarting suicide terrorists is a reaction, not an action. It is not an ab initio policy but the response to a policy, the program of deadly actions chosen by others, by suicide terrorists.

THE ENDEAVOR: THWARTING SUICIDE TERRORISTS

So, what is the appropriate response to the unique threat posed by undeterrable individuals? What can actually be done to thwart suicide terrorists? The crucial elements must be apparent from the preceding discussion and the new realities that the new model must accommodate.

We must devote sufficient resources to discovering just who are suicide terrorists. We must use our full range of intelligence-gathering capabilities, from orbiting satellites to aircraft overflights to electronic interceptions to the infiltration of terrorist groups. Again, the goal is not to study the abstraction of terrorism but to determine which individuals are suicide terrorists. And then we must devote sufficient resources to preventing those individuals from doing their evil deeds.

We can take—and are taking—measures to prevent attacks at the various sites of attack: airports and airliners, national monuments, power plants and grids, spent nuclear fuel rod storage facilities, chemical plants, reservoirs and aqueducts, the food supply, sporting events with dense concentrations of people, and so forth. The list goes on and on. But there are too many targets, too many modes of destruction, too few ways of interception. These measures are important—but insufficient.

When we discover individuals who are terrorists, who pose a clear and present danger to the United States, to U.S. interests abroad, or to allies and their interests, these individuals must be incapacitated. This has got to be the goal. And the harsh new reality is that incapacitation means killing or incarcerating. And incarcerating to incapacitate means incarcerating each individual until such time as that individual no longer poses a threat to U.S. interests, broadly construed. As a matter of practical fact, that could well be a life sentence. But as incipient mass murderers, they must remain incarcerated so long as they constitute a threat.

So here too the law model, the rule of law, is utterly inappropriate—as is the war model. The rule of law is aimed at punishing malefactors when the deterrent threat of the law fails to deter. In the case of suicide terrorists, the deterrent threat will indeed fail—but there will be no surviving malefactor to try and to punish.[13] Further, under the law model, the length of incarceration is to be proportionate to the offense—after which the malefactor is to be released. As regards suicide terrorists, however, if the offense has already occurred, then there is no one to incarcerate—much less for a proportionate term. On the contrary, if a terrorist is genuinely thwarted, is interdicted prior to a suicide attack—she or he must be incarcerated until no longer posing a threat. In practical terms, this may well mean for life. Once again, the proportionality of the law model is inapplicable. And there can be no prospect of repatriation, as in the war model, since there is no one authorized to declare an end to the hostilities and since there is no foreseeable end to the hostilities.

Indeed, what justification could there be for freeing an individual currently in custody who is undeterrable and still intent on death and destruction—regardless of how long he or she has been imprisoned? Freeing such a person would be morally irresponsible.

MORAL CONSTRAINTS ON THE ENDEAVOR: HUMAN RIGHTS?

In the second section, I argue that suicide terrorists are sui generis; in consequence, the threat they pose is sui generis, too. Near the beginning of the section is a long quotation from Luban; in the midst of that passage, as cited, is an ellipsis. What is omitted there, I provide here.

> Given the unique and heightened danger that suicide terrorists pose, a stronger response that grants potential terrorists fewer rights may be justified.[14]

I think this statement quite extraordinary in its hedging. In any case, I am of course here arguing for a "stronger response."

Luban hedges in part by using the term *potential*. We have to be cautious about the meaning of this here; it could mean anything from the distant to the imminent. Some have claimed that every infant born in a Palestinian refugee camp is a potential terrorist;[15] quite differently, an individual who is actively plotting an attack or is interdicted in the course of launching an attack prior to its "success" could be termed a potential terrorist. In what follows, I shall understand Luban as meaning something closer to the latter than the former: for the purposes of my argument, a potential terrorist is someone who is presently capable of performing an act of suicide terrorism and who is reasonably believed to intend to launch such an attack—for example, has committed at least one overt act that evidences a commitment to terrorism.[16]

But even with this reasonable reading of "potential," Luban's reticence is still obvious: a stronger response granting fewer rights only may be justified.[17] So we must take up, albeit briefly, the matter of human rights.

Theories of human rights abound in philosophy, political science, and diplomacy; the nature, extent, and grounding of human rights is a matter of controversy among scholars, politicians, United Nations officials, activists, and so forth. Let us consider two human rights documents.

Consider first the Universal Declaration of Human Rights, adopted by the UN in 1948. An array of rights is enumerated in this document. Some are quite fundamental and are couched in the language of the founding documents of the United States. According to Article 3, "Everyone has the right to life, liberty and security of person"; according to Article 20, "Everyone has the right to freedom of peaceful assembly and association." Other human rights specified in this document seem fanciful at best. According to Article 24, "Everyone has the right to rest and leisure"; Article 27 includes "Everyone has the right . . . to enjoy the arts."[18]

What are we to make of these proclamations? There is no institution positioned to grant these human rights, to guarantee them, or even to take interesting measures toward such a guarantee. As I see it, the declaration is the expression of a noble hope: a conception of how the world might be. It is to be understood as being the promulgation of a vision of a possible future. But it cannot be the granting of the numerous and enumerated human rights.

Now the declaration does serve a useful purpose as a recommendation that these rights be embodied in the constitutions of, and enforced by the courts in, various nation-states. As a set of aspirations, it provides guidance in the writing or amending of constitutions—South Africa is a compelling example. But many of the human rights that are identified in the declaration are not part of the positive law of many nation-states. And in some of those states, it is widely believed that the absence is a good thing: in some states, freedom of conscience is heresy, the claimed equality of the genders is blasphemy, and so forth.

The declaration, in my judgment, is a paradigm of what Joel Feinberg has called "manifesto rights."[19] They are not claim rights or valid claims that have correlative duties imposed on others—for example, the officials and institutions of a government that possesses the power and resources to protect or satisfy those rights. In consequence, there is no compelling argument that could be asserted by a suicide terrorist, moving from "I have human rights under the declaration" to "Your endeavor to thwart me is morally constrained by those human rights."

To be a human is, I take it, to be a member of the species *Homo sapiens sapiens*—to be able to reproduce. No rights bearing arises from this brute fact. Belief in universal human rights as something real, rather than an aspiration, used to be merely quaint. Now, I think, there is a lethal silliness to it, insofar as it impedes the endeavor to thwart suicide terrorists.

The French Revolution's Declaration of the Rights of Man and the Citizen claims that there were "natural and imprescriptible [unrevisable] rights." According to Jeremy Bentham, the claim that there are natural rights was "simple nonsense"; to claim that they were "imprescriptible" made the claim "nonsense upon stilts."[20] To continue the metaphor, the claim that suicide terrorists have human rights is nonsense upon stilts with vertigo.

Alternatively, one might think of human rights as being moral rights—that all human beings, taken together, constitute a single moral community and that each person has a set of symmetrical moral rights. Kant's "Kingdom of Ends" is a paradigm. Kant writes,

> All rational beings stand under the law that each of them should treat himself and all others never merely as a means but always at the same time as an end in himself. Hereby arises a systematic union of rational beings through common objective laws, i.e., a kingdom that may be called a kingdom of ends . . . inasmuch as these laws have in view the very relation of such beings to one another as ends and means.
>
> . . . Morality consists in the relation of all action to that legislation whereby alone a kingdom of ends is possible. This legislation must be found in every rational being and must be able to arise from his will, whose principle then is never to act on any maxim except such as can also be a universal law and hence such as the will can thereby regard itself at the same time the legislator of universal law.[21]

A world in which each person is rational and obedient to the categorical imperative is not self-contradictory. It is a possible world. It is a highly desirable world. But it is not our world. So we need to take very seriously Kant's parenthetical, following "kingdom of ends," which I omitted as cited: "certainly only an ideal."[22]

The fact of the matter—emphasized dramatically by the events of September 11—is that a significant number of people do not subscribe to universalism in ethics.[23] Furthermore, they are perfectly willing to kill and to die for that repudiation.

Earlier I argued that one does not become a bearer of human rights solely by being a member of the species. Here I argue that one does not become a bearer of moral rights solely by having the DNA of *Homo sapiens sapiens*.

I do believe that there are constraints on the endeavor to thwart terrorists and that some of these constraints are moral constraints. Dedicating oneself, one's nation-state, to thwarting suicide terrorists does not give one free rein, carte blanche, to adopt just any strategy, employ just any tactics, in that attempt. However, those constraints are not to be found by looking for the human rights or the moral rights of suicide terrorists. They are to be found in safeguarding one's own moral integrity and in respecting the constitutional rights of one's fellow citizens.

RIGHTS, COMMITMENTS, AND MORAL COMMUNITY

In his final work, *Justice as Fairness: A Restatement*, John Rawls gives full expression to his political philosophy as it bears on justice within bodies politic.[24] In many ways, this work is much more than a restatement; it develops several ideas not found in *A Theory of Justice* and only imperfectly expressed in *Political Liberalism*.[25] In any event, I want to draw from *Justice as Fairness* a philosophical framework for thinking about the ways in which our commitments to the rights of others might place moral constraints on us as we endeavor to thwart suicide terrorists.

People have values. Reflective and introspective people are able to articulate their values, but what is true of everyone is that their values are revealed in the actions they choose. An individual's set of values may well include judgments about the sacred and the profane; right and wrong conduct; good and bad character; and the scope, functions, and justifications (if any) of the state. The totality of one's values—broadly construed to include religion, morality, and government—is what Rawls terms a "comprehensive doctrine," or a "comprehensive position." People of like mind (like values) typically come to associate in a community—a group of people who subscribe to the same comprehensive position.[26]

In *Theory of Justice*, Rawls is open to the possibility that liberalism is a comprehensive doctrine, that it incorporates (or at least can accommodate) the full spectrum of value commitments. Although he later says that he never explicitly claims that liberalism is indeed a comprehensive position,[27] his speculation about a fully developed morality, reified with the name "goodness as fairness," has certainly inspired others to think in these ways.[28] In any event, Rawls explicitly holds that "justice as fairness," the best expression of liberalism, is not a comprehensive position.

Rawls quite accurately sees the United States—and there has never been any doubt but that Rawls is focused primarily on the United States and other Western democracies—as being a diverse and multicultural society. The landmass within its borders contains a vast array of communities in the technical sense: groups of individuals with a common commitment to some comprehensive position. These comprehensive positions, however, are to various extents inconsistent and even antagonistic. Those who subscribe to some comprehensive positions believe—as deeply as it is possible to believe—that the subscribers of certain other comprehensive positions are unjustified in their beliefs and wrong or blasphemous in their activities—and conversely, of course. (And those who subscribe to yet other comprehensive positions—for example, nonpracticing agnostics—might well think the adherents of both positions hysterical or at least overwrought. Chill!) Pluralism is a fact and a fact to be celebrated—but only if it is reasonable pluralism; that is, the various adherents are committed to toleration of one another's comprehensive positions.

The exceedingly important—yet more modest—function of justice as fairness is to provide a way to resolve political issues in a nation-state composed of a wide range of communities, the respective members of which are deeply committed to conflicting values.[29] The question then becomes, Can we agree on principles of justice, rights and duties, distribution of the burdens and benefits of civil society despite these enduring commitments to contrary views about the existence of god(s), divine commands, and so forth? The affirmative answer is justice as fairness. But for political issues to be resolved in this way, individuals must have "two moral powers"; the first of these is more relevant to my argument here: "the capacity for a sense of justice"—that is,

> the capacity to understand, to apply, and to *act from (and not merely in accordance with)* the principles of political justice that specify the fair terms of social cooperation.[30]

This gives rise to the concept of a "well-ordered society."

> First . . . it is a society in which everyone accepts, and knows that everyone else accepts, the very same political conception of justice (and so the same principles of political justice). Moreover, this knowledge is mutually recognized. . . . Second . . . society's basic structure—that is, its main political and social institutions

> and the way they hang together as one system of cooperation—is publicly known . . . to satisfy those principles of justice. Third . . . citizens have a normally effective sense of justice, that is, one that enables them to understand and apply the publicly recognized principles of justice, and for the most part to act accordingly as their position in society, *with its duties and obligations, requires*.[31]

To further emphasize the point of the italicized portion,

> The role of the principles of justice . . . is to specify the fair terms of social cooperation. . . . These principles specify the basic rights and duties to be assigned by the main political and social institutions, and they regulate the division of benefits arising from social cooperation and allot the burdens necessary to sustain it.[32]

There are great benefits to living in a well-ordered society—including the possession of genuine claim rights—but those benefits cannot be realized unless its citizens bear their fairly assigned burdens.

To live in a Rawlsian well-ordered society then requires a significant commitment on the part of each member: to distinguish political issues from other values that constitute one's "comprehensive position," to work for the resolution of those political issues in accord with the publicly affirmed principles of justice, to respect other citizens despite their subscribing to antagonistic comprehensive positions (so long as those others are tolerant of citizens who subscribe to comprehensive positions contrary to their own), and to do one's fair share in support of the well-ordered society. Again, this is a significant commitment. But nothing's got for nothing; being born within the boundaries of a particular nation-state does not entitle one to benefits—including rights—that result from others' fulfilling their commitments.

The Rawls of *Justice as Fairness* is quite conscious of the "dark side." If we fail to achieve an overlapping consensus on political principles, if our pluralism is not reasonable—if it is intolerant, if we are unable to quarantine our visceral objections to, say, the religious practices of the members of other communities—then civil strife or civil war is our inevitable future. If we cannot come together on political principles—acknowledging but deciding not to act upon divergences in other values—then civil society is not possible. Without the liberal metavalues of toleration and mutual respect—values essential to reasonable pluralism, which is necessary for achieving an overlapping consensus on principles of justice—human life is indeed doomed to be "solitary, poor, nasty, brutish and short."[33]

A well-ordered society must have a policy of open immigration.[34] To those who will commit to tolerance and mutual respect, who are willing to undertake the burdens, and who seek the benefits only in the context of undertaking those burdens (and the prior commitment to tolerance and mutual respect), we say, "Welcome!" But to those who repudiate tolerance and mutual respect, who wish to deny the constitutional rights that flow from them—to those who wish to impose their comprehensive positions upon us, by force of arms, we say, "Unwelcome!"

Now, suppose we push the foregoing Rawlsian analysis to a higher level of abstraction, applying it not just to justice but to morality itself. We can replace the nation-state of Rawls's position with the concept of the moral community. Of course, the members of the moral community will subscribe to different comprehensive positions. But to be a bearer of moral rights is to be a respecter of moral rights. Moral rights do not somehow arise from the biological ability to produce fecund offspring but from the commitment to be a member in good standing of the moral community.

Drawing from Rawls's account of a well-ordered society, we might describe the well-ordered moral community in the following terms. First, it is a community in which everyone accepts and knows that everyone else accepts the very same principles of morality. Moreover, this knowledge is mutually recognized; that is, people know everything they would know if their acceptance of those principles were a matter of public agreement. Second, the community's basic structure—that is, its main political and social institutions and the way they hang together as one system of cooperation—is publicly known to, or with good reason believed to, satisfy those principles of morality. And third, members have a normally effective sense of morality—that is, one that enables them to understand and apply the publicly recognized principles of morality and, for the most part, to act accordingly as their positions in the community, with their duties and obligations, require.

To be a member of the moral community is to be committed to conscientiously fulfilling one's moral obligations and duties—and to respecting the moral rights, as specified, of other members. In committing oneself to that, one becomes a bearer of moral rights. Members of the moral community have rights, "and there are things no person or group may do to them (without violating their rights)."[35] The crucial implication here is that the moral community does not automatically include as members the entirety of humanity.

When we look globally, the divergences in comprehensive positions and the passion with which they are held by their adherents are even greater than they are within the borders of the United States. And some peoples' acquaintance with toleration and mutual respect is fleeting or nonexistent. These facts are obstacles to membership in the moral community. And yet, I think the conditions of membership are fair.

Universalism—the position that we are all members of a single moral community in virtue solely of our being members of a single species—is, I think, implausible.

What is our relationship toward those who do not subscribe to tolerance and mutual respect, who are not members in good standing of the moral community? What is the relationship, for example, between the citizens of the United States and the terrorists of al Qaeda? I believe that we are in a Lockean "state of nature":

> Every man, in the state of nature, has a power to kill a murderer . . . to secure men from the attempts of a criminal, who having renounced reason, hath . . . declared war against all mankind, and therefore may be destroyed as a *lion* or a *tyger*, one of those wild savage beasts, with whom men can have no society nor security.[36]

Could there be, at some future date, universal subscription to a set of moral values—for example, the Universal Declaration of Human Rights? Certainly the idea is not self-contradictory. And the moral community, like the well-ordered society, must have an "open immigration" policy. I wish to be counted among those who would celebrate the day. But that day is not dawning. There are empirical grounds for believing that it may never arrive.[37] In any case, it is dangerous to pretend that it has arrived—for example, by conferring upon suicide terrorists a set of "human rights," despite their sworn intention to kill both those who do indeed have those rights and themselves in the process.

MORAL CONSTRAINTS ON THE ENDEAVOR REVISITED: INTEGRITY AND MORAL COMMUNITY

Suicide terrorists do not belong to our moral community, and the human and moral rights enjoyed by members of our community do not belong to them—and thus place no constraints on our treatment of them. But we are nevertheless constrained in what we may do in attempting to thwart suicide terrorists. Some of these constraints are practical, that is, political: we need to be sensitive to the ways that others, whether friend or foe, will view the actions we take. This includes the announced justification as well as the imputed justification.[38] I also believe, however, that some of these constraints are moral constraints. But we must ask, what is the locus of these constraints? Where should we look to determine the nature and foundation of these constraints? These constraints are not to be found by looking for the alleged human rights of suicide terrorists.[39] Rather, they are to be found in our need to be attentive to our own moral integrity. How can we ensure our own moral rectitude while endeavoring to thwart suicide terrorists?

As a starting point, we could consider treating suicide terrorists as if they were members of the moral community—pursuing courses of conduct that would not violate their rights, if they had the rights of a member of our moral community—despite the fact that they are not members and do not have those rights. This would specify parameters for humane treatment, from housing to hygiene. And it would have implications for broadly construed legal proceedings, including issues of due process, admissible evidence, and standards of proof. What must be borne in mind, however, is that the reasons for observing this code of conduct center on preserving one's own character and not on respecting the rights—human or moral—of suicide terrorists. They have no such rights.

Although this is the starting point, it will not be the finishing point. Even if we decide, ceteris paribus, that suicide terrorists should be treated as if they were the bearers of a certain set of rights, often ceteris are not in fact paribus. The paradigm, perhaps, is a captured terrorist who is reasonably believed to possess information about an imminent attack.

Luban writes,

> One striking example of the erosion of human rights is tolerance of torture. It should be recalled that a 1995 al Qaeda plot to bomb eleven U.S. airliners was thwarted by information tortured out of a Pakistani suspect by the Philippine police—an eerie real-life version of the familiar philosophical thought-experiment.[40]

What are we to make of this incident—and Luban's treatment of it?

There is a possible world at which this terrorist is not tortured. In consequence, the plot is not discovered and is not foiled—the terrorist attack is not, in fact, thwarted. Eleven airliners are destroyed; millions of dollars and thousands of innocent lives are lost. The crucial question that must be confronted is this: Is that possible world morally superior to the actual world? But Luban does not confront it; he evades it, moving on to other topics.[41] I believe that we are entitled to an answer and an argument for that answer: In context, was the torturing of this terrorist the morally superior course of action? Are we to eschew the erosion of the alleged human rights of a terrorist at a cost of the violently terminal transgression of the human rights of a host of innocents?[42]

What needs substantial philosophical investigation is this: How can I permit, countenance, or perhaps even engage in the torture of terrorists without sacrificing my moral integrity? We can hold that the actual world is the morally superior world on abstract utilitarian grounds and that judgment appears to be relatively antiseptic. Sufficient for its truth is that the pain inflicted on the tortured terrorist is outweighed by the pain to innocents that is thereby avoided. But if we are convinced that a world at which the planes and passengers are lost is morally inferior to the actual world, then there is torturing that has got to be done. Actualizing that world requires quite particular actions by particular individuals—and that raises a series of difficult questions.[43]

Let us think now in Aristotelian terms—and the better to grasp the moral magnitude of the issues, let us think in the first-person singular. How can I exhibit courage and not the cowardice that could be exhibited in light of the fact that the person being tortured is completely under my control—poses no threat to me, the torturer? How can I remain even-tempered when I know or strongly suspect that this person possesses knowledge of deadly plots against me or other members of the moral community? How can I avoid becoming anesthetized to the suffering of sentient creation? Even more of a worry, perhaps, how can I guard against intemperance—taking pleasure in hateful things? And more generally, how can I be involved in these activities and yet preserve my moral integrity, the integration of my core values?[44]

These are posed here as rhetorical questions, but they are in fact not rhetorical: they are excruciating challenges to one's character. And yet—morality may well demand the torture of suicide terrorists.

In my judgment, the worst critics of the endeavor to thwart suicide terrorists—both bad and befuddled—are those who claim that, if we do not respect the human rights of terrorists, if we violate their human rights, then we are no better than they are. Simply not true. What makes us morally superior to them is our respecting the rights of rights respecters and our willingness to respect their rights—provided that they become rights respecters. We are willing to accept them as members of the moral community, but they must realize that membership entails burdens as well as benefits and that the burdens include a commitment to freedom of conscience, tolerance, and mutual respect. Those who are unwilling to respect the moral rights of others are not themselves the bearers of moral rights. Treating suicide terrorists in certain ways while attempting to thwart their attacks does not reduce us to their level. We are willing to accord them rights and to respect those rights; they are not willing to respect the rights of others—indeed, they intend to kill and cannot be deterred from killing the bearers of those rights. Therein lies the vast moral difference.

Put another way, intolerance of the intolerant is in quite different a moral category than intolerance per se—especially murderous intolerance.

CONCLUSION

The central thesis of this chapter is that suicide terrorists are sui generis—and so too is the threat that they pose. Both the war model and the law model fail because suicide terrorists—though like criminals in some ways and like soldiers in some ways—differ from both soldiers and criminals in crucial ways. The hybrid model, an ad hoc construct of the Bush administration, does seem to me, as well as to Luban, morally facile. The appropriate response, however, is not to lament the death of human rights but to develop a new model, one whose goal is thwarting suicide terrorists without sacrificing moral integrity. I think it a philosophical blunder, however, to believe that constructing the new model must be done within the confines of human rights. Different humans believe wildly different things about human rights; this is hardly a settled area of philosophy. We must not mistake noble aspirations for universal commitment to a set of rights, including freedom of conscience, toleration, and mutual respect—and commitment to their correlative duties. So long as that universal commitment is lacking, we must be open to the idea that the moral constraints on our endeavor to thwart suicide terrorists are based upon a concern for our own moral status as members of a rights-respecting moral community and not the alleged human rights of suicidal mass murderers.

NOTES

1. The term has become ubiquitous—for example, CNN Headline News had a special segment, in virtually every news cycle, that bore that title.

2. For a critique of the war on drugs, both the metaphor and the endeavor, see Jonathan Schonsheck, *On Criminalization: An Essay in the Philosophy of the Criminal Law* (Dordrecht, The Netherlands: Kluwer Academic Publishers), 1994, pp. 227–229.

3. As cited by Richard Estrada, "Corporate Welfare Won't Help Poor." Available at www.thehollandsentinel.net/stories/071199/opi_welfare.html.

4. David Luban, "The War on Terrorism and the End of Human Rights," *Philosophy & Public Policy Quarterly*, Vol. 22, No. 3 (Summer 2002). Reprinted in *War after September 11*, ed. Verna V. Gehring (Lanham, MD: Roman & Littlefield), 2003, pp. 51–62.

5. They may well intend to prosper—but in the next life, not in this foreshortened life.

6. "To Western observers, the acts of suicide terrorism by adherents of Islam and Hinduism may be attributable to fanaticism or mental illness or both. From the perspective of the Islamic movement, however, such acts of self-destruction have a cultural and religious context. . . . According to scholars of Muslim culture, so-called suicide bombings . . . are seen by Islamists and Tamils alike as instances of martyrdom, and should be understood as such. The Arabic term used is *istishad*, a religious term meaning to give one's life in the name of Allah, as opposed to *inihar*, which refers to suicide resulting from personal distress. The latter form of suicide is not condoned in Islamic teaching. . . . Hamas or Islamic Jihad operatives sent the attackers on their missions believing they would enter eternal Paradise." Quoted from "The Sociology and Psychology of Terrorism: Who Becomes a Terrorist and Why?" Federal Research Division, Library of Congress, September 1999, p. 28. Available at www.loc.gov/rr/frd/Sociology-Psychology%20of%20Terrorism.htm.

7. The focus of this chapter is suicide terrorists, terrorists who are undeterrable. Terrorists who are not suicidal—who intend, like the bank robber, to "live long and prosper"—are, in principle, deterrable. In consequence, the endeavor to thwart them will be different—as will the moral justification of that endeavor.

8. Luban, *Philosophy and Public Policy Quarterly*, p. 12.

9. This and subsequent passages cited in this section are from Luban, *Philosophy and Public Policy Quarterly*, pp. 13–14.

10. I believe this prediction accurate. For a recent endorsement, see Michael Elliot, "Why the War on Terror Will Never End," *Time*, May 26, 2003, pp. 26–31. (As I have argued, however, it is not a war per se, and it is not against terror per se.)

11. Luban writes that "the War on Terrorism will be a war that can only be abandoned, never concluded." It could be concluded only if all suicide terrorists were captured or killed—an unlikely outcome. But I am perplexed by the option of abandoning the endeavor. What would it be like to abandon it—and could that option be morally responsible?

12. Luban, pp. 13–14.

13. Mohamed Atta, for example, was reduced to subatomic particles.

14. Luban, *Philosophy and Public Policy Quarterly*, p. 12.

15. This is a useful perspective when one is constructing broad, long-term foreign policy. What this is, of course, is a dramatic way of making the point that failing to justly resolve the Palestinian issues will have deleterious consequences into the future. (But that is distinguishable from the current and urgent endeavor to thwart suicide terrorists.)

16. Perhaps the paradigm overt act is undergoing training at a known terrorist camp, e.g., a camp run by al Qaeda. While the supporting argument is to be found in what follows, I want to state its conclusion now: a person who has (for example) begun training to become a suicide terrorist—who is committed to killing innocents and who is undeterrable—has forfeited one's rights, is not the bearer of rights. To join a group that proclaims "Death to America" is to justify one's death by America.

17. A question of the sort "What are the human rights of suicide terrorists?" sounds like the beginning of a rather tasteless joke.

18. See www.fourmilab.ch/etexts/www/un/udhr.html.

19. Joel Feinberg, *Social Philosophy* (Englewood Cliffs, NJ: Prentice Hall), 1973, p. 67. Feinberg is far more sympathetic toward manifesto rights than am I.

20. See www.xrefer.com/entry/552967.

21. Immanuel Kant, *Grounding for the Metaphysics of Morals*, trans. James W. Ellington (Indianapolis: Hackett Publishing Co.), 1981, pp. 39–40.

22. *Ibid.*, p. 39.

23. Jonathan Schonsheck, "Constraints on *The Expanding Circle*: A Critique of Singer," *Inquiries into Values: The Inaugural Session of the International Society for Value Inquiry*, ed. Sander Lee (Lewiston, NY: The Edwin Mellen Press), 1988, pp. 695–707. Large-scale genocide in Rwanda, Bosnia—and Afghanistan—have all happened since I published that piece.

24. John Rawls, *Justice as Fairness: A Restatement*, ed. Erin Kelly (Cambridge, MA: Harvard University Press), 2002.

25. John Rawls, *A Theory of Justice* (Cambridge, MA: Harvard University Press), 1971; and Rawls, *Political Liberalism* (New York, NY: Columbia University Press), 1993, reprinted with additional material, 1996.

26. What counts as the same comprehensive position will vary from community to community and from social context to social context. As I claim in "Rudeness, Rasp, and Repudiation: The Three 'R's' of Incivility" (forthcoming in *Civility and Its Discontents*, ed. Christine Sistare, University Press of Kansas), any particular individual will belong to an indefinitely large number of communities, of varying importance to that individual's life, with varying degrees of ease of entry/exit (or no such possibility [race; to some extent gender]). This complicates the exposition, and life. But did we really think it could be simple. . . .

27. *Justice as Fairness*, p. xvii.

28. See Charles R. Beitz, *Political Theory and International Relations* (Princeton: Princeton University Press, 1979). During these heady times, I myself contributed to this global extension of justice as fairness; see "Rights, Resources, and Redistribution," *Philosophy in Context*, Volume 15, 1985, pp. 44–51. I no longer believe it useful to consider the population of the earth as a single moral community. However, I do continue to believe that my analysis of the concept of a natural resource is both correct and useful. In particular, it provides a strong argument for holding that the fruits (i.e., earnings) of one's talents ought to be considered a community asset as well as an individual asset—and thus appropriately subject to principles of distributive justice.

29. Rawls cites, with approval, Robert Dahl, from *Dilemmas of Pluralist Democracy*: "today no unit smaller than a country can provide the conditions necessary for a good life, while no unit larger than a country is likely to be as democratically governed as a modern polyarchy." See *Justice as Fairness*, p. 13, n. 12.

30. Rawls, *JF*, pp. 18–19, italics added.

31. Rawls, *JF*, pp. 8–9, italics added.

32. Rawls, *JF*, p. 7.

33. Thomas Hobbes, *Leviathan*, Chapter XIII.

34. An open immigration policy is still an immigration policy and is consistent with maintaining national borders and preserving the interests of the nation-state. Open immigration policies may still be selective when the number of immigrant applicants exceeds the number that may be admitted without threat to national self-interest. What an open immigration policy never does is exclude immigrant applicants ab initio on the basis of ethnicity, religion, national origin, and the like.

35. Robert Nozick, *Anarchy, State, and Utopia* (New York: Basic Books), 1974, p. ix.

36. John Locke, *Second Treatise of Government*, ed. C. B. Macpherson (Indianapolis: Hackett Publishing Company, 1980), p. 11.

37. See my forthcoming "Rudeness, Rasp, and Repudiation: The Three 'R's' of Incivility," *supra*, for an overview of those reasons.

38. I consider some of these issues in "Thwarting Suicide Terrorists: The *Sui Generis* Threat and a Pseudo-Kantian Objection Dismantled," read to the Society for Philosophy in the Contemporary World, meeting with the American Philosophical Association, Central Division (Cleveland, OH; April 2003).

39. One can condemn, on moral grounds, the wanton destruction of beauty—for example, the vandalism of a natural scene or a microecosystem—without being committed to the rights of shrubbery.

40. Luban, *Philosophy and Public Policy Quarterly*, p. 13. Luban cites (p. 14) by way of a note an account of the torture from the *Washington Post*.

41. And thus provides another instance of ignoratio elenchi. What is Luban's position—all things considered? Was this torture warranted?

42. It is difficult to refrain from sarcasm here in specifying the position that must be defended: "Thousands of people have been killed, millions of dollars have been lost, the world economy has been staggered (consider the aftermath of 9/11, but on a global scale)—but at least we didn't torture the terrorist who possessed the information needed to thwart the attack."

43. Note the similarities with making credible nuclear deterrent threats. See Jonathan Schonsheck, "Wrongful Threats, Wrongful Intentions, and Moral Judgments about Nuclear Weapons Policies," *The Monist*, Vol. 70, No. 3, July 1987: *The Ethics of Nuclear Warfare*, pp. 330–356.

44. Aristotle, *Nicomachean Ethics*, Second Edition, trans. Terrence Irwin (Indianapolis: Hackett Publishing Co.), 1999, pp. 40–66.

Index

About the Editors and Contributors

David A. Reidy is assistant professor of philosophy at the University of Tennessee.

Mortimer N. S. Sellers is Regents Professor of the University System of Maryland and director of the Center for International and Comparative Law at the University of Baltimore School of Law.

David Duquette is professor of philosophy at St. Norbert's College.

Kenneth Henley is professor of philosophy at Florida International University.

Steven P. Lee is professor of philosophy at Hobart and William Smith Colleges.

Alistair M. Macleod is professor emeritus of philosophy at Queen's University, Canada.

Rex Martin is professor of philosophy at the University of Kansas and honorary professor at Cardiff University (UK).

Larry May is professor of philosophy at Washington University.

Stephen Nathanson is professor of philosophy at Northeastern University.

William Nelson is professor of philosophy at the University of Houston.

Lucinda Joy Peach is associate professor of philosophy at American University.

Jonathan Schonsheck is professor of philosophy at LeMoyne College.

Helen Stacy is senior research scholar at the Stanford Institute for International Studies and also a lecturer in law at Stanford Law School.